TYPES OF
JEWISH-PALESTINIAN PIETY
FROM 70 B.C.E. TO 70 C.E.

JEWS' COLLEGE PUBLICATIONS
No. 8

TYPES OF JEWISH-PALESTINIAN PIETY

FROM 70 B.C.E. TO 70 C.E.

THE ANCIENT PIOUS MEN

BY

ADOLPH BÜCHLER, Ph.D.

PRINCIPAL OF JEWS' COLLEGE

LONDON

1922

TO

THE EVER-CHERISHED MEMORY

OF MY MASTER

PROF. DR. W. BACHER

OF THE RABBINICAL SEMINARY

BUDAPEST

THIS VOLUME IS DEDICATED

IN REVERENCE AND GRATITUDE

S. B. N. — GB: 576.80135.6

Republished in 1969 by Gregg International Publishers Limited
Westmead, Farnborough, Hants., England
Printed in Israel

74-140

CONTENTS

SOME TYPES OF JEWISH-PALESTINIAN PIETY FROM 70 B.C.E. TO 70 C.E.

THE ANCIENT PIOUS MEN, חסידים הראשונים

In his comprehensive book on the religion of Jewry in the New Testament period,[1] Professor Bousset undertook the difficult task of a historical reconstruction of the religious life and thought that prevailed among the Palestinian Jews in the first century. That he grievously failed, was due not only to his insufficient knowledge of the rabbinic literature, the chief source of information on his subject, and even of its language. But not less to his unparalleled boldness in both the outlining and the painting of the enormous and complicated picture the essential parts of which had not even summarily been defined and elaborated by experts and specialists. In addition, he failed to consult the few, but valuable essays published by Jewish scholars in various periodicals, who, as e.g. Geiger, had investigated some of the important religious ideas and practices of the time in question. They would have supplied Professor Bousset with some correctly translated early rabbinic accounts unknown to him as dealing with some religious beliefs and their realization in life. As the wilful disregard of such and similar early rabbinic material naturally involved the absence from his book, as also from the works of other scholars about the first century, of many an essential feature of Jewish-Palestinian life, it must be stated here most emphatically that a history of any phase of Jewish religious

[1] *Die Religion des Judentums im neutestamentlichen Zeitalter*, 2nd edition, 1906.

life must be based on the same principles of research as that of the Assyrian, Indian, Greek, or Roman religions. Only an instructed and impartial collection of the available rabbinic data and their scientific analysis; a trained and objective examination and sifting of the individual statements, their authenticity, their dates, and their historical value for a reconstruction of actual concepts and practice; and only an unpreconceived appreciation of the underlying sentiments and beliefs will prepare the ground for a true account of the actual religious notions and conditions. The reverse method, especially if it is not checked in its free construction by a pertinent knowledge of the sources of information, must produce a caricature, a freak.

The present essay undertakes the modest task of collecting and re-examining the reports preserved in the rabbinic literature about the pious men, חסידים, who lived in Jerusalem in the period extending from 70 B.C.E. to 70 C.E.; of supplementing by a detailed examination of all the early records about the ways in which the pious men expressed their religious sentiments and ideas, the generalizing presentations by scholars of the rank of Jost, Grätz, Derenbourg, Geiger, Wellhausen, and Kohler, of the religious life of all the sections of Palestinian Jewry in the first century; of describing one representative class of typically pious individuals, and incidentally throwing some new light on the inner life of the Jews of Jerusalem, which hitherto has not been considered worthy of special attention. The standard of the ethical teachings of those pious men, a few of the central points of their theology, the purity and the depth of their religious sentiments, and the fundamental principles of their actions as reflected in early and authentic reports, will incidentally be tested, and allow an insight into a small, but important section of Jewish ethics and theology in the first century.

I

HILLEL, THE חסיד

1. THE word חסיד is well known from the Psalms as denoting a pious man who, in all adversity, put his trust in God; in the plural it refers in the same book to a group of men similarly distinguished by their attachment to God. The Oxford Gesenius, 339[b], has about it this: 'חסיד, kind, pious, so, as denoting active practice of חסד, kindness; its use as attribute of God, Jer. 3. 12; Ps. 145. 17, and the context Ps. 12. 2; Mic. 7. 2, &c., favour active sense. 2. Pious, godly, either as exhibition of "duteous love" toward God, or (in view of rarity of such passages as Hos. 6. 4, 6; Jer. 2. 2, and their possible ambiguity) because kindness, as prominent in the godly, comes to imply other attributes, and to be a designation of the godly character, piety. In Maccabean age, *συναγωγὴ Ἀσιδαίων* denoted, technically, the party of the pious who opposed the Hellenization of Judaea, 1 Mac. 2. 42; 7. 13; 2 Mac. 14. 6; so perhaps Ps. 116. 15; 149. 1, 5, 9.' On p. 338[b]: 'חסד affection of Israel to God, love to God, piety, Jer. 2. 2; Hos. 6. 4, 6.'[1] The active meaning of the word is specially interesting in Ps. 145. 17, The Lord is just in all His ways, and חסיד in all His works; for as צדיק designates God as employing justice, so חסיד describes Him as employing love towards His creatures,[2] and the word is identical with עושה חסד in Exod. 20. 6. The same words are used of men in parallel sentences in Isa. 57. 1: הצדיק אבד ואין איש שם על לב ואנשי חסד נאספים באין מבין, where איש חסד is the same as חסיד, as in Prov. 11. 17.[3] This also shows that חסיד in the case of man means the same as in that of God:

[1] See also Gesenius-Buhl, s.v. חסד and חסיד.

[2] See also Ps. 33. 5.

[3] See Delitzsch, Baethgen, and others, on Ps. 145. 17.

it is active, and not passive.[1] As, according to the critics, the date of the composition of Ps. 145 was very near the Maccabean rising, the Asideans of that period were also most probably men practising loving-kindness towards their fellow men.[2] The pious or holy men appear also[3] in the Psalms of Solomon as *οἱ ὅσιοι* which Greek word is in the LXX the translation of חסיד in the biblical Psalms; a special chapter will be devoted to the establishment of their religious character.

In rabbinic literature חסיד appears in connexion with Hillel[4] who died about the year 1: 'When once the elders (scholars) went into the house of the family of Gadia in Jericho, and a heavenly voice came forth and said to them, "There is among you a man worthy of the holy spirit,

[1] So also in the explanation in Sifré Deut. 49: מה הקב״ה נקרא צדיק שנאמר צדיק ה׳ בכל דרכיו אף אתה הוי צדיק, מה הקב״ה נקרא חסיד שנאמר וחסיד בכל מעשיו אף אתה הוי חסיד.

[2] 1 Macc. 2. 42; 7. 13 describes them as men of valour who were devoted to the law. This is all the information that we have; undoubtedly too little to justify the various theories about the relations of the Asideans to the Essenes, or the ascription to them of Enoch, the Book of Jubilees and other books, persistently advocated without a shadow of evidence in the sources. The identification of the Ḥasidim with the Essenes advanced again by Weinstein, *Beiträge zur Geschichte der Essäer*, Vienna, 1892, 13 ff. 61, 67, requires, owing to the unscientific nature of his arguments, no lengthy refutation. He starts from a corrupt reading in Sifré Num. 78, 20a, הם חסרים ממי ילמדו והוא חסר למי ילמד, באו חסרים ללמוד אצל חסר, where the parallel, quoted by Friedmann, in Mekhil. 18. 27, 60b: הם בקשו את הרב ויעבץ בקש חכמה, shows that the correct reading is not חסידים, but חסרים and חסר, meaning lacking. On such evidence is based also his derivation of the Essenes from the Rechabites in 1 Chron. 2. 55. See also Z. Frankel in his *Zeitschrift für die relig. Interessen des Judenthums*, III, 1846, 449 ff., and below; Asidaeans in *Encycl. Biblica*, Foakes Jackson and Kirsopp Lake, *Beginnings of Christianity*, I, 88-9.

[3] See Sirach 39. 24 compared with Hos. 14. 10.

[4] Baraitha jer. Sotah IX, 24 b. 29; Cant. r. 8. 9. 3; Tos. Sotah 13. 3; b. 48 b: מעשה שנכנסו זקינים אצל בית גדיא ביריחו ויצתה בת קול ואמרה להן יש ביניכם אדם אחד ראוי לרוח הקודש אלא שאין הדור כדיי ונתנו עיניהן בהלל הזקן. וכשמת היו אומרים עליו הוי עניו הוי חסיד תלמידו של עורא. Tos. has הי עניו הי חסיד, b. הי חסיד הי עניו, Cant. הא.

only the generation is not worthy of it", all eyes turned towards Hillel the elder. When he died, they bewailed him thus: 'Woe for the humble, the saint, the disciple of Ezra.'[1] The adjective עניו is well known from the Bible, and is applied to Moses in Num. 12. 3: 'Now the man Moses was very meek, above all the men that were upon the face of the earth.' Its meaning is taken by the rabbis for granted, and they emphasize that Moses was humble neither in money, nor in physical strength and beauty, but exceedingly humble in character.[2] Hillel's innate meekness and humility are described in several reports of some incidents in his life;[3] here instead of the biblical ענו its Aramaic equivalent ענוותן is applied to him which, it is true, sometimes means only modest, patient, but in this instance, as a short consideration of some of the characteristic details will show, denotes humility. In Jerusalem, at least in the last years before 70, men and women used to call on the teachers and to ask them questions of practical religious law;[4] and the rabbis were at all times at the caller's

[1] The form of the dirge is biblical (Jer. 22. 18), and was, as rabbinic accounts show, several centuries after Hillel still in use in Judaea. From the contrasting of Hillel's worthiness of the holy spirit with the unworthiness of his contemporaries it appears that his colleagues, constituting the authoritative religious body, did not sufficiently appreciate his great qualities and did not think him worthy of the position which he was holding. Perhaps it was at the beginning of his career as the president of the Beth-din, when he had quite accidentally, by answering the practical question about the admissibility of the Passover sacrifice on the Sabbath (Pesaḥ. 66 a; jer. IV, 33 a; Tos. IV, 1), been elected in the place of the sons of Bethera. These and their fellow members may have objected to the foreign scholar's presidency of the Beth-din. As a disciple of Ezra he is described as a great scholar who restored the knowledge and the right observance of the Torah.

[2] Sifré Num. 101; Sifré zuta on Num. 12. 3; ARN. 9, 21 a.

[3] Shabb. 30 b ff.

[4] Tos. Nid. V, 3; Baraitha b. 33 b bottom, the wife of a Sadducee said to a high-priest, 'Though we are Sadducee women, we ask (about our levitical purity) the (Pharisee) scholars.' R. Joḥanan b. Zakkai in Jerusalem said to a digger of pits, ditches, and caves, who declared himself as important as the teacher by his public work, 'If a man came to you with an academic or a practical question, could you tell him to drink of the water? or, if

disposal,[1] except perhaps on Fridays later in the afternoon, when they were preparing for the reception of the Sabbath.[2] Once a man who had wagered to make Hillel angry came on Friday afternoon, when Hillel was washing his head,[3] and called out for him in the street, and in a way displaying deliberate disrespect; though, as his high wager[4] shows, he belonged to the class of citizens of Jerusalem that knew manners. Ignoring it, Hillel wrapped himself, came out to meet him, and asked him what he desired. 'I have a question to ask'. 'Ask, my son, ask'. 'Why are the heads of the Babylonians not round?' Whereas other men or women submitted questions of religious law arising out of daily life, this man invented a subject of no consequence, nor concerning practical life, but one aiming at Hillel who was a Babylonian. 'My son, you have asked a great question'; and he answered it. The man left, but returned after a

a woman asked you about her purification, could you advise her to bathe in this pit, because its water could purify her?' (Kohel. r. 4. 17).

[1] When R. Ishmael and R. Simeon were about to be executed by the Romans (2 ARN. 41, 57 b), the first asked his friend, Has ever a woman come to you to ask a question about her purification, or a man about his vow, and they were kept waiting, because you were asleep or having a meal, or you were engaged, or perhaps the servant would not allow the person to enter? R. Simeon answered, The servant had the order not to stop anybody from entering, whether I was asleep or having a meal. Though in the parallel account in ARN. 38, 57 b R. Ishmael said to R. Simeon, 'Perhaps, when you were sitting and expounding on the Temple Mount and all the multitudes of Israel were sitting before you, you were conceited', the incidents referred to did not happen in Temple times, but in the year 117, when under Trajan an attempt was made to rebuild the Temple (see Schechter, Agadath Shir Hashirim 99, Grünhut, Midrash on Canticles 3 b, 7 a, and Baraitha Berakh. 58 a: When once ben Zoma saw a multitude on the stairs on the Temple Mount, he said, &c.), see Schlatter, *Tage Trajan's und Hadrian's*, 88 ff., Mekhil. Exod. 22. 22.

[2] Rabh reports in Shabb. 25 b how R. Jehudah b. Ilai washed every Friday his face, hands, and feet in warm water, and dressed in a white mantle in honour of the Sabbath. This happened between 137 and 160.

[3] In a parallel, but in many details different account of the incident in 2 ARN. 29, 30 b, the man waked him from his sleep, and put several additional questions.

[4] The amount of 400 Zuzs was, e.g. the double of the usual marriage settlement, or that of the daughter of a priest (Kethub. I, 5).

while in the same way as the first time, and put to Hillel the question as to why the eyes of the Palmyreans were half closed; when he returned the last time, he asked why the feet of the Persians were broad. Each time Hillel deliberately declared the question difficult, and answered it calmly. After the third explanation the man said to Hillel, I have many more questions to put, but, I am afraid, you might be angry. But Hillel wrapped himself, sat down opposite him, and said, 'Put any questions that you have to ask'. 'Art thou Hillel whom they call prince in Israel?' 'Yes'. 'If so, may not many be like thee in Israel!' 'Why, my son?' 'Because I have lost 400 Zuzs through thee'. Hillel replied, 'Take heed of thy spirit! Hillel deserves it that thou shouldst lose through him 400 Zuzs or even 800, and Hillel not be angry.' Not even after the last, extremely rude remark did he lose his calmness, but continued the discussion; and he finished up by emphasizing the value—in money that engrossed the mind of his questioner—of not turning angry. Such patience and calmness were born of and sustained by true humility. For the object of the man must have been clear to Hillel after the second, if not already after the first question; and still he treated them, by wrapping his head,[1] in the same solemn manner as any other serious

[1] If the wrapping meant merely a temporary dressing, there would have been no occasion for it before Hillel's entering into the fourth question, as he had not left his visitor, after he had called out the rabbi for his third question. When once R. Gamaliel II, accompanied by R. Ilai, travelled from Akko to K'zibh, and reached this town, a man asked him to dissolve a vow of his; but as the rabbi had drunk some wine, he, in accordance with Lev. 10. 9-11, refused to attend to a religious question, and asked the man to walk by his side for a time. When they reached the Ladder of Tyre, R. Gamaliel dismounted from his ass, wrapped himself, sat down, and dissolved the man's vow (Baraitha 'Erub. 64 b; Tos. Pesaḥ. I, 28; jer. 'AZ I, 40 a. 62). R. Ilai enumerated the rules which he had learned from R. Gamaliel's actions, among them ואין מפירין נדרים . . . אלא עטופין ויושבין, they do not dissolve vows except wrapped and sitting. In the account in 2 ARN. 29, 30 b Hillel each time admitted the man to his house, wrapped himself, sat down and asked the man to put his question.

point of religious law. And even after the third question, when the man said that he had many more to put, Hillel wrapped himself, and sat down to listen to him, with a deference due not to the man whom he might have ignored, but due to any matter of law to be submitted to a Pharisee teacher for explanation and decision. And also in the accounts about his conversations with three non-Jews who expressed the desire to become proselytes, but made very grave reservations, Hillel's humility is evident. One refused to accept the oral law, the second wished to learn the whole Torah while standing on one foot, and the third was prepared to adopt Judaism only if he could be made a high-priest. Hillel told the second that the whole Torah was contained in the principle: what is hateful to thee, do not to thy neighbour; the rest is its explanation, go and learn. Then he admitted him, just as the other two.[1] As he knew very well that the belief in the one God was most essential, and the worship of the Creator and of the Redeemer of Israel by the observance of the Sabbaths and festivals very important, his readiness to receive those men without further conditions must have rested on some principle. His eagerness for proselytes is nowhere stated. But he had a good opinion of human nature: a heathen who had made up his mind to join Judaism, to submit to the circumcision and to the fundamental laws of the Torah, was surely firm in his religious determination, and should not be refused. Any reservations advanced by him were due to ignorance that could be overcome by instruction, as also other statements of Hillel will show. Just as he, in his humility, patiently listened to those men, and entered into a discussion of Judaism with them, so he himself instructed the proselytes in the same spirit; and all three expressed their gratitude in the words: Humble Hillel, may blessings rest on thy head for bringing us near under the wings of God's glory![2]

[1] See Abrahams, *Studies in Pharisaism*, I, 23.

[2] The different attitudes of R. Eliezer and R. Joshua towards the

One of Hillel's few sentences preserved also emphasizes the importance of humility:[1] 'My humiliation is my elevation, my elevation is my humiliation'. The verbal nouns of the IVth form may, as the verb itself, be transitive, and mean the placing high or low of Hillel by others. And the sentence may, as also the whole context suggests, reflect his own experience, when, during the first years of his stay in Jerusalem, he was probably placed, in the school of Shema'yah and Abtalyon, in the last row of the disciples;[2] and again, when, after his abilities and his knowledge had been recognized, he was raised to the presidency of the Beth-din. Or the IVth form of the verbs may be intransitive, and, as

criticism by the proselyte Akylas of the reward, promised in Deut. 10. 18 to the proselyte (Gen. r. 70, 5 and parallels; Bacher, Tannaiten I^2, 106. 2), resemble those of Shammai and Hillel; אמרו אלולי אריכות פנים שהאריך רבי יהושע עם עקילס היה חוזר לסורו וקרא עליו טוב ארך אפים מגבור, R. Joshua's patient argument is described as slowness to anger, as in Prov. 16. 32. And the prospects held out by Moses to Ḥobab in Num. 10. 29, 'for the Lord hath spoken good concerning Israel', are interpreted in Sifré Num. 78, 21 a thus: God has ordered Israel to do good to proselytes, and to deal with them ענוה, gently, humbly. Here mere patience cannot be meant, as Ḥobab had not yet refused to go with the Israelites. A curious meaning of ענוותנות is to be found in Gittin 56 a in the report about the sacrifice for the emperor, the refusal of which on account of its blemish was the immediate cause of the revolution in 66. A certain bar-Kamṣa had, in order to revenge himself on the rabbis, deliberately caused the blemish. When the rabbis suggested that, for the sake of peace, the animal should exceptionally be offered, R. Zekhariah b. Abkulos objected, as some might infer that such a sacrifice was permissible. Others advised that, in order to prevent information, bar-Kamṣa should be killed; but R. Zekhariah objected, as it might lead to the error that one who caused a blemish on a sacrifice might be put to death. R. Joḥanan (in the name of R. José b. Ḥalaftha, Tos. Shabb. 16. 7) remarked: ענוותנותו של רבי זכריה בן אבקולס החריבה את ביתנו ושרפה את היכלנו והגלתנו מארצנו, the too great consideration of R. Zekhariah destroyed our House, burnt our Temple, and exiled us from our land (cf. *J.Q.R.*, VIII, 1896, 232 bottom).

[1] Lev. r. 1. 5; Bacher, Tannaiten I, 6. 1: השפלתי היא הגבהתי הגבהתי היא השפלתי, cf. 'Erub. 13b.

[2] Ḥull. 137 b; Menaḥ. 29 b, Rabbinovicz, and *J.Q.R.*, IX, 1897, 701.

the statements of other scholars suggest,[1] may refer to Hillel's own choice of a humble place or of a front seat among the scholars, reflecting his modesty or his pride. Or the first person of the suffix may not refer to his own experience at all, but only be his literary formulation of a rule and a sentence. In any case, his words state that humiliation or humility is merely an external experience that does not affect the soul of a man or his own estimation of the incident; for he may feel inwardly elevated, when outwardly he is placed low, or distinction or pride may be felt by his inner self a degradation or shame. The standard by which such outward experience is measured is that of the humble stoic. And with this may be connected another meaning of Hillel's epithet עניו, suggested by ben-Zoma's rendering of the same word in Num. 12. 3 by עלוב,[2] 'Who is the most submissive of all? He who is as submissive as our master Moses was, as it says, And the man Moses was very submissive.' He heard himself abused by his sister and his brother, and said nothing, following the principle of those described in the well-known Baraitha:[3] 'To such as are humiliated, but humiliate not, hear themselves reviled, but reply not, do all from love, and rejoice at their sufferings, Judges 5. 31 applies: Those who love Him (God) are as the sun, when he goeth forth in his might.' We have no knowledge of actual insults by words or actions against

[1] Lev. r. 1. 5; ARN. 25, 41 a; 2 ARN. 22, 23 b, R. Akiba in the name of Simeon b. 'Azzai (see Bacher, I, 413. 1), in commenting on Prov. 25. 7: כי טוב אמר לך עלה הנה מהשפילך לפני נדיב אשר ראו עיניך, says, Withdraw from thy place two or three seats and sit down, till thou art told to go higher up; but go not too high up, in order not to be told to go down. It is better that they tell thee, Come up, come up, than that they should tell thee, Go down, go down; and so Hillel said, &c.

[2] ARN. 23, 38 a; Bacher I, 427. 5: איזהו עלוב שבעלובים זה שהוא עלוב כמשה רבינו שנאמר והאיש משה ענו מאד.

[3] Shabb. 88 b: תנו רבנן עלובין ואינן עולבין שומעין חרפתן ואינן משיבין עושין מאהבה ושמחין ביסורין עליהן הכתוב אומר ואהביו כצאת השמש בגבורתו.

Hillel; though as a Babylonian he was publicly disparaged,[1] and his sentence may have referred to such an experience of his.[2]

2. As to Hillel's description as חסיד, it should be noted that, as in Jer. 2. 2 חסד and אהבה are synonyms and signify, as לכתך in the parallel sentence shows, Israel's active love of God, it follows that חסיד and אוהב are synonyms, and that the meaning of חסיד is the same as is expressed in R. Meir's statement about him who studies the Torah for its own sake:[3] he loves God and loves men. Hillel's attitude towards God is only incidentally described. It is related how his colleague Shammai thought, throughout the week, of the coming Sabbath and the food by which to honour it, and reserved the best meat which he could acquire, for that day; 'but Hillel had another way, for all his doings were in the honour of God, as it is written (Ps. 68. 20), Blessed be the Lord day by day.'[4] No doubt,

[1] Jer. Pesaḥ. VI, 33 a. 22: אמרו לו כבר אמרנו אם יש תוחלת מבבלי, 38: מי גרם לכם לצרך לבבלי הזה; ARN. 12, 28 a: בבלאה טפ״ואה.

[2] After his election to the presidency of the Beth-din, he began to chide the sons of Bethera for their inability to answer the question of religious law, due to their refusal to attend the school of Shema'yah and 'Abtalyon (Pesaḥ. 66 a; jer. VI, 33 a. 38). By his chiding, of which the Baraitha disapproves, it accounts for his inability to answer the next question. Though of the first half of the third century, the statement of R. Alexandri in Midr. Ps. 86. 1 is an interesting illustration of the Baraitha in the text: He who hears himself cursed, and keeps silence, though he has the means to stop it, becomes a partner of God who hears Himself blasphemed by the nations, and keeps silence. So David heard himself cursed, and kept silence; therefore he calls himself חסיד, as God is called חסיד in Jer. 3. 12. Those whom the Baraitha and ben-Zoma term עלוב, R. Alexandri calls חסיד.

[3] Aboth VI, 1: אוהב את המקום אוהב את הבריות.

[4] Mekhil. R. Simeon, p. 107; Baraitha Beṣah 16 a; Pesik. r. 23, 115 b: אבל הלל הזקן מדה אחרת היתה בו שכל מעשיו לשם שמים דכתיב ברוך ה׳ יום יום. In Mekhil. 20. 8, 69 a the practice of Shammai is quoted as one commended by Eleazar b. Ḥananiah b. Ḥizkiah b. Ḥananiah b. Garon, see Friedmann, note 18. Another Baraitha in Beṣah 16 a ascribes the two practices to the two schools of the Shammaites and the Hillelites: תניא נמי הכי בית שמאי אומרים מחד שביך לשבתיך ובית הלל אומרים

Hillel honoured the Sabbath not less than did Shammai; but he was not absorbed throughout the whole week by the thought of that one duty, as every day claimed the fulfilment of its own religious and moral obligations in the honour of God, which he considered just as important. He applied once the expression 'doings in the honour of God' to an action of his wife.[1] Once, when she had prepared a meal for a guest invited by her husband, a poor man called at the door and stated that he had to bring his bride to his house that day, but had no food whatever; she gave him the whole dinner, and quickly prepared other food, and brought it into the room. When Hillel asked her, why she had not brought it in sooner, and she told him the reason, he said, My daughter, also I have judged you with an inclination in your favour and not your disfavour, for all the deeds which you have done you have done in the honour of God. Though an act of charity, her deed might have been prompted by considerations of a different nature: she might have accidentally spoiled the food by burning it, and might not have liked to be criticized; or she disliked the visit or the visitor, or felt annoyed at her husband, or had delayed the dinner for some other, quite human reason. But Hillel knew his wife, and his own kind heart never allowed him

ברוך ה׳ יום יום. What Hillel did, is not expressly stated, and the meaning of the verse, and its connexion with the preceding statement are not clear. Rashi says, Hillel trusted that a nice portion would be found for the Sabbath. Samuel Edels elaborates this, and adds: Hillel ate his food every day, trusting that God would supply a portion for the Sabbath; he did so, not from greediness, for just as all his doings were in the honour of God, so this action was dictated by his faith in God. We have to bless God daily for his provision of food, and to trust that He will supply us with such also in the future. The verse has accordingly to be quoted to the end. Weiss, I, 160 explains it differently: Hillel's statement proves the strength of his faith; he used to say, Blessed be the Lord day by day: if he had sufficient for the needs of the day, he did not trouble about the next day, but trusted in God. But this explanation, though it is supported by the other Baraitha, does not take into account the important sentence: for all his doings were in the honour of God.

[1] Derekh ereṣ VI: שכל המעשים שעשית לא עשית אלא לשם שמים.

to assume any but a favourable motive for the actions of others; and he had no hesitation in saying that this time, just as ever, she was actuated by one thought only: the honour of God, to help the poor man in his distress immediately, and as effectively as possible, without weighing the consequences for herself too long and too seriously. Her deed was not only unselfish, but had demanded of her self-sacrifice in the performance of duty dictated by the unwritten will of God; she had obeyed that without hesitation, and thereby acted in the honour of God.[1]

When once R. Gamaliel II and R. Joshua were on the way, they availed themselves of a privilege, instituted by Joshua,[2] and walked, on account of the hard mud in the road, by the side of the cultivated fields. On noticing a man walking towards them in the mud, R. Gamaliel angrily asked R. Joshua who the man was who so ostentatiously exhibited his strict observance. R. Joshua replied that it was R. Jehudah b. Pappos, all doings of whom were in the honour of God.[3] It was said of R. Jehudah b. Baba that all his doings were in the honour of God, except that (against the accepted prohibition) he reared goats; the physician had advised him to drink naturally warm milk, and so he kept a goat tied to his bed. When, on his death, the scholars entered into an examination of his deeds, they found no other sin but that one.[4] The meaning of the

[1] When Herod built the Temple, so Sifra Lev. 26. 4, 110 d reports, it rained at night, and in the morning the sun shone, the wind blew, and the earth was dry, so that the workmen could go to their work; this showed them that their doing was לשם שמים, in the honour of God. The support of God demonstrated to them that the building of the Temple by the sinful king was not disapproved of by God as soiled and unholy, but was, at least as far as the share of the workmen was concerned, carried on with pure intentions, in the honour of God. Cf. R. Nathan in Sifré Deut. 11. 14. 42, 80 a; Mekhil. Exod. 12. 11, 7 b.

[2] Baba kam. 81 a.

[3] jer. Berakh. II, 5 d. 5; in the parallel Baba kam. 81 b Rabbi and R. Ḥiyya met in the same circumstances Jehudah b. Nekosa.

[4] Tos. Baba kam. VIII, 13; in the parallel Baraitha Baba kam. 80 a, cf. Themur. 15 b, no name is mentioned, but instead an unnamed חסיד.

sentence that all his deeds were in the honour of God is clear in both instances. R. Jehudah b. Pappos did not act with the idea of exhibiting to the looks of others his self-imposed strictness of observance; but, as the contrast clearly shows, he considered, in his actions, God only, and the deed itself as well as its quality were determined by his thought of God. The pious man in the other Baraitha not only avoided all sin,[1] which in itself is only a negative virtue; but, whenever he acted, his only motive was God whose will he was thereby carrying out. And when the disciple of R. Joḥanan b. Zakkai, R. José the priest (Aboth II, 12) said, 'Let all thy deeds be done for the sake of God', he intended to impress the highest principle to guide a man's actions: God should ever be present in his mind; and, whatever he does, whether it is great or small, important or indifferent, religious or moral, he should, like Hillel, think of God, and measure his deed by the will and honour of God;[2] not his [illegible] benefit or pleasure, nor his own ambition and glory, but only God's honour. מעשיך refers to positive actions; and, as the incidents referred to show, not merely to biblical positive commandments of a moral or ritual character, but to every kind of service to the fellow-man, as will be more fully shown presently. Whether it was this his religious attitude to God, that made Hillel's contemporaries term him a חסיד, is not evident.

An instructive instance of Hillel's way of thinking and

As R. Jehudah b. Baba was killed in the Hadrianic religious persecutions by the Roman police (Synh. 13 b ff.), the name of the scholar who died a natural death cannot be correct; and we would have, according to the canon in the passage of the Talmud, to substitute R. Jehudah b. Ilai.

[1] Apoc. Baruch 9. 1: Jeremiah whose heart was found pure from sin. In *Antiquit.* XIX, 6. 4. 315, Jonathan, Ananos' son, described to King Agrippa I his brother Matthias as worthy of the high-priest's office, as he was free from all sin against God and the king.

[2] Cf. Baraitha Baba meṣ. 59 b: When, after putting R. Eliezer in the ban, R. Gamaliel was overtaken by a violent storm at sea, he saw in it a punishment for that act. He rose, and prayed, Master of the Universe, it is known to Thee that I did it not for my honour, nor for that of my family, but for Thy honour, &c. Here the word used is לכבוד, not לשם.

of his religious reflection on ordinary actions of his has fortunately been preserved. When once Hillel had taken leave of his disciples (in the school), he went with them; to their question as to where he was going, he replied, 'To perform a religious duty'; and this he explained to mean bathing in a public bath. To their further question as to whether that was a religious duty, he said, 'The man appointed to the duty of scouring and rinsing the statues of the king set up in the theatres and circuses is for that paid by maintenance, and, in addition, he is one of the government officials. As I was created in the image and after the likeness (of God), as it says (Gen. 9. 6), 'for in the image of God made He man': how much more so (have I to wash my body)'.[1] It need hardly be pointed out that a man with that conception of his body—for to this and not to the soul does the image of God here refer—ever present in his mind, kept his body clean not only physically, but also morally, free from any kind of pollution; and even his physical use of it for natural functions, as at easying it or in sexual intercourse, was hallowed, even though he was not an Essene. The perfection and the beauty of the human organism would be described by him in words of admiration for God's greatness as the Creator, and in

[1] R. Aḥai in his שאילתות, section בראשית, refers this to Hillel's regular bathing on the Friday in honour of the Sabbath; but he had no other source for that statement, and it was merely his own, hardly correct interpretation of the above report, see Reifmann in המגיד X, 367. Reifmann points to the parallel in Tos. Berakh. IV, 1: לא ישתמש אדם בפניו ידיו ורגליו אלא בכבוד קונהו שנאמר כל פעל ה׳ למענהו, a man should not employ his face, his hands, and his feet but for the glory of his Creator, as it says in Prov. 16. 4: The Lord hath made all things for Himself. The parallel Baraitha in Shabb. 50 b is different: תניא רוחץ אדם פניו ידיו ורגליו בכל יום בשביל קונו משום שנאמר כל פעל ה׳ למענהו, a man should wash his face, his hands, and his feet every day for the sake of his Creator, &c. In both versions Hillel's idea is applied. In the parallel account in 2 ARN. 30, 33 b Hillel also declared his going to the water-closet a religious duty, as it was to prevent the body from becoming spoiled; Shammai, on the other hand, said, Let us do our duty to our body. See Bergmann in H. Cohen's *Festschrift* I, 161–62.

praise and gratitude for the preservation of the body in health.

The report continues: 'When once Hillel had taken leave of his disciples (in the school), he went with them; to their question as to where he was going, he replied, To do loving-kindness to the guest in the house. To their further question as to whether he had a guest every day, he said, Is not my poor soul a guest in the body, as it is this day here, and to-morrow no longer here?' While these reports incidentally give very interesting information about Hillel's method of teaching, they are more important for his plain observations about the soul. Its transitory stay in the body would naturally urge him on to use every day for its cultivation, as his disciple, R. Joḥanan b. Zakkai, illustrated that thought by the preparations and the clean garments for the king's banquet.[1] Its return to God would remind him of the soul's duty to render account of all that he did during his life on earth, and of the advisability of keeping the soul as pure as it had left God, so that it might return pure to God; as R. Joḥanan b. Zakkai on his deathbed explained to his disciples his fear of having to appear after death before God for eternal judgment.[2] The soul is immortal, and will receive its reward or punishment. The epithet poor or grieved given to the soul suggests the Greek idea of its removal from the holy regions of heaven and its habitation in the uncongenial house, the body.[3] As it requires the attention of loving-kindness, it is dependent on what man does for it; but what attention did Hillel offer it? Was it retirement and solitary meditation intended for comforting it, and deeper thought about its heavenly origin and nature? Or was it the lifting up of the depressed soul to God by prayer, its temporary rise to the heights of its fountain? And was it this attitude of Hillel's to his body and his

[1] Shabb. 153 a. [2] Berakh. 28 b.

[3] See Josephus, *Wars*, II, 8. 11 about the same view of the Essenes, and VII, 8. 7. 346; Contra Apion. II, 24. 203.

soul that merited for him the attribute of חסיד?[1] Or was it his true trust in God, manifested on an occasion accidentally reported? 'When he was once on his way home, and heard a cry of anguish in the town, Hillel said, I feel reassured that it is not in my house.'[2] He wa snot afraid of evil tidings, his heart was fixed, trusting in the Lord. Or was it his unusual consideration for the sensitiveness of the poor that had come down in life? For it is reported that he bought for a poor man of good family a horse for riding, and a slave to run before him; and when once he found no slave for that purpose, he ran himself three miles before the poor man.[3] As Hillel was at that time evidently a man of means, his action was dictated not only by the desire to relieve the man of care, but, by self-sacrifice and public self-abasement in the service of true humanity, to make him forget his present circumstances.[4] This act of humility probably constitutes one of the deeds which he performed in the honour of God. There was no written law that prescribed it, nor any fixed rabbinic rule to be followed; it was Hillel's own way of interpreting the duty of Jewish charity, and of translating it into reality. Such extension of a positive commandment by a rabbinic authority is an interesting instance of rabbinic exegesis by which its author imposed in the first instance upon himself the onerous moral duty deduced; and it was understood that the rabbi had to be the first to obey such additions to the biblical law. Thereby he set an example of charity and of humility

[1] In neither incident did he quote any passage of the Bible. Prov. 11. 17: גמל נפשו איש חסד is quoted at the head of each paragraph by the later Haggadist who interpreted the verse and illustrated it by Hillel's statements; and it is the Haggadist who in this way proved Hillel to have been an איש חסד, see Bacher, I, 7. 4.

[2] Baraitha Berakh. 60 a: and to him applies Ps. 112. 7; in jer. Berakh. IX, 14 b. 5: הלל הזקן אומר משמועה רעה לא יירא Hillel himself quoted the verse: he shall not be afraid of evil tidings.

[3] Baraitha Kethub. 67 b; in the parallel in Tos. Pe'ah IV, 10 and jer. VIII, 21 a. 55 the last part of the account is missing.

[4] Cf. Testam. Zebulun 7. 4.

to his disciples, and to such as knew him personally and were prepared to imitate his action. Whether, in carrying it out, they were able to grasp the ideal that guided Hillel, and were actuated by the same unselfish love and humility, may rightly be doubted; it was given only to a few to attain to it.

3. A different side of Hillel's character is revealed by his rule,[1] 'If I am not for myself, who is for me? But if I am only for myself, what am I? and if not now, when?' He justifies egoism as necessary; for in practical life nobody cares really for his fellow-man, or goes so far as to work for another person's maintenance, and so the latter would starve and perish. But such egoism, though necessitated by the realities and exigencies of human existence, and therefore irreproachable, must not fill out a man's whole thought; for he is not a human being, if he thinks only of himself and of his own needs. Only by thinking of others and by working for others, while busy with his own needs, does he rise to be a man. This principle and its realization must be watched during every hour of one's life, for the latter is short and quickly passing, and, once finished, allows of no further work. Here on earth is the only time available for it, not after death; and it is no special merit, it is a plain duty. And in another sentence Hillel enjoined on his hearer not to judge his fellow-man, until he himself is in his position.[2] The neighbour is not, as it seems, in financial difficulties, and unable to pay a debt or keep a promise on a date stipulated; but more probably he is in some trouble brought about by neglect or by a moral lapse, and help is neither solicited nor perhaps possible. In such or similar circumstances, Hillel urges on his follower the restraint of a very forward in-

[1] Aboth, I, 14: אם אין אני לי מי לי וכשאני לעצמי מה אני ואם לא עכשיו אימתי.

[2] Aboth, II, 4: הלל אומר אל תפרוש מן הצבור ואל תאמין בעצמך עד יום מותך ואל תדין את חבירך עד שתגיע למקומו.

clination in man, ready not so much to help and to offer sympathy, as to rush forth with blame against the neighbour who is depressed by his failure and disappointment. As we see the calamitous result only, we are quick in condemning our fellow-man on the result before us. And not only by deed must we not wrong him, but not even by undeserved words, nor censure him hastily even in our thoughts. This warning is merely a practical application of Hillel's rendering of Lev. 19. 18: what is hateful to thee, do not to thy neighbour,[1] which he declared to the non-Jew to be the whole Torah: not only to think oneself into the position of the fellow-man and refrain from reproaching him, but to wait till one is actually in the same trouble. Considering man's bent, Hillel's demand is very heavy, as it requires a strong moral sense and powerful mental restraint. The same claim seems to underly the warning in the same sentence, not to believe in oneself to the last day of life. When, by hard struggle, we have overcome a momentary temptation, and even our passions from prevailing over us, we should not yet think our moral hold firmly established and secure against any unexpected sally of a sinful or immoral character; for how easily does even a strong mind succumb unawares to the beauty of women and to lust! [2] Hillel appeals here to men whose minds were trained to watch their wills, evidently his disciples whom such consciousness of human weakness should fill with humility.

To the same are addressed his words of teaching, 'Be of the disciples of Aaron: love peace and pursue peace, love men, and bring them near to the Torah'.[3] To *keep* only the peace, especially in contrary circumstances, presupposes patience, yielding, self-effacement, Hillel's meekness and

[1] Shabb. 31 a.

[2] jer. Shabb. I, 3 b. 64; Midr. Abkir, p. 11; Gaster, מעשיות 93 ff.; Tanḥ. מקין B. 15; Bacher, I, 384. 3 about R. Matthia b. Ḥarash.

[3] Aboth, I, 12: הלל אומר הוי מתלמידיו של אהרן אוהב שלום ורודף שלום אוהב את הבריות ומקרבן לתורה.

humility. But to *seek* peace[1] demands active intervention, to reconcile men who quarrelled, to restore harmony between husband and wife, between neighbours and partners, and others, as Hillel's disciple, R. Joḥanan b. Zakkai, explained the same duty.[2] In such unsolicited intervention, not only has disappointment to be expected, but rudeness, repulsion, offence, and abuse have to be faced. Indifference towards the fellow-man, which would appear preferable, is not the proper attitude of the religiously cultured and the learned to whom, as the concluding words of Hillel's warnings show, he addressed his teachings. He had, at the same time, those in view who stood far away from the Torah either in knowledge or in practice, the עם הארץ, who should be approached with love.[3] To love one who is of our mind and shares our religious convictions is not difficult, and requires no exertion; but love for the religiously ignorant or indifferent is difficult, but due to him as a creature of God who should be raised to a higher level. We have to ignore his mental attitude and his religious state for which he is not responsible: while as God's creature he has a claim to our sympathy and love.[4] These will attract him to the learned men; and as he attributes their love to their learning, he will be drawn to the Torah which, in fact, represented general moral and religious culture. This principle of Hillel taught active humanity in its highest manifestation, possible only in a man of standing and of learning, and dictated and sustained by loving-kindness, חסד. And as such attitudes of mind and action are not contained in, nor covered by, his description as a disciple of Ezra, nor by his meekness and humility which are not *active* qualities of the character, they seem to have been the effluence of his third characteristic, חסיד. If this is correct, the word described the relation of man's

[1] Ps. 34. 15.

[2] Mekhil. Exod. 20. 25, 74 a.

[3] Testam. Issachar, 7. 6: I loved the Lord, likewise also every man with all my heart.

[4] See Heinemann, *Poseidonios' metaphys. Schriften*, I, 1921, 138.

active love not to God, but to man, as the noun חסד in rabbinic literature invariably does. And so Hillel in his sentence enjoined on his disciples the duty of realizing loving-kindness as lovers and promoters of peace, and thereby proving themselves disciples of Aaron,[1] and of extending love to the ignorant and the indifferent. Humility and love were Hillel's prominent qualities of character, and expressed the spirit of his ethical teachings.

In a sentence in which Hillel himself used the word חסיד[2] its meaning is at first sight not clear: 'An empty man cannot be a sin-fearing man, nor can an ignorant person be pious, nor can a shamefaced man learn, nor a passionate man teach, nor can one who is engaged overmuch in business grow wise'. As the middle part of the sentence refers to the learner and the teacher, Hillel dealt here with the school; he encouraged the new disciple not to be ashamed to admit that he did not follow the details of the instruction, as, if he refrained from asking for additional information and explanation, he would not make sufficient progress. On the other hand, the teacher whom frequent questions make impatient and angry is not fit for his task, as he discourages the beginner and the slower mind. Nor should young men who, before joining the school, had carried on, and are still engaged in, trade, think themselves too experienced, learned, and wise to require the theoretical wisdom taught in the school. The first part of the sentence refers to men who before joining the school considered themselves possessed of the religious qualifications which in Hillel's opinion were the results of a life-long study of the Torah. One of those men is described as totally devoid of all knowledge and

[1] There must have existed an early exposition of Mal. 2. 6 referring to Aaron's activities as a peacemaker.

[2] Aboth, II, 5: הוא היה אומר אין בור ירא חטא ולא עם הארץ חסיד ולא הביישן למד ולא הקפדן מלמד ולא כל המרבה בסחורה מחכים ובמקום שאין אנשים השתדל להיות איש. In 2 ARN. 33, 36 b, the sentence is quoted as that of R. Akiba, and has חסיד פרוש, see p. 49 ff.

education;[1] the other had some home education, as he belonged to the landowning, wealthy class. When either of them asserted that he could in the practice of religion or in his moral conduct attain to the same degree of perfection, Hillel emphatically denied the fact and its possibility;[2] as the context suggests, only attendance at the school enabled a man to become sin-fearing and pious, for such high qualities could be taught. Innate kindness and love, even though strengthened by natural tact, will, in an uneducated person, never reach the degree of moral excellence to which Hillel's instruction in the Torah and his example could train and guide them. In another sentence[3] he expressed it clearly and forcibly, 'He who acquires the words of the Torah, acquires the life in the world-to-come', that the only means for obtaining a share in that life is the acquisition of knowledge. Hillel places here the highest aim and purpose of man's life before his eyes, and defines the way, open to everybody, by which he can safely reach that

[1] Cf. Kidd. I, 10: כל שישנו במקרא ובמשנה ובדרך ארץ לא במהרה הוא חוטא, שנאמר והחוט המשולש לא במהרה ינתק. וכל שאינו לא במקרא ולא במשנה ולא בדרך ארץ אינו מן היישוב; and bar-Kappara in Kidd. 40 b ff.: וכל שאינו לא במקרא ולא במשנה ולא בדרך ארץ דור הנאה ממנו שנאמר ובמושב לצים לא ישב, מושבו מושב לצים, a man who knows Bible, Mishnah, and manners, does not easily sin; but he who knows none of those is not of civilization. Bar-Kappara advises total separation from such a man, as his company is that of a scoffer. See R. Eliezer b. Jacob in 2 ARN. 35, 44 a.

[2] In 2 ARN. 26, 27 b it is reported that Hillel once stood at the gate of Jerusalem, and asked some men who were going out to work, how much they would earn that day. On hearing the amount, he asked them how they would use the money; and on learning that they would spend it on their daily necessities, he asked them whether they would not come, acquire Torah, and thereby acquire life in this world and in the world to come. Hillel acted in this way throughout his life, and brought men under the wings of God. See further.

[3] Aboth, II, 7: מרבה בשר מרבה רמה מרבה נכסים מרבה דאגה מרבה נשים מרבה כשפים מרבה שפחות מרבה זמה מרבה עבדים מרבה גזל מרבה תורה מרבה חיים מרבה ישיבה מרבה חכמה מרבה עצה מרבה תבונה מרבה צדקה מרבה שלום קנה שם טוב קנה לעצמו קנה לו דברי תורה קנה לו חיי העולם הבא.

goal. But it must be kept in mind that the object of the ordinary man's attendance at the school of the rabbi was not to listen to the halakhic interpretation of the legal portions of the Pentateuch, nor to learn by heart the rules deduced; but only practical instruction of the kind evident in Hillel's sentences, to guide him gradually to an improvement of his moral and religious conduct. It was probably based on a full exposition of selected chapters of the Pentateuch like Lev. 19, applied to the requirements of daily life, and illustrated by the sayings and the lives of the patriarchs and the ancient leaders of Israel. By that method the ordinary man who attended the lessons only in the evening was taught first to avoid all that was wrong and sinful, and then the positive duties of the Jew towards his fellow-man, as Hillel understood and interpreted them. And it is, for a proper understanding of his teachings, of great importance to establish the class of men to which his words were addressed. He said,[1] 'He who increases flesh increases worms (in the grave), he who increases possessions increases care, he who increases wives increases witchcraft, he who increases maidservants increases immorality, he who increases slaves increases robbery.' We see here how some wealthy men of Jerusalem invested some of their substance in one or the other form of property, and enjoyed themselves, and showed to the outside world their wealth in the number of wives and of servants, and in their own physical appearance. Their ideal was purely gross materialism; and, by pointing to the dark sides of the various manifestations of wealth, Hillel endeavoured to deter the thinking man from making such objects the only goal of his life. The enumeration of the destructive results inherent in every one of them only served to enhance the contrast which follows: 'The more Torah, the more life; the more sitting, the more wisdom; the more counsel, the more understanding; the more charity, the more peace; he who has acquired a good name has acquired it for

[1] See note 3, p. 26.

himself; he who has acquired for himself words of Torah has acquired for himself life in the world-to-come'. When Hillel commended to the wealthy twice and in two different aspects the value of possessing Torah, he did not urge them to become scholars, but only to make the acquisition of Torah as important a task of their lives as that of riches. Knowledge will, in the first instance, have the great and desirable effect of prolonging their lives on earth; and secondly, by transforming their moral and religious standards of activity, it will procure for them a share in the future world. During life the greatest of treasures, peace, can be obtained by charity, which, at the same time, brings a lasting good name.[1]

4. The two terms used by Hillel for the two kinds of pious men, the sin-fearing and the saint, were employed also by his disciple R. Joḥanan b. Zakkai in his characterization of his five prominent disciples. 'He used thus to recount their praise: José the priest is a pious man, Simeon, the son of Nethanel, is a fearer of sin.'[2] It would be a mistake to think a sin-fearing man to be one of only a negative virtue, one who merely avoids sin, that is, the transgression of one of the prohibitions in the Pentateuch. For there is a reference to a chamber of the silent in the Temple, where sin-fearing persons privately deposited their contributions from which the poor of good families were

[1] Before these two there are mentioned as valuable objects wisdom and discretion which, compared with the rest, cannot mean scholarship, but, just as תבונה, practical wisdom, so often emphasized in the Book of Proverbs. Consequently, ישיבה by which it is acquired cannot mean, as the commentators suggest, keeping a school, but probably the sitting in the company of scholars or of men of culture, as in the sentence of R. Dosa b. Harkinas in Aboth, III, 10: ישיבת בתי כנסיות של עמי הארץ it is the sitting in the meeting-places of ignorant men.

[2] Aboth, II, 8: הוא היה מונה שבחן . . . רבי יוסי הכהן חסיד רבי שמעון בן נתנאל ירא חטא, in ARN. 14, 29 b: חסיד שבדור, Shabb. 19 a top, Baraitha: תנו רבנן . . . אמרו עליו על רבי יוסי הכהן ואמרי לה על רבי יוסי החסיד שלא נמצא כתב ידו ביד נכרי מעולם, Tos. Shabb. 13. 13; jer. I, 4 a. 70 only רבי יוסי הכהן.

secretly supported.[1] No doubt, those sin-fearing persons possessed some positive piety, not only that of charity, but other high qualities, as they in their acts of benevolence also observed one of the essential requirements of charity, the careful avoidance of publicity. Men who considered even the deposition of their gift in a collecting-box in the presence of others among whom possibly were some needy in receipt of support from that collection, a sin, must have had a high conception of the duty of helping the poor, and of the way in which even the shadow of an offence to his feelings should be avoided. The sin-fearing quality would then refer to the deliberate avoidance of an action that constituted an offence only for the very sensitive donor, but was for the average and observant Jew not approaching a sin. And the well-informed recorder of incidents of the last decades of Temple times, R. Jehudah b. Ilai, remarked of ʽAkabia b. Mahalalel, ‘God forbid that he should have been put in the ban! For the inner forecourt of the Temple never closed behind a man in Israel like ʽAkabia in learning and in the fear of sin’.[2] That R. Jehudah intended to describe that scholar as most learned and most pious, is clear from his exaggerated praise; and it is inadmissible to think merely of ʽAkabia's avoidance of sin, even if the latter were of a very subtle degree. And R. Joḥanan b. Zakkai himself was once asked, ‘If a man is learned and sin-fearing, to what could he be likened?’ He answered, ‘He is like a skilled workman with his tools in his hand; the learned man who is not sin-fearing is like

[1] Shekal. V, 6; Tos. II, 16: לשכת חשאים יראי חטא נותנים לתוכה בחשאי ועניים בני טובים מתפרנסים מתוכה בחשאי.

[2] ʽEduy. V, 6: שאין העזרה ננעלת בפני כל אדם מישראל בחכמה וביראת חטא כעקביא בן מהללאל. Cf. in the two Baraithas in Taʽan. 28 a, the description of the exploits of בני גונבי עלי ובני קוצעי קציעות, and of בני סלמאי הנתופתי, all of whom a third Baraitha declares identical: מה עשו יראי חטא שבאותו הדור, see Rabbinovicz. The parallel in jer. Taʽan. IV, 68 b. 55 has: כל מי שהיה כשר וירא חטא באותו הדור היה מביא את בכוריו ונותנן לתוך הסל . . .

a skilled workman without tools; a sin-fearing man who is not learned is like an unskilled man with tools in his hand'.[1] Again it is clearly the very pious man that is referred to, and, as the illustrations show, one that is not only guarding himself against sin, but one that is using his learning for carrying it into effect. The fear of sin is the tool with which the man who knows the law carries out the will of God: it is the religious readiness of the mind to realize the law. And as the tool of the skilled workman does visible, positive work, the fear of sin is actively carrying out positive commandments, and it is not merely passively refraining from transgressions.[2]

And R. Gamaliel II said to R. Joshua who, against his conviction, submitted on a point of the calendar to the ruling of the patriarch and, to signify his submission, appeared before him, 'Come in peace, my master, my disciple: my master in learning, my disciple in the fear of sin who carries out all that I order him to do'.[3] Here also the

[1] ARN. 22, 37 b: אמרו לפני רבן יוחנן בן זכאי חכם וירא חטא מהו. אמר להם הרי זה אומן וכלי אומנותו בידו. חכם ואין ירא חטא מהו. אמר להם הרי זה אומן ואין כלי אומנותו בידו. ירא חטא ואין חכם מהו. אמר להם אין זה אומן אבל כלי אומנותו בידו. A contemporary of R. Joḥanan b. Zakkai, R. Ḥaninah b. Dosa in Aboth, III, 9, says, He in whom the fear of sin comes before learning, his learning shall endure; but he in whom learning comes before the fear of sin, his learning will not endure. Cf. the sentence of R. Eleazar b. 'Azariah in Aboth, III, 17, Agad. Shir. Hashir. Schechter, line 26; Bacher, I, 222. 1; and ARN. 29, 45 a: R. Isaac b. Pinḥas said, He who possesses a knowledge of Midrash, but not of the rules deduced by it has not tasted of learning; in the reverse case he has not tasted of the fear of sin.

[2] In the parallel in 2 ARN. 31, 34 a, instead of the sin-fearing man appears one who has done good deeds; accordingly, the sin-fearing man is one who practises loving-kindness towards his fellow-man.

[3] jer. Rosh haShan. II, 58 b. 55: בוא בשלום רבי ותלמידי רבי בחכמה ותלמידי ביראת חטא, רבי בחכמה ותלמידי, שכל מה שאני גוזר עליו הוא מקיים, the text has not been preserved intact. In the parallel Mishnah, II, 9, it reads only: רבי ותלמידי רבי בחכמה ותלמידי שקבלת עליך את דבריי, nor has the Baraitha in RH. 25 b the fear of sin. In ARN. 26, 41 b, R. Akiba says: סייג לקדושה טהרה, סייג לענוה יראת חטא, in the parallel 2 ARN. 33, 36 a that part is missing.

fear of sin is explained as the active execution of positive orders, as suggested by the previous passages, and there is no trace of an avoidance of prohibited things. Again, in the sad picture of the years that will immediately precede the coming of the Messiah, R. Gamaliel II says, 'The learning of the scholars will be corrupted, and the sin-fearing men will be despised';[1] meaning clearly such as distinguish themselves by a life strictly in accordance with the will of God, in which the fulfilment of the positive commandments of the Torah naturally occupies a more prominent place than the refraining from the transgression of prohibitions. And also another teacher of the same period, between 90 and 135, used the same term to describe the very pious man. When Moses said to Joshua, 'Choose for us *men*' (to fight against Amalek), he meant according to R. Joshua mighty men, but according to R. Eleazar of Mode'im they were to be sin-fearing men.[2] The idea of the latter rabbi was that it was not might that won the war, but piety;[3] as R. Eleazar himself, during the siege of Betthar, prayed, in sackcloth and in ashes, for the success-

[1] Derekh ereṣ zuta, X; in Synh. 97 a R. Jehudah appears as the author, evidently the name of R. Gamaliel in whose name he handed down this sentence, as several others, has fallen out; anonymous in Sotah, IX, 15; Bacher, I, 92. 3: וחכמת סופרים תסרח ויראי חטא ימאסו ופני הדור כפני כלב. See also R. José's statement about the appointment of judges to the various courts in Temple times in Tos. Synh. VII, 1: ומשם שולחין ובודקין כל מי שהוא חכם ושפוי ויירא חטא ופרק טוב ורוח הבריות נוחה הימנו עושין אותו דיין בעירו, when they found a learned, calm, and sin-fearing man with an untainted youth and liked by the people, they appointed him judge in his own town. The parallel in jer. Synh. I, 19 c. 33 reads: חכם עניו שפוי עין טובה נפש שפלה רוח נמוכה לב טוב יצר טוב חלק טוב, qualifying the man to become a judge of the lowest court on the Temple Mount; b. 88 b.

[2] Mekhil. 17. 9, 53 b: בחר לנו אנשים, רבי יהושע אומר בחר לנו אנשים גבורים, רבי אלעזר המודעי אומר בחר לנו יראי חטא, cf. Sifré Deut. 323; Midr. Tan. Deut. 32. 33, 200

[3] Cf. Sifré Num. 157, 59 a ff.: וימסרו מאלפי ישראל . . . רבי נתן אומר אחרים מכ׳.ם, איש פלוני כשר יצא למלחמה איש פלוני צדיק יצא למלחמה.

ful defence of the fortress by bar-Kokhba.[1] Very instructive is the way in which an anonymous colleague of R. Eliezer and R. Ishmael rendered the fear of the Lord in the Bible by the fear of sin.[2] Though it is, therefore, clear that the sin-fearing man was as pious as the חסיד, as he also was faithfully practising God's positive commandments, it is certain that there was some difference between them. For not only did R. Joḥanan b. Zakkai call one of his disciples sin-fearing and another a saint, but in one sentence [3] R. Joḥanan b. Nuri is described as a man of the fear of sin, and ben-'Azzai as one of piety.[4] And in the list of R. Pinḥas b. Yair, which will be considered below, humility leads to the fear of sin, and this to saintliness; so that the first is

[1] jer. Ta'an. IV, 68 d. 60.

[2] Midrash Tannaim Deut. 14. 23, 77 ff.: למען תלמד ליראה את ה׳, מגיד שהמעשרות מביאין את האדם לידי יראת חטא. The same rendering is found in jer. Sotah, V, 20 c. 39 of Deut. 10. 20: . . . את ה׳ אלהיך תירא עשה מיראה שאם באתה לבעט אין ירא מבעט, 'fear the Lord thy God', do so from the fear of God, so that, if thou shouldst feel tempted to kick against Him, a sin-fearing man does not kick against God. So also in the explanation of the sentence of R. Pinḥas b. Yair, the fear of the Lord is rendered by R. Isaac by fear of sin in jer. Shekal. III. 47 c. 68; Midr. Tannaim Deut. 23. 15, 148. In Baraitha Nedar. 20 a bottom, Mekhil. 20. 20, 72 a: תניא בעבור תהיה יראתו על פניכם לבלתי תחטאו, מלמד שהבושה מביאה לידי יראת חטא, 'in order that His fear may be on your faces, that ye sin not': that teaches us that shame leads to the fear of sin; the fear of God is rendered by בושה, and לבלתי תחטאו by the fear of sin.

[3] ARN. 40, 64 b; here the book of Psalms is stated to indicate humility, in 2 ARN. 46, 64 b, fear of sin, and R. Akiba is described as sin-fearing, in 65 a ben-Zoma.

[4] In פרקי רבינו הקדוש, ed. Grünhut, 33: שבעה דברים צוה רבינו הקדוש את בנו שלשה על יראת חטא וארבעה על דרך ארץ. של יראת חטא אמר לו אל תישן על מטתך עד שתקרא את שמע ותתפלל ואל תכנס באחרונה לבית המדרש ואל תשב לאכול בשבת עד שתגמור את הפרשה, the three things of יראת חטא which Rabbi is alleged to have ordered his son to obey, refer to prayers, to the reading of the weekly portion of the Torah, and to the attendance at the school. But what has it to do with the fear of sin? See Friedmann's Mekhil. 121 a.

only preparatory for the second.[1] The identity of the fear of sin with the fear of God suggests that the first referred to the very strict observance of the duties expressing the honour, love, and worship of God, while, as was shown above, the חסיד was most particular in the practice of the love of man; but both, it is understood, observed conscientiously all the commandments to be kept.

A few instances of such strictness observed by the pious are specially recorded. The ancient pious men fixed the blue cord of the fringes, prescribed in Num. 15. 38, as soon as the cloth for the garment woven had reached the breadth of three fingers, and they did not wait till it was finished.[2] The same are reported to have had marital intercourse only on Wednesdays, so that their wives should not, at childbirth, come to the necessity of a desecration of the Sabbath.[3] Such scrupulousness in the observance of the Sabbath was considered by some scholars a peculiarity of the Essenes, so that they identified the pious men with the Essenes.[4] Rabbinic law permitted without hesitation any action or work to be performed on the Sabbath in order to avert any danger to a human life, to assist a woman in childbirth, or to kill poisonous snakes. But, just as the stricter Jews in 1 Macc. 2. 35 ff. would not defend themselves on the Sabbath against the attacks of a Syrian army, so the ancient pious men tried to obviate, if at all possible, a desecration of the Sabbath; but they would still, if the necessity arose, assist their wives in every way on the

[1] It is true that the Tractate known as דרך ארץ זוטא, and containing high ethical rules for the conduct of scholars, was in the tenth century quoted by Joseph Kirkisani as יראת חטא, but in 2 ARN. 26, 26 b as מגלת חסידים (see Abrahams in *J. Q. R.*, X, 1898, 660 and in Steinschneider's *Festschrift*, 75), which would show the identity of חסיד and ירא חטא. See also Poznański in *MGWJ*. 61, 1917, 229 ff.

[2] Menaḥ. 40 b.

[3] Niddah 38 a ff.

[4] See a later instance in Shabb. 121 b: The scholar employed in the school of the Babylonian teacher Rabha b. R. Huna to cite Baraithas bearing on the subject just under discussion, once quoted a Baraitha of an unknown date, Of him who kills serpents and scorpions on the Sabbath the pious men do not approve.

Sabbath, as permitted by the law. In neither case is there a trace of Essenes or Essenic observance. And the same applies to the strictness of the pious men in the case of the early fixing of the fringes; for nothing whatever is known of any special rigour of the Essenes in the practice just of that commandment. It is true, Abba Saul b. Batnith whom Dr. Kohler without any justification, only on account of his title, declares to have been an Essene,[1] or his father, wore on his garment the blue thread of the fringes, and asked his children to remove it after his death.[2] But did not his friend, R. Eleazar b. R. Ṣadok, report expressly[3] that only very few men in Jerusalem had fixed the blue thread to their *linen* garments, clearly implying that on woollen garments many, certainly every teacher, wore the blue thread? And did not the schools of the Shammaites and the Hillelites in Jerusalem deal with the details of the law concerning the fringes?[4] Were they all Essenes? Besides the two observances mentioned, only the strict practices of two pious priests are recorded. José b. Joëzer[5] who is described as חסיד שבכהונה observed the rules of levitical purity very conscientiously.[6] As in connexion with their

[1] *J.Q.R.*, XIII, 1901, 572 ff.

[2] Semaḥ. XII; מסכת ציצית, ed. Kirchheim, 23: אין מתירין ציצית על המת. אבא שאול בן בטנית אומר אבא אמר לי כשאמות התר לי ציציות שיש בה משום קדושה. וחכמים אומרים אין בה משום קדושה אלא עושה אותה תכריך למת ומרדעות לחמור. Kirchheim refers to the variants in Naḥmani's תורת האדם, ed. Venezia 32 c bottom: אבא שאול בן בטנית מתיר. אמר אבא שאול. . . Cf. Derenbourg, *Essai*, 172.

[3] Menaḥ. 40 a.

[4] Sifré Num. 115, 34 a; Menaḥ. 40 a, 41 b.

[5] Ḥagigah II, 7.

[6] In 'Eduy. VIII. 4 the evidence of R. José b. Joëzer on three points of levitical purity is recorded. As not only his name and that of his father, but that of his place are the same as those of José b. Joëzer of Ṣeredah of the Maccabean rising in Aboth, I, 4, scholars identify the two and also that in Ḥagigah II, 7. Against the identification should be considered (1) the place of his evidence in the list of the evidence of scholars who appeared before the school in Jamnia about the year 100, among them a few who had survived the destruction of the Temple; (2) the title of rabbi attached to the name of José b. Joëzer in the Cambridge Mishnah and many early editions (see Rabbinovicz). Kohler in *Jew. Encyclop.*,

sacrificial meals, taken within the Temple, all priests had to observe those rules, it is not clear in what José's strictness consisted. In their homes, the priests, as far as is known, did not apply the same levitical laws to their ordinary food. The rabbis, however, required the priests to handle their heave offering, תרומה, given to them of various kinds of produce by the farmers, as being of a holy character, also at home in due levitical purity. José b. Joëzer not only submitted to such strictness, but guarded even his ordinary food in ever higher purity, and was, for that observance, called a pious man among the priests. This interpretation of his rigour is borne out by the instance of the intended strict observance of levitical purity by a noble, but ignorant priest who lived in the days of R. Joḥanan b. Zakkai in Ramath-beth-ʿAnath. Sent by his master, R. Joshua went to see the ways of that priest who, by keeping the rules of levitical purity in connexion with his heave offering, is stated to have behaved as a pious man. The scholar entered into a conversation with him about the pertinent rules of a pious man, meaning those of levitical purity, and soon established the priest's ignorance even of the relevant biblical law.[1]

5. On the evidence just adduced the question could reasonably be founded as to whether Hillel was not called a pious man on account of his strict observance of the law

V, 225 b, quotes the Mishnah about the ancient Ḥasids: 'Especially rigorous were they in regard to Levitical purity.' But strange to say, the passage deals not with what José b. Joëzer observed, but with the purity *not* observed in certain instances in the Temple; and, as his evidence was throughout testifying to leniency, the scholars called him José the permitting teacher. How could this be quoted as an instance of rigour in levitical purity? Cf. J. Levy in אוצר נחמד, III, 1860, 29.

[1] ARN. 12, 28 b: שהיה נוהג בעצמו מדת חסידות, or, as another version quoted by Schechter in note 77 reads: שנהג סלסול בעצמו ומדת פרישות. In 2 ARN. 27, 28 b: והלך רבי יהושע לדבר עמו והיו עוסקים בהלכות חסידים, see also the wording p. 72 a top. It may be added here that in such strictness there is no trace of Essenic observance, as assumed by Z. Frankel in *Zeitschrift für die relig. Interessen des Judenthums*, III, 1846, 454, and by Geiger in *Jüd. ZS.*, IX, 1871, 54; see Derenbourg, *Essai*, 166.

of levitical purity, and not for his conduct towards his fellow man, his trust in God, and his cultivation of his soul and his body. But apart from the fact that the two incidents quoted concerned priests and the priestly food, and Hillel was not a priest, only academic discussions of his about points of levitical purity,[1] but not a single practical occurrence of that nature, are reported. And, in addition, it is sufficient to remember the juxtaposition of the two adjectives עניו חסיד describing Hillel, to cause us to admit that the quality denoted by the second word was closely related to his humility; as also in the sentence of R. Pinḥas b. Yair, humility leads to the fear of sin, this to piety, and this to the holy spirit of which, as we have seen, a heavenly voice declared Hillel worthy. Again, the few references preserved to the practical conduct of pious men in the first century and the first half of the second century in no case deal with the observance of levitical purity, though by that time it had begun to be adopted by a few non-priests. A pious man bought an article from one of two men both of whom claimed the purchase-money, but he himself did not know from which of them he had obtained the goods. R. Tarfon, before whom he brought the case, advised him to put the money in front of both claimants, and to withdraw. The man then went to R. Akiba who replied, 'There is no other remedy for you but to pay both claimants.' R. Tarfon's decision which exempted the purchaser from double payment was, no doubt, based on strict law, but evidently did not satisfy the conscience of the pious man, and so he submitted his scruples to another authority. As the opening words of his judgment, אין לך תקנה show, R. Akiba did not base it on strict law, but went beyond its letter, and satisfied the scruples of the pious man.[2] A man was clearing his field of stones

[1] Shabb. 15 a; 17 a.

[2] Baraitha Baba kam. 103 b. The judgment reminds us of Tos. Shebu'oth III, 1; jer. Baba kam. VI, 5 b. 38; b. 55 b. bottom, Baraitha: R. Joshua says, 'In four cases a man need not, by law, pay compensation, but God will not forgive him till he has paid such.' There is again

which he threw into the main road. A pious man who passed by and saw his action asked him why he threw stones from the field which was not his into land which was his; indicating thereby that, as a punishment, he would soon lose his property.[1] From the discussion of the matter in the Tosiftha we learn that, unlike R. Akiba, R. Joshua declared the procedure followed by that farmer permissible; and, it seems, the accepted rule did not prohibit the landowners from throwing the stones, removed from their fields, into the main road. But the pious man did not point to any law that could be enforced by the authorities, but warned the moral trespasser on a purely moral consideration of the eventual danger arising for the users of the road; and as human punishment was not warranted by the law, he prophesied to him a severe visitation by God in the form of the loss of his property. So the Ḥasid not only acted himself beyond the requirements of the law, even when it implied a monetary loss, but whenever the welfare of the fellow-man was concerned, expected others also, and tried to persuade them, to follow the same principle. The same rule underlies the action of the ancient pious men who hid thorns and glass in the soil of their fields three hand-breadths deep, so that the ploughshare might not be hindered,[2] or, as the better wording of the passage has it, that the ploughshare should not bring those up to the surface (and cause damage or injury).[3] The consideration, even regarding one's own property, of

nothing Essenic in that principle; it represents a point of view in the application of civil law, which the rabbis termed לפנים משורת הדין, as beyond the line of law, and which, according to R. Eleazar of Mode'im, Jethro advised Moses to teach the children of Israel, Mekhil. 59 b on Exod. 18. 20; Baba kam. 99 b. ff. What Dr. Kohler in Berliner's *Festschrift*, 199 ff., without any evidence assigns to the Essenes, would lead this discussion too far.

[1] Baraitha Baba kam. 50 b top; Tos. II, 13.

[2] Baraitha Baba kam. 30 a; Tos. II, 6.

[3] Jer. Baba kam. III, 3 c. 44; cf. Midr. Samuel on 2 Sam. 7. 5, 63 a the Baraitha. A virgin field is one that has never yet been cultivated; R. Simeon b. Gamaliel says, One in which there is no potsherd.

possible harm to others made the pious man act more strictly than the adopted custom demanded.[1] An anonymous Mishnah[2] enumerates four different characters of men: 'One who says, What is mine is mine, and what is thine is thine, his is a neutral character; some say, this is a character like that of Sodom. He who says, What is mine is thine, and what is thine is mine, is an 'Am-ha'areṣ; he who says, What is mine is thine, and what is thine is thine, is a pious man; he who says, What is thine is mine, and what is mine is mine, is a wicked man.' We see that one and the same action, attitude or declaration may be judged by two different standards, one being that of everyday life, the other that of high morality. As long as an action is not encroaching on the neighbour's interest, the first mentioned standard terms it indifferent; to call it an average action, is already above commercial and legal morality. Hillel's standard, on the other hand, was, 'If I am only for myself, what am I?'[3] It is man's bounden duty to place himself and all his belongings at the service of his fellow-man, so that the rule, 'What is mine is mine', though legally correct, is not only selfish, but wrong to the degree of Sodom's selfishness. In the opposite statement, 'What is mine is thine, and what is thine is thine', where a man not only claims no benefit from his neighbour, but places his own property at his disposal, the principle is that of the

[1] In the middle of the third century, R. Joshua b. Levi defended before Elijah the prophet his extradition of a Jew who had fled to Lydda, resolved only in order to save the city from the enemy; he had based his action on the Mishnah Tos. Terum. VII, 20; jer. VIII, 46 b. 45, but the prophet retorted, Is it a Mishnah of the pious men? (jer. Terum. VIII, 46 b. 50; Gen. r. 94 end, Bacher, *Pal. Amoraër I*, 188 ff.; Friedmann, Hebrew Introduction to his *Seder Eliahu*, 48). In his conduct towards a fellow-man, a rabbi must not follow the letter of the law laid down in a Baraitha, but must act in accordance with the highest principles of humanity taught and practised by the pious men.

[2] Aboth, V, 10.

[3] If it might be assumed that the sentence in 2 ARN. 27, 28 a top, 'Since that which I possess is not mine, what for do I require that which belongs to others?' was Hillel's (see Schechter's note, and G. Klein, *Der älteste christl. Katechismus*, 87), the beautiful principle would account for his unselfishness.

חסיד. As Hillel was admittedly no Essene, there is not the slightest foundation for looking in the Ḥasid for an Essene; it was nothing but high Jewish morality, as expressed by Hillel in his sentence, consistently applied.

Another anonymous Mishnah[1] says: 'There are four kinds of tempers: he whom it is easy to provoke and easy to pacify, his loss disappears in his gain; he whom it is hard to provoke and hard to pacify, his gain disappears in his loss; he whom it is hard to provoke and easy to pacify is a חסיד; he whom it is easy to provoke and hard to pacify is a wicked man.' Taking Hillel's meekness and his deliberate resistance to provocation as the standard, we find here an additional reason why also from this point of view he was rightly called a pious man; just as the directly opposite disposition and the failure of deliberate self-control stamped a man as a sinner. At the same time it is evident that for his mere natural disposition no man could justly deserve to be called pious or wicked; but it is his deliberate and active self-control that constituted the merit, as the deliberate neglect of its application formed the sin. In the next anonymous Mishnah[2] the principle underlying the use of the same two terms is not at all clear. It says: 'As to almsgiving there are four dispositions: he who desires to give, but that others should not give, his eye is evil towards what appertains to others; he who desires that others should give, but will not give himself, his eye is evil against what is his own; he who gives and wishes others to give is a Ḥasid; he who will not give and does not wish others to give is a wicked man.' In rendering the explanations given by the Jewish commentators, Professor Taylor says,[3] 'The first character has an evil or grudging eye with respect to the things of others. He is unwilling that they should share with him the credit of liberality, or he is a misanthrope who is jealous lest his neighbours' possessions should be blessed

[1] Aboth, V, 11. [2] Ibid., V, 13. [3] *Sayings*², 90.

by their almsgiving, and lest they should enjoy favour with God and man. The truly liberal, on the contrary, is he who "counsels" liberal things (Isa. 32. 8): who is not only liberal himself, but moves others to be so (Abarbanel).' In fact, however, there is no need for interpretations introducing foreign thought, as the two middle parts expressly state grudge to be the only source of the man's conduct. When a poor man appeals for assistance to one person in the presence of others, say in the synagogue or the school, the person appealed to recognizes the claim to apply not only to him, but to all present, and gives himself and induces the others to contribute; this is the pious, truly charitable man. But if he refuses help himself, and even dissuades others from giving, he is wicked. If he himself supports the poor man, but thinks his own assistance to be sufficient, so that the money of others would be wasted, he is grudging the poor the help of others; in the reverse case, when he allows him to receive only the money of others, and grudges him his own assistance, his meanness refers to his own support. But even with this plain interpretation of the sentence, it is not evident why his slight consideration for the helpless fellow-man should be sufficient to merit for him the distinctive name of a Ḥasid. And even more difficult is it in the next Mishnah,[1] 'There are four characters among those who attend the house of study: he who goes and does not practise secures the reward for going; he who practises, but does not go, secures the reward for practising; he who goes and practises is a Ḥasid; he who neither goes nor practises is a wicked man.' Even the mere attendance at the house of learning is accounted meritorious; for, by listening to the teaching, he receives useful guidance for his moral and religious conduct, and its effect will in the end not fail, though, for the present, he evinces no inclination to realize the principles of conduct taught there. But if he keeps away from the school altogether, he exhibits an attitude of slighting or even contempt for its spirit; and by

[1] Aboth, V, 14.

adding the failure of practice, he deliberately turns away from the religious tendency represented by the school, and proves himself a sinner. Attendance and practice prove him a pious man. Though here, naturally, the conduct towards the fellow-man is not referred to, the sentence could still be understood as dealing with such conduct, as the subject of instruction in the school, as suggested above (p. 27), was, in the first instance, morality applied to practical life. But apart from the fact that the plain wording does not justify such an interpretation, Dr. Hoffmann[1] has shown from the text of the Mishnah Aboth underlying Aboth di R. Nathan that V, 10 was the last paragraph of Aboth known to the author of that midrashic commentary, and all subsequent parts of the chapter were later additions. After the year 135, the rabbis made an extensive use of the term חסיד, and, in imitation of earlier sentences composed before that year in the schools of Judaea, formed new rules in which חסיד merely designated a good, law-abiding man who conscientiously practised the moral duties.[2] All this tends to confirm the result of the previous examination that חסיד designated Hillel as a man filled with true love to his fellow-man.

[1] *Die erste Mischna*, 27–31, especially p. 28.

[2] Of a different kind appears to be the case reported in Baraitha Baba kam. 80 a, referred to above, p. 17, about a Ḥasid who coughed blood, and was advised by the physicians to drink naturally warm milk every morning. Against the rabbinic prohibition that declared sheep and goats robbers of other men's plantations (see Büchler, *'Am-ha'areṣ*, 191 ff.), he kept a goat tied to his bed; and on his death-bed he stated that that was the only sin of which he was conscious, and his fellow scholars also admitted that he was free from any other sin. Whether his comparative sinlessness earned him the title of a Ḥasid, is not stated. It was mentioned above that the name of the scholar given in Tos. Baba kam. VIII, 13, cf. Themur. 15 b, R. Jehudah b. Baba, is incorrect, though it is stated here that all his deeds were in the honour of God, as in Tos. Sotah XIII, 4; jer. IX, 24 b. 39; b. 48 b, and that he was to be bewailed in the same words as Hillel as humble and pious. His sin was committed against a rabbinic decree, which, in the case of a scholar, was considered very grave. When imprisoned by the Roman authorities in Caesarea, R. Akiba would rather die from thirst than eat without having before washed his hands, and thereby act against the view adopted by his colleagues, 'Erub. 21 b.

6. As in the definition of the Ḥasid and of the sin-fearing man reference had several times to be made to the sentence of R. Pinḥas b. Yair on the gradual acquisition of humility and piety; and as its contents throw important light on the whole question of the Ḥasid, though its author taught in the second half of the second century, a short analysis of his statement will be useful. It reads:[1] 'Care leads to cleanness, this to purity, this to holiness, this to humility, this to the fear of sin, this to piety, this to the holy spirit, this to the quickening of the dead, and this to Elijah the prophet.' This is preceded by a Baraitha: 'Keep thee from every evil thing' (Deut. 23. 10) warns us to suppress in the daytime every thought of a sexual nature, so that no pollution should ensue in the night; hence R. Pinḥas b. Yair inferred, &c. Granted that this was his starting-point for the whole sentence, is the list of the various graduated virtues in agreement with that warning, and is the meaning of each link clear? And if, by following faithfully the instruction of R. Pinḥas, anybody can, by self-control and self-education, attain to holiness, what does such holiness that leads up to humility really represent?

[1] Midr. Tannaim Deut. 23. 15, 148; jer. Shekal. III, 47 c. 59; Cant. r. 1. 1. 9; Midr. Prov. 15. 32, 41 a; Sotah IX, end; 'Ab. zar. 20 b, see Rabbinovicz: מיכן היה רבי פנחס בן יאיר אומר זריזות מביאה לידי נקיות נקיות מביאה לידי טהרה טהרה מביאה לידי קדושה קדושה מביאה לידי ענוה ענוה מביאה לידי יראת חטא יראת חטא מביאה לידי חסידות חסידות מביאה לידי רוח הקדש רוח הקדש מביא לידי תחיית המתים תחיית המתים מביאה לידי אליהו ז״ל. In Sotah only in the editions, but not in the Cambridge Mishnah (in the text of the Mishnah of the Palestinian Talmud the whole sentence is missing), there is an additional link: וטהרה מביאה לידי פרישות ופרישות מביאה לידי קדושה, b. has it between נקיות and טהרה. The introductory word מיכן does not refer to והצנע לכת עם אלהיך quoted immediately before from Micah 6. 8, but, as it is expressly stated in b., to Deut. 23. 10: תנו רבנן ונשמרת מכל דבר רע, שלא יהרהר אדם ביום ויבא לידי טומאה בלילה מכאן אמר רבי פנחס בן יאיר תורה מביאה לידי זהירות זהירות מביאה לידי זריזות . . , and to the whole group of verses interpreted in Midr. Tannaim. Cf. Ḥull. 37 b; Grünhut, ספר הלקוטים, II, 20 b, note; ס׳ האורה, 3.

Should not the sequence more naturally be reversed? and even so, how can the preparatory steps enumerated bring a man to either quality of character? Or did R. Pinḥas address himself to a class of men specially trained in the preliminary qualities, e.g. the Essenes, and could only such hope to attain to those distinctions of holy men? As far as the scanty material in rabbinic literature at my disposal suggests, holiness commended to be striven for or actually practised referred to sexual life. To the question of some Alexandrian Jews, what a man should do to obtain male children, R. Joshua b. Ḥananiah replied, 'Let him marry a wife worthy of him, and let him sanctify himself during his marital intercourse.[1]' He did not, however, explain his meaning,[2] though it is clear that he recommended chastity; as his colleague, R. Gamaliel II, stated that he liked the chastity of the Persians observed at three actions: at their meals, when easying their bodies, and at their marital intercourse.[3] Unfortunately, other remarks on this feature

[1] Baraitha Nidd. 70 b: מה יעשה אדם ויהיו לו בנים זכרים, אמר להן ישא אשה ההוגנת לו ויקדש עצמו בשעת תשמיש, cf. Shebu'ōth 18 b: אמר רבי בנימין בר יפת אמר רבי אלעזר כל המקדש את עצמו בשעת תשמיש הויין לו בנים זכרים שנאמר והתקדשתם והייתם קדושים וסמיך ליה אשה כי תזריע.

[2] An anonymous statement in Tanḥ. נשוא, B. 13: כל אשה שמתייחדה עם בעלה בקדושה describes a woman who, during her marital intercourse, thinks of no other man but her husband, as having with him intercourse in holiness. Compare the precautions of R. Eliezer in Baraitha Nedar. 20 b top, to prevent himself from thinking of another woman, as such *thought* would stamp his children as born in adultery. Note his idea of adultery committed by a mere thought; his colleague R. Joshua may have meant the same. See also Baraitha Baba meṣ. 107 b: תנו רבנן י״ג דברים נאמרו בפת שחרית. . . ונזקק לאשתו ואינו מתאוה לאשה אחרת. . .

[3] Baraitha Berakh. 8 b: תניא אמר רבן גמליאל בשלשה דברים אוהב אני את הפרסיים הן צנועין באכילתן וצנועין בבית הכסא וצנועין בדבר אחר. This is explained in Kethub. 48 a to mean that they performed it dressed, as the wife of R. Eliezer said of her husband in Nedar. 20 b, מגלה טפח ומכסה טפח, which is explained by Asheri as avoiding קירוב בשר contact of the bodies, as in Kethub. 48 a: תני רב יוסף שארה זו קרוב בשר שלא ינהג בה מנהג פרסיים שמשמשין מטותיהן בלבושיהן, and as it is reported of R. José b. Ḥalaftha in jer. Yebam. I, 2 b. 12: סדין בעל ודרך סדין where

of holiness designated by the word קדש belong to the middle of the third century;[1] but as the underlying ideas are, as will be seen, the same as those in the earlier statements, a reference to them will be useful.[2] R. Joshua b.

means the sheet, as in Nidd. 5 a top. In Nidd. 16 b ff. R. Simeon b. Yoḥai says, 'There are four things which God hates and I do not like: him who enters his house unexpectedly, and all the more his neighbour's house,' והאוחז באמה ומשתין מים ומשתין מים ערום לפני מטתו והמשמש מטתו בפני כל חי. The last sentence reads in some texts (see Tosafoth s.v. משתין) והמשמש מטתו ערום, cf. פרקי רבינו הקדוש, ed. Grünhut 47: אמר רבי שמעון בן יוחאי שלשה שהקב"ה שונאן ואני איני אוהבן המשמש מטתו ערום והאוחז באמתו ומשתין והאומר דברים שבינו לבין אשתו, p. 41: שלשה דברים שאין הגוים נהנין מהן . . . וכשהן משמשין פושטין את בגדיהם ומשמשים לפיכך אין נהנין. The word צנוע 'chaste', is a synonym of קדוש, see below; but in jer. Berakh. II, 5 b. 56 R. José described R. Meir to the inhabitants of Sepphoris as אדם גדול אדם קדוש אדם צנוע, both words being applied to him, while the parallel passage in Gen. r. 100. 7 has only אדם קדוש, see Bacher, *Tannaiten*, II, 5. 1. In Gen. r. 33. 3 the patriarch Jehudah I praised R. Ḥiyya as a great and holy man.

[1] Already Testam. Joseph, 4. 1 has: 'Often therefore did she flatter me with words as a holy man, and guilefully in her talk praise my chastity before her husband, while desiring to ensnare me when we were alone.'

[2] Jer. Yebam. II, 3 d. 24: אמר רבי יודה בן פזי ולמה סמך הכתוב פרשת עריות לפרשת קידושין, ללמדך שכל מי שהוא פורש מן העריות נקרא קדוש שכן שונמית אומרת לאישה הנה נא ידעתי כי איש אלהים קדוש הוא, אמר רבי יונה קדוש הוא ואין תלמידו קדוש, רבי אבין אמר שלא הביט בה, ורבנן אמרין שלא ראה טיפת קרי מימיו. אמתיה דרבי שמואל בר רב יצחק אמרה מן יומוי לא חמית מילה בישא על מנוי דמרי. In the parallel in Lev. r. 24. 6: אמר רבי יהודה בן פזי מפני מה נסמכה פרשת עריות לפרשת קדושים, אלא ללמדך שכל מקום שאתה מוצא בו גדר ערוה אתה מוצא קדושה, ואתיא כהדא דרבי יהודה בן פזי דאמר כל מי שהוא גודר עצמו מן הערוה נקרא קדוש. רבי יהושע בן לוי מייתי מן שונמית . . . אמר רבי יהושע בן לוי מפני מה נסמכה פרשת עריות לפרשת קדושים, אלא ללמדך שכל מקום שאתה מוצא גדר ערוה אתה מוצא קדושה ואית ליה קריין סגיין . . .; the parallel in Berakh. 10 b: מנא ידעה, רב ושמואל חד אמר שלא ראתה זבוב עובר על שולחנו וחד אמר סדין של פשתן הציעה על מטתו ולא ראתה קרי עליו. In Gen. r. 98. 4; Agg. Gen. 82. 1; Tanḥ. ויחי, 9; Yebam. 76 a, Jacob said to his son Reuben, I am eighty-four years old ולא ראיתי טפת קרי.

Levi says, 'Why are the chapters about prohibited intercourse (Lev. 18) and holiness (Lev. 19) put close to each other? To teach us that where we find a guard against immorality, we find holiness; and there are many passages in the Bible to prove it. R. Jehudah b. Pazzi in the name of R. Joshua b. Levi says, Whoever separates himself from immorality is termed holy, as the Shunammite woman called Elisha a holy man of God in 2 Reg. 4. 9.' An older contemporary of R. Joshua b. Levi, the Babylonian scholar Samuel, says that she called the prophet holy, because she had never noticed a stain of semen on his sheet; and a later Amora, R. Abin, suggests as the reason, because he had never looked at her.

But it is of importance for our examination that already a Baraitha dealt with the prohibition to look at women, and suggested the reason of it: 'Keep thee from every evil thing (Deut 23. 10): one should not look at a fair woman, even if she is unmarried, nor at a married woman, even if she is ugly, nor at the coloured dress of a woman, nor at an ass, a swine, or a fowl, when they are pairing.'[1] While we learn incidentally from an illustration of R. Gamaliel II

[1] 'Abod. zar. 20 a, b; Midr. Tann. Deut. 23.10, 147: מיתיבי ונשמרת מכל דבר רע, שלא יסתכל אדם באשה נאה ואפילו פנויה באשת איש ואפילו מכוערת ולא בבגדי צבע של אשה ולא בחמור ולא בחמורה ולא בחזיר ולא בחזירה ולא בעופות בזמן שנזקקין זה לזה ואפילו מלא עינים כמלאך המות. In jer. 'AZ. I, 40 a. 73; b. 20 a, a Baraitha reports how R. (Simeon b.) Gamaliel I, when he once saw a beautiful non-Jewish woman on the Temple Mount, spoke a blessing over her; the Talmud is surprised that he should have looked at a woman. Joseph in Egypt would not look at the princesses who threw rings and ornaments at him to attract his attention, and God rewarded him for it, Gen. r. 98. 18. Two Babylonian disciples of R. Joḥanan in Tiberias, R. Ḥaninah and R. Osha'ia, were bootmakers, and worked for immoral women; when the latter looked at them, the scholars did not raise their eyes to look at the women. For this they were called in Babylonia רבנן קדישי 'the holy scholars of Palestine', Pesaḥ. 113 b top; Bacher, *Paläst. Amoräer*, III, 551. 1. In פרקי רבינו הקדוש, ed. Grünhut, 37: משום שמואל הקטן אמר לו ואם בקשת לישמר מכל דבר רע אל תסתכל באשה נאה ולא באשה המקושטת בבלי צבעונין ולא בבהמה חיה ועוף בשעה שנזקקין זה לזה.

that in his time, about the year 100, nobody looked at a married woman,[1] but anybody at an unmarried one,[2] the honour of women demanded it that they should not be looked at by men.[3] In explanation of Job 31. 1 it is specially stated that Job imposed upon himself the strict moral obligation, not even to look at a girl.[4] If a man counts money into the hand of a woman or from her hand into his, in order to look at her, even if he be like Moses who received the Torah on Sinai, he will not escape the punishment of hell.[5] R. Aḥai b. Joshiah said, 'He who looks at women will, in the end, come to immorality; and he who looks at the heel of a woman will have unworthy children'.[6] The reason is here clearly stated: it is to pre-

[1] Tos. Kidd. I, 11; in jer. Ḥagigah, II, 77 d. 38 ff., in a legendary report, R. Jehudah b. Tabbai blamed his disciple for having looked at the married woman with whom they were staying in Alexandria. Cf. Brüll, *Jahrbücher*, III, 52, note 129, and Midr. Cant. ed. Grünhut 4 b.

[2] R. Matthia b. Ḥarash was a God-fearing rabbi who never looked at a married, nor even at any other woman, Tanḥuma Num. B. p. 66 a; Midr. Abkir, 11, § 30; Gaster, ס׳ מעשיות, 93 ff.; Bacher, *Tannaiten*, I, 384. 3.

[3] Jer. Synh. II, 20 b. 44 states that at funerals, according to one opinion, they walked behind the men מפני כבוד בנות ישראל שלא יהו מביטין בנשים.

[4] ARN. 2, 7 a top, 2 ARN. 2, 4 b, because next day she might become the wife of another man. See R. Samuel b. Naḥman in Tanḥ. וישלח 5; B. 13, cf. Bab. bath. 16 a.

[5] Baraitha 'Erub. 18 b; slightly different in Berakh. 61 a: Even if he possess learning and good deeds as Moses did.

[6] Nedar. 20 a; Derekh ereṣ I: כל הצופה בנשים סופו בא לידי עבירה וכל המסתכל בעקבה של אשה הויין לו בנים שאינן מהוגנים. To look at the nakedness of a woman is a sin, as the Israelites who had fought against the Midianites, brought in Num. 31. 50 an offering to the Lord; תנא דבי רבי ישמעאל מפני מה הוצרכו ישראל שבאותו הדור כפרה, מפני שזנו עיניהם מן הערוה, according to the school of R. Ishmael they required atonement, because their eyes had looked with pleasure at nakedness, Baraitha Shabb. 64 a, b. Cf. the additions to Derekh ereṣ in Maḥzor Vitry 724: There are twenty-four obstacles in the way of repentance &c., 5. he who looks at nakedness. R. Miasha in Pesik. r. 24, 125 a; Lev. r. 23 end; Derekh ereṣ I says, 'He who sees a thing of nakedness and does not derive pleasure from the sight of it, merits to see God's glory.' Cf. Synh. 92 a bottom: ואמר רבי אלעזר כל המסתכל בערוה קשתו ננערת שנאמר עריה תעור קשתך with Rashi's explanation.

vent lust and immoral desires. But the extension of the prohibition even to looking at the coloured dress of a woman or at animals is based on an additional consideration. In connexion with the examination of a man who shows symptoms of a running issue, R. Jehudah b. Ilai says that the sight of animals pairing or that of the coloured dress of a woman excites sexual desires, and causes a pollution.[1] A teacher of the third century, introduced as רבנן, says, as quoted above, that Elisha was called a holy man, because he had never experienced a pollution, and that meant to say that sexual desires had never entered his mind; but already earlier teachers warned emphatically against any action that might have such an effect. Carnal thoughts should not be excited even by looking at one's own membrum. And such a sight was actually avoided by holy men like the patriarch R. Jehudah I, and before him by R. José b. Ḥalaftha whose great chastity at the marital intercourse was mentioned before; the first never put his hand even below his belt.[2] If this explanation of holiness

[1] Zabhim, II, 2: אפילו ראה בהמה חיה ועוף מתעסקין זה עם זה אפילו ראה בגדי צבע האשה.

[2] Jer. Megil. III, 74 a. 38: Antoninus who had submitted to the circumcision asked Rabbi to look at his membrum; but Rabbi replied, I have not looked at my own, how much less should I look at yours! And why was Rabbi called our holy teacher? Because he never looked at his membrum. R. José in Shabb. 118 b bottom, stated the same of himself; but ברבי מלתא אהריתי הוה ביה שלא הכנים ידו תחת אבנטו. Such extraordinary precaution is reported of teachers of the end of the first and the beginning of the second centuries in a Baraitha Nidd. 13 a: רבי אליעזר אומר כל האוחז באמתו ומשתין כאילו מביא מבול לעולם. אמרו לו לרבי אליעזר והלא ניצוצות ניתזין על רגליו ונראה ככרות שפכה ונמצא מוציא לעז על בניו שהן ממזרים. אמר להם מוטב שיוציא לעז על בניו שהן ממזרים ואל יעשה עצמו רשע שעה אחת לפני המקום. (וכל כך למה, מפני שמוציא שכבת זרע לבטלה, דאמר רבי יוחנן כל המוציא שכבת זרע לבטלה חייב מיתה). ואמר רבי אליעזר מאי דכתיב ידיכם דמים מלאו, אלו המנאפים ביד. תנא דבי רבי ישמעאל לא תנאף לא תהא בך ניאוף בין ביד בין ברגל. תנו רבנן הגרים והמשחקין בתינוקות

is correct, the first stages enumerated in the sentence of R. Pinḥas b. Yair as leading up gradually to holiness would mean this: if a man takes deliberate care to restrain himself from thinking of women, it will bring him to the state of cleanness; he will not be defiled by pollution in the day, he will not dream of women by night, and so keep himself in continuous purity. Gradually he will free himself from irritating thoughts of sexual intercourse in the day, and from all that even approaches immorality in any form or degree.

7. In the wording of the passage in the Talmud, as stated above, נקיות, cleanness, leads up to פרישות, and this to purity. The word פרישות generally means separation, abstinence;[1] but the thing from which one undertakes to

מעכבין את המשיח. תניא רבי טרפון אומר יד לאמה תקצץ ידו על טבורו. אמרו לו ישב לו קוץ בכריסו לא יטלנו, אמר להן לא. והלא כריסו נבקעת, אמר להן מוטב תבקע כריסו ואל ירד לבאר שחת. In Tos. Nidd. II, 8: כל היד המרבה לבדוק בנשים הרי משובחת ובאנשים תקצץ. רבי טרפון אומר תיקצץ על טיבורו. אמרו לו הרי כריסו נתפתחת, אמר להם אף אני לא נתכוונתי אלא לכך, משלו משל למה הדבר דומה לנותן אצבע בעין כל זמן שהוא דוחק הרבה מוציא דמעה. במה דברים אמורים בשכבת זרע אבל לזיבה כל היד המרבה לבדוק הרי זו משובחת. R. Eliezer and R. Tarfon, followers of the Shammaite school, who had before 70 lived in Jerusalem and later taught in Lydda, declared it a grave sin, if the hand, even in a case of urgent need or danger, touched the membrum or even came near it, because, as the Baraitha explains it, it irritates, and may produce pollution. Cf. פרקי רבינו הקדוש, ed. Grünhut, 45 ff. יד לאמה תיקצץ מפני שהיא מחממת אותו ומוציאה שכבת זרע לבטלה, and R. Jehudah in the Baraitha Shabb. 108 b bottom יד לאמה תיקצץ.

[1] For instance, in R. Akiba's sentence in Aboth, III, 13: נדרים סייג לפרישות סייג לחכמה שתיקה, vows are a fence to abstinence, a fence to wisdom is silence. Here, as the other parts of the list show, fence means advancement: vows advance self-imposed abstinence. If the vow were that of a Nazirite, his abstention from wine, strong drink, and defilement would prepare him for a more extensive abstinence. In ARN. 26, 41 b the order of the words is inverted: סייג לנדרים פרישות סייג לקדושה טהרה סייג לענוה יראת חטא, and, as a comparison with the sentence of R. Pinḥas

separate in order to be led to holiness is not indicated, and could naturally be one of several matters or conditions. One is idolatry;[1] and holiness is attained by a complete divorce of the mind from all ideas and practices connected with, and arising out of, Palestinian heathen worship. This includes in lists given by teachers of the second century theatres, circuses, stadia, superstitious practices, the heathen way of growing the hair, &c.[2] Even to look at idols was included in the prohibition; and Naḥum b. Simai was called a most holy man, because he never looked at the figure (the head of the emperor) on a coin.[3] Or פרישות may be the separation from levitical impurity,[4]

shows, they mean: the result of vows is abstinence, that of purity holiness, and that of humility fear of sin.

[1] Sifra Lev. 20. 7, 91 d: והתקדשתם והייתם קדושים, זו קדושת פרישות עבודה זרה . . או אינה אלא קדושת כל המצות. כשהוא אומר קדושים תהיו הרי קדושת כל המצות אמורה, ומה תלמוד לומר והתקדשתם והייתם קדושים זו קדושת פרישות עבודה זרה.

[2] Sifra Lev. 18. 3, 86 a. Mekhil. 19. 6, 63 a: וגוי קדוש, קדושים ומקודשים פרושים מאומות העולם ומשקוציהם; Sifré Deut. 85: ובו תדבקון, הפרישו עצמכם מעבודה זרה ודבקו במקום.

[3] Jer. 'Abod. zar. III, 42 c. 1; Pesaḥ. 104 a: אל תפנו אל האלילים . . . רבי יהודה אומר אל תפנה לראותן ממש. כד דמך רבי נחום בר סימאי חפון איקוניתא מחצלן, אמר כמה דלא חמתון בחייוי לא יחמינון בדמכותיה . . . ולמה נקרא שמו נחום איש קדיש קדשים שלא הביט בצורת מטבע מימיו. just as the Zealots, on patriotic grounds, see Hippolytus, *Refutatio haeres.* ix. 26.

[4] Sifra Lev. 11. 44, 57 b; 11. 45, 57 b; 19. 2, 86 c: כי אני ה׳ אלהיכם והתקדשתם והייתם קדושים כי קדוש אני ה׳ כשם שאני קדוש כך אתם קדושים, כשם שאני פרוש כך אתם היו פרושים. Though it does not suggest from what God separates Himself, the connexion between separation and holiness is expressly stated, and the biblical basis suggests separation from everything impure and defiling; see Schechter, *Some aspects of Rabbinic Theology*, 205. In Tos. Shabb. I, 15; jer. I. 3 c. 3; b. 13 a: בית שמאי אומרים לא יאכל זב פרוש עם זב עם הארץ ובית הלל מתירין, the Shammaites say, A man with a running issue, if he is otherwise keeping away from levitical impurity, shall not eat with a man who has the same complaint, but is as an 'Am ha'areṣ not separating from levitical impurity; the Hillelites permit it. Ḥagig. II, 7: בגדי עם הארץ מדרס לפרושין, בגדי פרושין מדרס לאוכלי תרומה, בגדי אוכלי תרומה

which would lead to a withdrawal from human society as complete as that of the Essenes. A third possible kind is the abstention from meat and wine,[1] producing Nazirites of a strict order. A fourth kind of separation is the partial or complete forbearance of marital intercourse,[2] which is in fact designated as holiness.[3] From the remark of

מדרס לקודש, the garments of the ʻAm ha'areṣ are a defilement for the separating (who eat their ordinary food in levitical purity, Rashi); the garments of the separating are a defilement for the priests who eat the priestly heave offering; the garments of the priests are a defilement for the sacrifices. See also Tohar. IV, 12: ספק החולין זו טהרת פרישות, R. José says, The food of a separating man concerning the practical impurity of which any doubt exists is impure, and such observance is only the scruple of far-going purity (see Büchler, *ʻAm ha'areṣ*, 166).

[1] Baba bath. 60 b; Tos. Sotah, XV, 11: תנו רבנן כשחרב הבית בשנייה רבו פרושין בישראל שלא לאכול בשר ושלא לשתות יין, נטפל להם רבי יהושע אמר להם . . ., when the second Temple was destroyed, many Jews abstained from meat and wine; but R. Joshua argued with them, &c. Cf. the Baraitha Sotah 22 b, 31 a; jer. Berakh. IX, 14 b. 54.

[2] Sotah, III, 4: רבי יהושע אומר רוצה אשה בקב ותפלות מתשעה קבין ופרישות, R. Joshua said, A woman prefers to receive from her husband as her sustenance only one Kabh of corn, but licence (frequent marital intercourse), to nine Kabhs of corn and abstention (from intercourse). תפלות can here mean neither obscenity, nor frivolity, just as in the same Mishnah: Ben-ʻAzzai said, It is the duty of a man to teach his daughter Torah, so that, if she should have to drink the bitter waters of Num. 5, she should know that a merit of hers suspends their effect; R. Eliezer said, If a man teaches his daughter Torah, it is as though he taught her תפלות. As the commentators explain, it means: he teaches her to think of sexual relations. R. Joshua continues in the Mishnah: חסיד שוטה ורשע ערום ואשה פרושה ומכות פרושין הרי אלו מבלי עולם, a foolish pious man, a subtle sinner, an abstaining woman, and the plagues (or stripes) of abstaining men (or Pharisees) are destroying the world. Geiger in אוצר נחמד, II, 100; Bacher, *Tannaiten*, I, 158. 2, quotes a variant אשה פרוצה, a licentious, loose woman. In Yoma 74 b, in a passage quoted from the Passover-Haggadah: ונילף מעינוי דמצרים דכתיב וירא את עניגו ואמרינן זו פרישות דרך ארץ, it means forced separation from marital intercourse. Cf. Apoc. Ezra 7, 125: qui abstinentiam habuerunt, and v. 122.

[3] According to Gen. 7. 13 Noah and his sons, while in the ark, lived separate from their wives; when God in 8. 16 permitted them to rejoin their wives, Noah in 8. 18 did not avail himself of the permission. R. Neḥemiah, in the middle of the second century, remarks on this in

R. Joshua it is evident that פרישות meant not total abstention from, but, as the contrast shows, merely a reduction of, such relations. On the other hand, Moses is in rabbinic sources stated to have completely given up marital intercourse with his wife,[1] in order to be ready

Gen. r. 35. 1: הוסיף על הצווי ונהג בקדושה, Noah extended the original command, and continued observing holiness. He designated the abstention from marital intercourse as holiness, just as the order of God in Exod. 19. 10 to sanctify the people was understood by Moses in verse 15 to mean keeping away from the women. As in the passages on p. 43, 3 צנוע 'chaste', was used for holy, so we read in a Baraitha Shabb. 53 b of a man who married a woman with a mutilated limb, and never had marital intercourse with her. Rabbi praised the woman as צנועה 'chaste', but R. Ḥiyya remarked, זו דרכה בכך אלא כמה צנוע אדם זה שלא הכיר באשתו, that it was woman's nature, while the husband's chastity deserved praise. 'Chaste' is hardly sufficiently strong for the context, as it should express very strong self-restraint. In Cant. r. 6. 6 an anonymous teacher says, Just as a ewe is chaste, so the Israelites in the war against Midian in Num. 31 were chaste and pure. R. Aḥa adds that they entered the houses of the Midianite women, blackened their faces, and took down their earrings in order to remove their attractive features, and not one of the Israelites was suspect of immorality. See Gitt. 57 a and p. 46, note 6.

[1] Baraitha Shabb. 87 a; ARN. 2, 5 b top, 2 ARN. 2, 5 b, Moses did three things of his own accord, and God later approved of them: he added a day to the two prescribed by God in Exod. 19. 10, 15, he ceased his marital intercourse with his wife, and broke the tablets. As to his intercourse, he argued thus, God commanded Israel before the revelation of the Decalogue on Mount Sinai to keep away from their wives, though He spoke to them on one short occasion only, and fixed the time of it: to me God speaks at any time, and it is not fixed beforehand, how much more must I keep away from my wife. In ARN. R. Jehudah b. Bethera, between 90 and 135, dealt with the same question. In Sifré Num. 12. 1. 99, 27 a, and Sifré zuta Num. 12. 1, 81 ff.: And Miriam and Aaron spake against Moses; whence did Miriam know that Moses was abstaining from begetting children? When she noticed that Ṣipporah was not adorning herself in the way of women, she asked her for the reason; Ṣipporah replied, Thy brother cares not for it. R. Nathan said, Miriam was standing near Ṣipporah, when the young man came running to Moses and told him (Num. 11. 27) that Eldad and Medad were prophesying in the camp; Ṣipporah, hearing this, said, Woe to their wives! Accordingly, all the seventy elders, at least for a time, had to abstain from marital intercourse, since God's spirit rested on them. It is interesting to find that already Philo, *Vita Mosis*, II, 68, M. II, 146, pointed out Moses' abstention as required for his readiness at all times to receive God's revelation.

at all times for receiving God's revelation,[1] to be pure and holy.[2]

If we now apply the various meanings of פרישות to the words of R. Pinḥas, we find that only two of them point to ways of separation that lead up to holiness: from idolatry with its branches, and partial abstinence from marital intercourse; and as the first cannot be connected with the

[1] In Apoc. Ezra 6. 32, For the Mighty One has seen thy purity (rectitude), yea the holiness (*pudicitiam*) which hath been thine from thy youth. Dr. Box remarks, Chastity, like fasting, intensifies the power of prayer, and prepares the way for a revelation, cf. 1 Enoch 83. 2. This would agree with Philo and the rabbis concerning Moses' chastity. But Gunkel in Kautzsch, *Pseudepigraphen*, 366, in adopting Hilgenfeld's retranslation into Greek σεμνότης, gives for *pudicitia* piety. As to the fasting, R. Akiba in Synh. 65 b; Midr. Tannaim, 110, in his explanation of one who inquires of the dead, Deut. 18. 11, refers to a man who starves himself and spends the nights in a cemetery, so that the spirit of impurity may rest on him, and attains it; how much more should a Jew who starves himself, so that the spirit of purity may rest on him, succeed in attaining it; but what can we do, since our sins are preventing such success. The spirit of purity is the holy spirit of prophecy, as in Hillel's case. Fasting and abstinence from marital intercourse appear together as signs of repentance or mourning in Baraitha 'Erub. 18 b: R. Meir says, Adam was a great Ḥasid: when he learned that through him death was decreed as a punishment, he fasted for 130 years, separated from his wife for 130 years, and clothed himself in garments of fig leaves for 130 years. Cf. Pseudo-Philo in *J. Q. R.*, X, 1898, 317, James, *Biblical Antiquities of Philo*, 100: When Pharaoh ordered that all new-born boys of the Israelites be thrown into the river, the elders of Israel wished the people to resolve to deny themselves intercourse with their wives. The same in Sotah 12 a, and in the advice of R. Ishmael in the Hadrianic persecutions in Baraitha Baba b. 60 b; Tos. Sotah, XV, 10. In the Elephantine Papyri, the Jews of Jeb mourned, fasted, and had no intercourse with their wives, when the priests of Jeb destroyed the Jewish Temple. R. Eleazar b. Pedath calls a man who is fasting holy, R. Simeon b. Lakish terms such pious, Ta'an. 11 a, b bottom; but see Tosafoth s. v. נומל. See also Sifré Deut. 18. 12. 173.

[2] Mekhil. R. Simeon on Exod. 19. 14, 98: As the words of the Torah require purity and holiness, it says, He sanctified the people. See the whole page. Pure and holy are found together in Mekhil. 15. 2, 37 a, b, Mekhil. R. Simeon, 61: Israel said, I am a queen, a daughter of kings, beloved, a daughter of beloved men, קדושה בת קדושים טהורה בת טהורים; in Sifré Deut. 214 of the captive woman in Deut. 21. 14: If she is ill, he shall wait, until she recovers; how much more so in the case of Jewesses who are holy and pure; cf. Shabb. 105 a; Mekhil. 14. 15, 29 a.

preceding cleanness, nor with the following purity, only the abstinence remains. In fact, it fits the context best, as established before: cleanliness from pollution by day leads to the moderation of intercourse, this to perfect purity from self-defilement by night, and this to freedom from all impure thought of a sexual nature.[1] Only it is difficult to see, if all the parts of the sentence so far considered refer to sexual life and thought, how marital moderation and chastity can lead up to humility. Before a definition of its meaning here can be attempted, attention must be drawn to the intimate connexion noticeable in rabbinic thought between the reverse of humility, haughtiness, and immorality. Already Gen. 39. 7, 'And it came to pass after these things that his master's wife lifted up her eyes to Joseph, and she said, Lie with me,' contains the immoral lifting up of the eyes, which is identified in a statement of R. José the Galilean with the haughty eyes in Prov. 6.17: 'Seven things are stated about the adulteress: high looks, for the adulteress raises her eyes to another man, as it says in Isa. 3. 16, Because the daughters of Zion are haughty, and walk with stretched forth necks and wanton eyes, &c.'[2] But already Sirach 26. 9 has the same

[1] We find, however, separation following after purity in Sotah IX, 15: On the death of R. Gamaliel the glory of the Torah ceased, and purity and separation died. Brüll, *Introduction to the Mishnah* I, 51, refers both expressions to levitical purity, while Levy, *NHW.*, IV, 144 a, translates them by purity and abstention from evil. In Sifré zuta Num. 6. 8, 38: All the days of his separation he is holy unto the Lord, מפני שנזר דרך פרישות וטהרה נקרא קדוש, because he abstained (from wine and strong drink) and observed levitical purity, the Nazirite is called holy. But this order merely follows that of Num. 6. A peculiar meaning of purity may be quoted in support of the above interpretation. R. Samuel b. Naḥman, in the name of R. Jonathan, in Menaḥ. 110 a, interprets the pure offering in Mal. 1. 11 to refer to him who studies the Torah in purity, by marrying first and then turning to study; in Yalkut, Mal. 1. 11 R. Neḥemiah, in Yoma 72 b, bottom on Ps. 9. 10 R. Ḥaninah is the author. Cf. Kidd. 29 b. bottom; Tos. Bekhor. 6. 10. A married man is not diverted by impure thoughts, has no pollution, and is clean and pure for the Torah.

[2] Tanḥ. נשא 1; B. 3; Num. r. 9. 11. In Midr. Samuel on 1 Sam. 9. 13,

thought: 'The whoredom of a woman is the lifting up of her eyes, and it shall be known by her eyelids.'[1] Similarly of men the Testaments of the twelve Patriarchs, Issachar 7. 2 say, 'Except my wife I have not known any woman; I never committed fornication by the uplifting of my eyes.' And Didaché 3. 3 has, 'Raise not thine eyes high, for from all that arises adultery.'[2] Rabbi saw in Acco a man whose father he had known to be a priest, walk on ground containing human corpses; when he asked the man why he acted against the law of priestly levitical purity, he replied, My father raised his eyes high, and married a divorced woman, and thereby disqualified me from the priesthood.[3] R. Joḥanan said, A man in whom there is haughtiness ultimately stumbles over a married woman.[4] And a woman said to her immoral husband, What was the cause of your action? that you are haughty.[5] Conversely, a man who never lifts up his eyes to another woman, never looks even at an unmarried girl, but keeps his looks down to restrain in him all desire for women, will be termed humble; therefore the absence of such lust and of sexual thought, which is holiness, will lead to that feature of humility. When such

43 b, R. Jehudah says that the girls who met Saul looked at his beauty without becoming satiated; to this R. José remarks, נמצאתה עושה בנות ישראל כך, which reads in Yalkut: אם כן עשיתה בנות ישראל כזונות, you describe girls of Israel as having been immoral.

[1] Cf. Menander's sentences in *ZATW*. 32, 1912, 213, § 43: Walk with a stretched forth neck in straightforwardness, and be chaste in thy thought, and consider and see that, as thou wouldest not like thy wife to commit adultery with someone else, also thou shouldst not desire to commit adultery with the wife of another man. In Psalms of Solomon 4. 4: His eyes are upon every woman without distinction (Syriac: immodestly); with his eyes he talketh to every woman of evil compact. In Gen. r. 41. 7 on Gen. 13. 10, And Lot lifted up his eyes, R. José b. Ḥaninah said, The whole verse deals with immorality, as Gen. 39. 7 and other parallels show.

[2] R. Simeon b. Yoḥai in Pesik. r. III, 10 a explains Lot's lifting up of his eyes as immorality, Gen. 13. 10; Bacher, *Tannaiten* II, 116. 1.

[3] Jer. Shebi'ith VI, 36 c. 20 Rabbi, in Synh. 5 b R. Ḥiyya; see Tosafoth s. v. רבי.

[4] Sotah 4 b.

[5] Num. r. 9. 3.

desires have been entirely eliminated from the mind of the pious man who is consistently striving after perfection, he is able to turn his attention undivided to God's will and to all the duties expressing the fear of sin, the submission of man to God's commands, and he will endeavour to fulfil them in humility. This will bring him to the practice of unselfish love to his fellow-man, to piety.[1]

Piety leads to the possession of the holy spirit which means the gift of prophecy.[2] Hillel was declared worthy of it; and though it is not expressly stated by what he merited it, the praise of his humility and piety in the same account strongly suggests those traits of his character as the qualifications for it. In the continuation of the

[1] In Synh. 19 b ff. humility means moral self-restraint : אמר רבי יוחנן תוקפו של יוסף ענותנותו של בועז תוקפו של בועז ענותנותו של פלטי בן ליש . . . אמר רבי יוחנן מאי דכתיב רבות בנות עשו חיל ואת עלית על כלנה, רבות בנות עשו חיל זה יוסף ובועז, ואת עלית על כלנה זה פלטי בן ליש. אמר רבי שמואל בר נחמן אמר רבי יונתן מאי דכתיב שקר החן והבל היפי, שקר החן זה יוסף, והבל היופי זה בועז, יראת ה׳ היא תתהלל זה פלטי בן ליש. The self-control of Joseph in Gen. 39. 8–12 is described as תוקף, moral strength ; that of Boaz in Ruth 3. 13, and of Palti b. Laish in 1 Sam. 25. 44 ; 2 Sam. 3. 15, who never touched his wife, is termed ענוותנות 'humility'; the latter evidently means even greater self-control, the total absence of all carnal desires and of lust. In Lev. r. 23. 11 and Ruth r. 3. 13, VI. 4 R. José says that the same three men whom passion tried to overpower restrained themselves by an oath. It is of special interest that R. Meir in Aboth VI, 1 attributes to the study of the Torah for its own sake the following effects on the character : he is called friend, beloved, lover of God, lover of men ; it clothes him in meekness and fear (of God), it fits him to become just, pious, upright, and faithful, it keeps him far from sin, and brings him near to virtue, . . . he becomes chaste, long-suffering, and forgiving of insults.

[2] Tos. Sotah 13. 2 ; jer. IX, 24 b. 23 ; b. 48 b : Since the death of the last prophets, Haggai, Zechariah, and Malachi, the holy spirit ceased in Israel ; also in several other passages, like Tos. Sotah 12. 5. In Mekhil. 12. 1, 2 b top, Simeon b. 'Azzai puts into the mouth of Baruch, Jeremiah's disciple, the complaint, Why should I be different from other disciples of the prophets? Joshua served Moses, and the holy spirit rested on him ; Elisha served Elijah, and the holy spirit rested on him. The parallel Baraitha about Hillel in Sotah 48 b has : He is worthy of God's presence, שכינה, to rest on him ; this also means the gift of prophecy.

report, Samuel the Small was, among the scholars assembled in an upper room in Jamnia, designated by a heavenly voice as the only one worthy of the holy spirit. He was called the Small, because he made himself small (was humble); according to others, because he was a little smaller (more humble) than Samuel of Ramah. On his death they bewailed him thus: Woe for the humble, the pious, a disciple of Hillel the old. While dying, he said in Aramaic, 'Simeon and Ishmael for destruction, and the rest of the people for plunder, and great distress will come'; but they understood not what he meant. Humility was his outstanding quality, as it became evident on a certain occasion. Once R. Gamaliel II[1] invited seven elders to the upper chamber to deliberate upon, and to resolve, the intercalation of a thirteenth month into the year. When he found eight scholars present, and inquired as to who had come unauthorized, Samuel the Small rose and said, I have come in order to obtain information about a difficulty of law. R. Gamaliel then said to him, 'O Eldad and Medad, if I had invited only two, all Israel knows it, you would have been one of them.'[2] Eldad and Medad considered

[1] Several texts have R. Simeon b. Gamaliel (see Rabbinovicz); and Dr. Ginzberg in *R. É. J.*, 66, 1913, 300. 3 assumes that Samuel was a member of the Beth-din under Simeon b. Gamaliel I in the days of the Temple. See also Halévy, דורות הראשונים, I e, 100 a ff.

[2] Baraitha jer. Synh. I, 18 c. 11; b. 11 a top; in Semaḥ. VIII, אלדד ומידד שכל ישראל יודעין. In b.: Sit down, my son, sit down, you are worthy to intercalate in any year; and it is added in an Aramaic statement that the scholar who had come in unauthorized was not Samuel, and that he rose only to avert shame from the intruder. When Samuel died, Semaḥ. VIII reports, his key and his writing-tablet were hung on his coffin, because he had no son. R. Gamaliel and R. Eleazar b. 'Azariah bewailed him publicly and said, For this man it is proper to weep, for this it is proper to mourn: kings die and leave their crowns to their sons, wealthy men die and leave their riches to their sons, Samuel the Small has taken all the treasures of the world and is gone. As he was invited to the deliberations on the intercalation, he must have been a great scholar, and the praises mentioned may have referred to his learning as well as to his humility. In jer. Sotah IX, 24 c. 37; Bacher, *Tannaiten*, I, 83. 4, R. Joshua b. Levi quotes the whole Baraitha about

themselves unworthy of the prophetical spirit, and were for their modesty in making themselves small distinguished over all the other elders by the gift of life-long prophecy.[1]

It is to be noted that some of Hillel's disciples were declared worthy of the holy spirit. Of his eighty scholars thirty were worthy that God's glory should rest on them as on our teacher Moses, (only their generation was not worthy of it), thirty were worthy that the sun should stop for them as it stopped for Joshua (or of intercalating a month in a year), and twenty were men of average capacity; the eldest of all was Jonathan b. ʿUzziel, the youngest Joḥanan

Hillel and Samuel differently: מעשה שנכנסו זקנים לעליית בית גדיא ביריחו ויצאת בת קול ואמרה להן יש ביניכם שנים ראויין לרוח הקדש והלל הזקן אחד מהן ונתנו עיניהן בשמואל הקטן. ושוב נכנסו זקנים לעלייה ביבנה ויצאת בת קול ואמרה להן יש ביניכם שנים ראויין לרוח הקדש ושמואל הקטן אחד מהן ונתנו עיניהן ברבי אליעזר בן הורקנוס והיו שמחין שהסכימה דעתן לדעת המקום. It is hardly doubtful that Samuel the Small as a contemporary of Hillel is a mistake for another Samuel or perhaps another unknown colleague of Hillel; see Brüll, *Jahrbücher*, I, 36, note 73. The inclusion of R. Eliezer b. Hyrkanos next to Samuel as worthy of the holy spirit is very instructive, as his teacher R. Joḥanan b. Zakkai also declared him the most distinguished of his disciples, Aboth II, 8, though we know nothing of his humility and piety. The suggestions of G. Klein, *Der älteste christl. Katechismus*, 111 ff., 113 ff. appear to have no foundation whatever. As to Samuel's supposed Essenism, the only point in favour of it seems to be his prophecy, which arose from the political unrest in Judaea in the year 117; but R. Eliezer also prophesied on his death-bed a violen end to R. Akiba and his fellow-scholarst, Baraitha Synh. 68 a. Of the characteristic traits of the Essenes enumerated by Josephus none are mentioned in the life of Samuel.

[1] Sifré Num. 95; Baraitha Synh. 17 a R. Simeon. Mekhil. 20. 21, 72 a says of Moses that his humility brought him the distinction of being permitted to draw near to the thick cloud where God was, as it says in Num. 12. 3, The man Moses was very humble. This verse tells us that he who is humble will ultimately cause God's glory to rest with men on earth, as it says in Is. 57. 15, For thus saith the High and Lofty One that inhabiteth eternity, whose name is Holy . . . with him also that is of a contrite and humble spirit, &c. And it says in Is. 61. 1, The spirit of the Lord is upon me . . . to bring good tidings to the humble; and it says in Is. 66. 2, For all those things hath mine hands made, &c. . . . but on this man will I look, even on him that is humble and of a contrite spirit, &c. And it says in Ps. 51. 19, The sacrifices of God are a broken spirit.

b. Zakkai.[1] The numbers may be exaggerated; but the connexion between the learning of the disciples and their characters on the one hand, and their worthiness of the prophetical gift and their ability to work miracles on the other, is evident. Now, accidentally, we learn some interesting details about their character. 'The Shammaites said, One should not teach but a wise, humble, and wealthy man, descended from a good family; the Hillelites said, One should teach everybody, for there were many transgressors in Israel who were brought near to the study of the Torah, and there proceeded from (among) them righteous, pious, and perfect men.'[2] The object of the study of the Torah was according to the Hillelites to make the scholar righteous, pious, and perfect; in the opinion of the Shammaites that goal could only be reached by such as had brought with them, when joining the school, good breeding, wisdom, and humility as the foundation on which to build.[3] The Hillelites relied on the cultivating influence and the force of the study of the Torah; and its effect combined with the influence of the spirit of Hillel was indeed

[1] Baraitha Sukkah 28 a; 2 ARN. 28, 29 a: תנו רבנן שמונים תלמידים היו לו להלל הזקן שלשים מהם ראויים שתשרה עליהן שכינה כמשה רבינו ושלשים מהן ראויים שתעמוד להם חמה כיהושע בן נון, עשרים בינונים, גדול שבכולן יונתן בן עוזיאל קטן שבכולן רבן יוחנן בן זכאי; ARN. 14, 28 a different: שמונים תלמידים היו להלל הזקן שלשים מהן ראויין שתשרה שכינה עליהן כמשה רבינו אלא שאין דורן ראוי לכך, שלשים מהן ראויין לעבר שנה ועשרים בינונים. . .

[2] ARN. 3, 7 b ff.: והעמידו תלמידים הרבה, שבית שמאי אומרים אל ישנה אדם אלא למי שהוא חכם ועניו ובן אבות ועשיר. ובית הלל אומרים לכל אדם ישנה שהרבה פושעים היו בהם בישראל ונתקרבו לתלמוד תורה ויצאו מהם צדיקים חסידים וכשרים; cf. 2 ARN. 12, 15 b: שמא לא זכו לך אבותיך, jer. Ber. IV, 7 d. 9.

[3] In Agadath Shir Hashir. 8. 9, Schechter, an otherwise unknown scholar, Abba Eleazar b. Gigi of Barak emphasizes the necessity of learning and humility in the scholar, אבא אלעזר בן גיגי איש ברק אומר למה הדבר דומה לאחד שהיו אומרים עליו איש פלוני חכם ואין ענווה בידו איש פלוני עניו ואין חכמה בידו אמר לו הכתוב הריני נותן לו חכמה וענווה.

evident: for the Hillelites were kind and humble,[1] thus making up for the initial absence of the qualities demanded of the disciples on their admission by the Shammaites. Some of the exceptionally gifted in humility and piety qualified under Hillel for attaining to the holy spirit.[2]

8. Here attention must be drawn to a statement of Dr. Kohler's about the qualifications required of one to be initiated into various mysteries. In the introduction to his paragraph on the 'chaste' whom, without a shadow of evidence, he identifies with the Essenes, he writes:[3] 'Upon the observance of the highest state of purity and holiness depended also the granting of the privilege, accorded only to the *élite* of the priesthood, of being initiated into the mysteries of the Holy Name and other secret lore. The Name of twelve letters was, after the Hellenistic apostasy, entrusted only to the Zenuʿim, the chaste ones among the priesthood. The Name of forty-two letters was entrusted only to the Zanuʿa and ʿAnaw, the chaste and the humble, after they had passed the zenith of life and had given assurance of preserving the Name in perfect purity, Kidd. 71 a, Eccl. rabb. III. 11; Yer. Yoma 40 d, 41 a'. To my great regret, I have not succeeded in finding in the passages indicated the evidence for the many striking assertions. The Baraitha[4] reports: 'At first they handed down the name of twelve letters to everybody; since, however, the impudent became numerous, they handed it down to the modest among the priests, and even the modest among the priests let it be drowned in the chant of their brethren, the priests.' Here the priesthood of the Temple of a certain date is, from a certain point of view, religious or moral, divided into three groups: insolent, modest, and

[1] 'Erub. 13 b: מפני שנוחין ועלובין היו.

[2] In Nedar. 38 a, R. Joḥanan says, God does not rest His glory but on a physically strong, wealthy wise, and humble man, as is evident in the case of Moses. His requirements of a prophet are nearly identical with those laid down by the Shammaites for a disciple of their school.

[3] *Jew. Encycl.*, V, 225 b ff.

[4] Kidd. 71 a.

non-descript; but there is in צנוע no trace of purity and holiness, no *élite* of the priesthood, no initiation into the mysteries of the holy name, no secret lore, and no Hellenistic apostasy. צנוע denotes a positive quality, probably nothing else but discretion or modesty,[1] and was chosen in contradistinction to פריץ. Other similar statements about priests and others, where none of the qualifications suggested by Dr. Kohler could possibly fit, bear it out. When at the distribution of the loaves of the 'Omer, the bread-offering of the Pentecost, and of the shewbread, only as much as the size of a bean was given to each priest, the modest withdrew their hands, but the greedy took and ate it; once a priest took his and his fellow's portions, and he was called for that a grabber.'[2] Here צנוע is opposed to גרגרן. R. Joḥanan b. Nuri relates that he once met an old man, a descendant of the beth-Abtinas, at one time the makers of the incense in the Temple, who told him, In the past when my father's family were discreet, they handed down the scroll (of the prescription for the incense) one to the other; but now that they are no longer trusted, take the scroll and keep it carefully.[3] Similar is its meaning where used of non-priests. 'The Shammaites say, One should sell olives only to one who observes levitical purity, the Hillelites permit to sell also to one who observes only the law of tithing; the discreet among the Hillelites acted according to the Shammaites.[4] Dealers in garments made of mingled materials may sell their goods by carrying them on themselves in the usual way; but the discreet carry them on the end of a staff behind them. Sewers of garments of mingled materials may sew them on their laps in the usual way; but the discreet sew them on the ground.[5] In order to prevent the poor who receive produce on the threshing-

[1] The passage in jer. has instead of צנועים the word כשרים.

[2] Baraitha Yoma, 39 a ff.; jer. VI, 43 c. 65; Tos. Sotah, XIII, 7, 8.

[3] Baraitha jer. Yoma III, 41 a. 73; Tos. II, 7; but b. 38 a bottom has קיימין.

[4] Damm. VI, 6.

[5] Kil. IX, 5, 6.

floor from eating it untithed, discreet farmers give them money and food'.[1] In connexion with the redemption of the fruit of a vineyard in the fourth year, the discrcet owners put the money down and said, All that will be gathered from here, shall be redeemed by this money.[2] In all these cases the word צנוע denotes such as were more careful in carrying out a religious duty; and even Dr. Kohler remarks that it is not always clear whether the same denotes the Essenes or simply the modest ones as a class. In fact, however, there is no trace of Essenism; and only in one case could any doubt arise. Simeon, the chaste, told R. Eliezer that he had entered the space between the altar and the porch of the Sanctuary without having previously washed his hands and his feet.[3] As there is no comparison intended between him and other priests, nor between his past and his present conduct, the word describes a special quality of his, either his chastity or his continence in conjugal life. As this conversation took place several years after the destruction of the Temple, Simeon may have lived, as a sign of mourning, a life of abstention, as the פרושים are reported to have, on the same ground, abstained from meat and wine.[4] But צנוע does not describe him as an Essene.[5]

9. The individual terms used by R. Pinḥas b. Yair in their technical meanings were, as was shown, familiar already to earlier rabbis: חסיד and עניו to Hillel and his contemporaries, ירא חטא to Hillel and R. Joḥanan b. Zakkai,

[1] Tos. Pe'ah, II, 18.

[2] Ma'as. sheni, V, 1.

[3] Tos. Kelim 1. I. 6.

[4] Baraitha Bab. bath. 60 b; Tos. Sotah, XV, 11.

[5] Dr. Kohler., *J.E.*, V, 226 a bottom, says: 'R. Simeon the Zanua', who, while disregarding the Temple practice, shows a certain contempt for the high priest, appears on all accounts to have been an Essene priest.' As we have no information about that practice in the Temple, and R. Eliezer only represents the stricter view in a dispute (as also his disciple R. Jehudah who is quoted as R. Meir's opponent as חכמים), it is not correct to say that Simeon disregarded the practice. How does his silence, which certainly was the most dignified answer to R. Eliezer's vehemence, show contempt for the high priest?

פרישות to R. Joshua b. Ḥananiah, טהרה ופרישות to R. Gamaliel II's contemporaries, and קדושה in its special signification to R. Joshua b. Ḥananiah, and more definitely to R. Neḥemiah; and continence, and abstention from conjugal relations as preparatory steps for the prophetical calling of Moses were known to Philo and to rabbis before 135. Also care and restraint towards women in general, and particular strictness in meeting, and speaking to, married women had found expression in many an emphatic warning. Again, the possession of the holy spirit as the highest goal of good and pious men was known, at least, from the days of Hillel who was declared worthy of it as of a recognition by God of his high virtues. In the absence of earlier parallels, it appears that the originality of R. Pinḥas lay in the systematic gradation of the various moral qualities to lead up the pious, by a natural progress in self-education, to the highest perfection, the possession of the holy spirit. On the other hand, as in Hillel's case piety and humility were known to be the qualifications for it, it is not improbable that already at the beginning of the first century the individual rungs of the ladder leading up to the holy spirit were named and described. As to the first stages, a sentence of R. Akiba, though differently expressed, seems to offer a parallel: 'Jesting and levity lead a man on to lewdness; the Masorah is a fence to the Torah, tithes are a fence to riches, vows are a fence to abstinence, a fence to wisdom is silence.'[1] The fence to the Torah and to wisdom indicate that R. Akiba was speaking to scholars. If by the fence to the Torah he meant the same as the men of the Great Assembly,[2] the fence in his opinion would seem to have been constituted either by the oral tradition, or by the detailed rules about the words and the letters of the

[1] Aboth, III, 13: רבי עקיבא אומר שחוק וקלות ראש מרגילין את האדם לערוה מסורת סייג לתורה מעשרות סייג לעושר נדרים סייג לפרישות סייג לחכמה שתיקה; Bacher, I, 268, 1.

[2] Aboth, I, 1.

Torah, which were essential for his consistent demonstration of an even remote biblical basis of all Halakhahs.[1] If fence meant protection also in the next sentence, tithing, while reducing the produce, actually protected wealth, as the sayings of teachers of the third century, adduced by the commentators, pointed out. Similarly, silence, as in Prov. 10. 19; 17. 28, was a protection of wisdom. But how vows protected abstinence, and to what the latter referred, is not clear. Maimonides refers it to the separation from levitical impurity, according to the technical meaning of פרוש.[2] But to my knowledge no vow of that tendency is reported in rabbinic literature, except in the case of the Nazirite, and among the requirements of a Ḥaber, as formulated by his disciple, R. Jehudah b. Ilai, who, in partly repeating R. Akiba's sentence, included in his list abstention from the gravest levitical defilement by a corpse and from frequent vows.[3] If it means voluntary abstinence from things otherwise permitted, as meat, wine, and other similar articles of food, as in the case of those who abstained on account of the destruction of the second Temple (above, p. 50), a vow to the same effect would have lent it religious and moral sanction. The reason for such a self-imposition may, however, have been different. In a discussion as to whether articles of food might be exported from Palestine, R. Jehudah b. Bethera permitted the export of wine, because thereby levity, תפלות, was reduced.[4] This may, in the first instance, as above (50, note 2), refer to immorality, as the impressive confession in the Testament of Judah, 14–16, forcibly shows; and wine also promoted pollution.[5] Abstinence from wine was not a rare occurrence, as the remarks of R. Simeon b. Yoḥai[6] and of R. Eleazar haKappar about its sinfulness suggest.[7] It is, however, difficult to assume that R. Akiba

[1] Bacher, *Terminologie*, I, 108.
[2] Hagig. II, 7.
[3] Damm. II, 3.
[4] Baraitha Baba bath. 90 b; Tos. 'Ab. z. IV, 2.
[5] Yoma, 18 a bottom; jer. I, 39 a. 46.
[6] Baraitha Nedar. 10 a; Tos. I, 1; jer. I, 36 d. 48.
[7] Sifré Num. 6. 11. 30; Baraitha Nazir 19 a.

should have approved of such abstention, and thereby have encouraged vows.[1] If, according to another meaning of פרישות, R. Akiba referred to a separation from every kind of immorality,[2] an iteresting parallel would account for the vow. R. José says, 'Three men in the Bible kept down their passion by an oath, when it threatened to overpower them: Joseph, Gen. 39. 9, David, 1 Sam. 26. 10, and Boaz, Ruth 3. 13.'[3] Here, instead of a vow, a solemn oath by God was uttered to counteract quickly and strongly the moment's rushing temptation; whereas a vow by its extension over a longer period supported and sustained the self-imposed separation from immorality. In the same way the vow extending over at least a month served the purpose of an oath in the instance of a Nazirite, in the days of the high-priest Simeon the Just, to check in the young man the sudden attack of vanity at the beauty of his hair, and to force him, after a short time, to cut his locks.[4] On the other hand, in the parallel version of R. Akiba's sentence,[5] levitical purity appears to lead up to sacrificial meals which required a higher degree of such

[1] In ARN. 26, 41 b, in a sentence introduced by הוא היה אומר, R. Akiba warns against too frequent vows, as they may lead to trespassing against oaths; in 2 ARN. 33, 36 b top, it is inverted. In Derekh ereṣ I end, Abba Ḥilfai, in the name of his father Abba Ḥagra, is the author of the same warning; in Nedar. 20 a it is an anonymous Baraitha. In 2 ARN. 35, 43 a R. Akiba commends the annulment of the vows (of the wife), הפרת נדרים, as the reading is also in Baraitha Yebam. 109 a by bar-Kappara, and in Gen. r. 93. 1 by R. Ḥaninah; in the anonymous Baraitha jer. Yebam. XIII, 13 c. 39 היתר נדרים, dissolution of vows by scholars.

[2] See R. Isaac b. Reuben in Joseph ibn 'Aknin's ספר המוסר, 97: Men who impose upon themselves the vow never to do anything immoral, דבר ערוה.

[3] Lev. r. 23. 11; Ruth r. 3. 13, VI end; in Sifré Deut. 33 on 6. 6 R. Josia quotes Abraham's and Elisha's refusal to accept any gift, Gen. 14. 22; 2 Reg. 5. 16, Boaz's opportunity of immoral intercourse with Ruth, and David's opportunity to kill Saul; Bacher, II, 360, 6.

[4] Baraitha Nedar. 9 b; Tos. Nazir, IV, 7; jer. I, 51 c. 40; Sifré Num. 22.

[5] 2 ARN. 33, 36 a: רבי עקיבא אומר סייג לחכמה שתיקה סייג לכבוד שלא לשחוק סייג לקדשים טהרה סייג לנדרים פרישות סייג לתורה מסורת.

purity;[1] and this would support Maimonides' reference of R. Akiba's words to levitical abstinence. But, apart from the difficulties against it mentioned before, R. Akiba evidently intended to give in all parts of his sentence advice for practical life, whereas in his days there were no sacrifices. In the wording of another parallel[2] is found, instead of sacrificial meals, the more correct and fitting holiness next to purity, the latter leading up to, and protecting, holiness. On the other hand, a new point here is the fear of sin as a protection of humility both of which are moral qualities, and would demand next to them moral and not levitical purity. But it has been suggested that the last two moral qualities were added later from R. Pinḥas b. Yair's list of graduated virtues; and the mere fact that they were placed at the end of the sentence strongly favours that suggestion, though it is not at all clear why only two parts and not more should have been selected for addition to R. Akiba's sentence. Evidently the version in the Babylonian Talmud which alone contains the part about abstinence in the list supplied it as a continuation to R. Akiba's words on abstinence.

R. Akiba's sentence in its earliest form included as its first point the statement that jesting and levity lead man on to sin; and it is only natural to expect some connexion between the warning against the two failings and the commendation of the qualities following. שחוק refers in the cases of men in the first instance to jesting with women which gradually leads to immorality. As many of R. Akiba's disciples were young men between twenty and thirty, and others, like Ḥaninah b. Ḥakhinai and Simeon b. Yoḥai, had left their wives at home and stayed in the school for several years in succession,[3] the teacher had to impress upon them as scholars the great duty of being most careful

[1] Ḥagig. II, 1.

[2] ARN. 26, 41 b: רבי עקיבא אומר סייג לכבוד שלא לשחוק סייג לחכמה שתיקה סייג לנדרים פרישות סייג לקדושה טהרה סייג לענוה יראת חטא.

[3] Kethub. 62 b; Lev. r. 21. 8; Bacher, Tannaiten, II, 71. 1.

in their association with women. While Abba Ḥilfai, in the name of his father Abba Ḥagra, in his unmeasured pessimism about the levity of women,[1] warned everybody not to speak too much with them, for all the talk of a woman was only immorality,[2] R. Akiba demanded only restraint in conversation and association. שחוק denotes immoral advances already in Gen. 39.14, 17. And in the rabbinic sources it is stated that when the high court in Jerusalem addressed the woman suspected of adultery, the judge said, 'My daughter, wine does much, שחוק does much, youth does much, bad neighbours do much'.[3] R. Akiba himself, in interpreting Gen. 21. 9, 'And Sarah saw the son of Hagar the Egyptian, which she had borne unto Abraham, mocking', said that where צחק occurs, as in Gen. 39. 14, 17, it means immorality.[4] Levity has the same meaning; when, at the joyous Feast of Water-drawing held on the Temple Mount, men and women took part in the entertainments together, the authorities found that they had come to levity, and made the necessary arrangements for their separation.[5] And so R. Akiba's educational principles for his disciples were that these should first refrain from jesting and levity, then

[1] Cf. פרוצה בשחוק in Tanḥ. נשא 2; B. 4.

[2] Derekh ereṣ I end; in Baraitha Nedar. 20 a anonymous. Dr. Kohler who sees in the title Abba a characteristic of the Essene would find in this opinion which agrees with that of Josephus, *Wars*, II, 8. 2. 121 about the Essenes (see also Hippolytus), a confirmation of his view.

[3] Sotah, I, 4, *MGWJ.* 47, 1903, 339. 1.

[4] Gen. r. 53. 11; in Tos. Sotah, VI, 6 R. Eliezer, the son of R. José the Galilean, is the author: אין מצחק אלא גלוי עריות היאך מה דאת אמר בא אלי העבד העברי אשר הבאת לנו לצחק בי, מלמד שהיתה אמנו שרה רואה אותו לישמעאל מכביש גנות וצד נשי אנשים ומענה אותם, Bacher, I, 243, 3. In a simile in Deut. r. 3. 17, R. Joḥanan b. Zakkai says, A king married a woman; when he once noticed that she jested with one of his slaves, he became angry and divorced her.

[5] Tos. Sukk. IV, 1; b. 51 b. In Derekh ereṣ zuta III, תחלת קלות ראש בנשים פתח לניאוף; in 2 ARN. 33, 36 a ff., in R. Akiba's sentence: אל תבוא לידי שחוק שלא תבוא לידי עבירה, come not to jesting, that you may not come to immorality. R. Jehudah, his disciple, requires the Ḥaber not to vow too much and not to jest too much, Damm. II, 3.

strive to abstain also from things permitted, as too frequent conjugal intercourse, and to support its gradual reduction by a vow: strict discretion and high morality in the association with women, and moderation and abstinence in family life should be the rule for scholars. Some of R. Akiba's colleagues, like R. Yeshebabh[1] and Simeon b. 'Azzai,[2] the Ḥasids, and R. Joḥanan b. Nuri, the sin-fearing man, may have urged the same principles even more emphatically by their own lives and their practice; and so R. Pinḥas b. Yair had undoubtedly precursors for his rules of gradual self-sanctification.

[1] Midr. Cant. ed. Grünhut 7 a.
[2] Berakh. 57 b; ARN. 40, 64 b; see p. 71.

II

THE ANCIENT PIOUS MEN

WHILE the reports about Hillel's piety dealt mainly with his relations to his fellow-man, the records about his contemporaries to be analyzed in this chapter refer, in the first instance, to the relations of those pious men with God. Their approach to Him was frequently expressed by sacrifices of a special kind not to be found in the sacrificial worship of the first century, and in fervent prayer and meditation. Their religious sentiments include true devotion at prayer, repentance, and trust in their Father in heaven; and their belief in a reward for the righteous after death gave them strength to bear patiently visitation and calamity. Though Köberle [1] devoted hundreds of pages of his book to the post-biblical conception of sin and atonement, the early statements about the sacrifices of the pious men, and their ideas of sin and atonement, are not even mentioned. For his ignorance of the original sources and of their value and their dates, coupled with a remarkable consistency of prejudice, made an objective consideration of Jewish religious sentiment and a recognition of rabbinic religious sincerity impossible. Also O. Schmitz [2], who exhausted the information about sacrifices and the underlying ideas contained in the Apocrypha and the Jewish-Hellenistic literature, and objectively weighed all the evidence, knew nothing of the valuable material about the sacrifices of the pious men, because it has been preserved in halakhic parts of the rabbinic literature. As Bacher, in his unique way, dealt only with the haggadic sayings and interpretations of the first century, and there exists no similar work written in

[1] *Sünde und Gnade*, 1905.
[2] *Die Opferanschauung des späteren Judentums*, 1910.

a European language on the non-haggadic statements of the scholars and the pious men before the year 70, Christian and some Jewish scholars who are unable to study the unwieldy Talmud are dependent on helps. They have, therefore, insufficient knowledge of the valuable, old information relating to the time when the Temple still stood, and when the feeling of gratitude and the burden of sin of the individual Jew were spontaneously expressed before God in prayer and sacrifice in front of the altar, and when these, according to the intensity of the sentiment and the capacities of the worshipper, were filled with, and sustained by, true devotion and repentance. The occasions for special sacrifices show best the religious emotions of the Jew, and allow an insight into the minds of the section of the people, of which the worshipper was typical.

1. 'When once a pious man forgot a sheaf of corn in his field, he told his son to go and to bring for him a bull as a burnt-offering and another bull as a peace-offering. When his son asked, why he rejoiced at the fulfilment of that commandment more than at that of any other duty imposed by the Torah, the father said, While God gave us all the other commandments to carry them out with intent, this one is to be fulfilled without intention; for had we acted before God with deliberation, the duty would not have offered itself to us. Now it says, Deut. 24. 19, When thou reapest thine harvest in thy field, and hast forgot a sheaf, &c.: the verse has fixed a blessing for it.'[1] This

[1] Tos. Pe'ah, III, 8; Midr. Tann. Deut. 24. 19, 161: משעה בחסיד אחד ששכח עומר בתוך שדהו ואמר לבנו צא והקריב עלי פר לעולה ופר לזבחי השלמים. אמר לו אבא מה ראית לשמוח במצוה זו יותר מכל מצות שבתורה. אמר לו כל מצות שבתורה נתן לנו המקום לדעתנו זו שלא לדעתנו שאילו עשינו ברצון לפני המקום לא באת מצוה זו לידינו אלא הרי הוא אומר כי תקצור קצירך ושכחת עמר בשדה וגו׳ קבע לו הכתוב ברכה. In Sifra Lev. 5. 17, 27 a; Sifré Deut. 283, 124 b, R. Eleazar b. 'Azariah, in commenting on Deut. 24, 19, expresses the same thought, and applies it to one who accidentally drops a coin which a poor man finds and uses for his maintenance; God assigns a blessing to him as to one who forgot a sheaf in his field.

wealthy landowner who could afford to offer as an occasional, voluntary sacrifice two bulls at a time, representing in those days a considerable sum of money, is in many respects an interesting Jew. He knew the passage of the Pentateuch that applied to the particular incident before him, and, in addition to the detail of the blessing promised which he might have looked up first, he knew even the special characteristic of the precept; but no scholarship is manifested in his remarks. His genuine joy at his unintended fulfilment of the law in question should specially be noted; though, at the same time, his mind, after the performance of the duty, fixed itself on God's blessing promised as a reward. It presupposes not only his conviction that the words of the Torah are those of God, but he had the fullest trust in His promise, though its realization might be far off. The joy of this farmer is an instructive instance of the pleasure that rose in the heart of the Jew in carrying out or after the fulfilment of an injunction of the law, in this case even one that implied a loss. The son had noticed in his father similar joy on previous occasions in connexion with the performance of other religious obligations; but no thanks-offerings had then marked the intensity of his satisfaction. The sacrifices which he now offered were prescribed neither in the Pentateuch nor by the rabbis, but were the spontaneous expression of his pleasure, and of his gratitude to God for having granted him the opportunity to carry out a commandment and to merit His blessing. He was not contented with merely offering up a prayer of thanksgiving in his own words or with reciting an appropriate psalm, but felt moved to express his sentiments by readily giving up to God a part of his wealth. Whether he represented a type of pious Jews in Jerusalem or not, this incident of the first century constitutes a most instructive instance of the spontaneous Jewish religious feeling, of an occasion of its manifestation, and of the form of its visible expression. A more thorough analysis of it may perhaps throw more light on the religious thought of its time.

The description of the farmer as חסיד in the account does not, as far as we know, represent him as the member of any organization brought and held together by a definite form of piety; but the term is intended, as it seems, to characterize his personal action in this one instance. It was not, however, his accidental observance of the one commandment which was, no doubt, readily obeyed by many other farmers, that merited for him the distinctive attribute, but his exceptional and conscious attitude to God, and his active and vigorous expression of it. But who called him a Ḥasid for that? If it were certain that a contemporary who learned of the incident before 70 applied the adjective to him, as Hillel's contemporaries described the great teacher as Ḥasid, it would have denoted a man distinguished by certain virtues and by definite moral and religious deeds. But what these were it is difficult to establish. The author of the statement about R. Yeshebabh, one of the several scholars who died as martyrs in the Hadrianic religious persecutions, described him as one of the last of the pious men,[1] and was consequently conscious that that type of man had become rare before 135; and we found that before 117 Samuel the Small, an older contemporary of R. Yeshebabh, was described as humble and pious, as also Simeon b. 'Azzai.[2] And in those persecutions, R. José b. Kisma said to R. Ḥaninah b. Theradyon, 'Knowest thou not that God made this nation (the Romans) to rule, though it destroyed His House, burnt His Temple, killed His pious men, destroyed His good men, and it still exists?'[3] Here the most precious, and in R. José's opinion the most prominent men of Judaea's

[1] Midr. Cant. ed. Grünhut 7 a: העשירי רבי ישבב מישארית החסידים.

[2] Berakh. 57 b; ARN. 40, 64 b; in Ḥagig. 14 b; jer. II. 77 b. 11; Tos. II, 3; Cant. r. 1. 4: בן עזאי הציין ומת עליו הכתוב אומר יקר בעיני ה׳ המותה לחסידיו, when he died, Ps. 116. 15 was applied to him: The death of His saints is precious in the sight of the Lord.

[3] 'Ab. zar. 18 a: אי אתה יודע שאומה זו מן השמים המליכוה שהחריבה את ביתו ושרפה את היכלו והרגה את חסידיו ואיבדה את טוביו ועדיין היא קיימת.

population before 70 are divided into God's pious and His best men, meaning probably the religious and the political leaders.[1] While it is almost certain from R. José's words that he did not refer to the Essenes, nor to any special group of pious men, it is hardly doubtful that the few rabbis singled out as Ḥasids represented a definite type of piety with distinctive virtues. Of R. Yeshebabh an extraordinary trait of character is reported: he distributed *all* his possessions among the poor, against the rule of the rabbis quoted to him by R. Gamaliel II that only a fifth part of one's property should be given to charity.[2] Though we find that King Monobazos of Adiabene, in a year of drought, distributed his and his father's treasures among the poor,[3] the act of R. Yeshebabh was one of remarkable self-sacrifice, and may well account for the title of Ḥasid given to him; though it is possible that his peculiar piety lay in a different direction. Nothing similar is recorded of Samuel the Small, Simeon b. ʿAzzai, or R. Jehudah b. Baba. Of Simeon, on the other hand, the unusual fact is related that he remained unmarried, and that he excused it by his attachment to the study of the Torah.[4] Had he been known, however, as an Essene, his single state would not have struck R. Eleazar b. ʿAzariah as strange. Of R. Jehudah b. Baba a late source reports that from his eighteenth to his eightieth year he never slept longer than a horse, which would describe him as an ascetic.[5] But not all these qualities were to be found combined in every one of the

[1] Apoc. Baruch 66. 2 says of King Josiah: 'He raised the horn of the holy, and exalted the righteous and glorified all that were wise in understanding.' The author applied the categories of his own time to those early days.

[2] jer. Pe'ah, I, 15 b. 39; Baraitha Kethub. 50 a.

[3] Baraitha Baba b. 11 a; Tos. Pe'ah, IV, 18; jer. I, 15 b. 63; Pesikt. rab. 25, 126 b.

[4] Tos. Yebam., VIII end; b. 63 b; Gen. r. 34.14. Cf. Rabh's statement in Berakh. 43 b (the correct wording in Rabbinovicz and Naḥmani on Exod. 24. 5) about young men who, in the messianic times, would not taste of sin, that is, would never touch any woman.

[5] מדרש אלה אזכרה.

pious men; as the Ḥasid whose thanks-offering and joy at the fulfilment of a commandment were described, kept his possessions, was married and had a son, and also Samuel the Small of whom it is stated that he had no children[1] must have been married. The gratitude to God of the farmer of Jerusalem rested on his humility and general piety; and this was totally different from the deeds of piety of all the men just enumerated, and in no way supports the assumption that חסיד represented members of the Essenic or any other order.

2. As his personality is unknown, any generalization of his case would be hazardous. But the sacrifice of another pious man is expressly stated to have been characteristic of his fellow-Ḥasids. R. Eliezer says, 'One may every day and at any time, whenever one likes, bring voluntarily a trespass offering brought for a doubtful sin; it was called the guilt-offering of the pious men. It is said of Baba b. Buta that he voluntarily brought every day a guilt-offering for a doubtful sin, except on the day after the Day of Atonement, and that he said, By this Temple, I should bring one, if they allowed me to do so; but they tell me to wait till I have come to a doubt.'[2] R. Eliezer knew many details of the sacrificial laws, not only from the traditions taught in the schools, but probably from the priests of the Temple and from scholars; for he had lived for some years before 70 in Jerusalem as a disciple of R. Joḥanan b. Zakkai, and may have had an opportunity for learning the facts about the special sacrifices of the pious men in the schools in Jerusalem and in the Temple. In his Halakhah he was later a follower of the Shammaites; and here also he agreed concerning the sacrifice with the practice of Baba b.

[1] Semaḥ., VIII.

[2] Kerith. VI, 3; Tos. IV, 4: רבי אליעזר אומר מתנדב אדם אשם תלוי בכל יום ובכל שעה שירצה, הוא היה נקרא אשם חסידים. אמרו עליו על בבא בן בוטי שהיה מתנדב אשם תלוי בכל יום חוץ מאחר יום הכפורים יום אחד, אמר המעון הזה אילו היו מניחים לי הייתי מביא אלא אומרים לי המתין עד שתכנס לספק. The Cambridge Mishnah has ביטי.

Buta who was a disciple in the school of Shammai.[1] Baba was a wealthy man. On a certain occasion he wanted, by a public act, to demonstrate that the Shammaites whose lead he as one of them generally followed, were wrong in prohibiting on the festival the laying of the hands upon a private sacrifice. For that purpose he brought at his own expense many costly rams to the Temple Mount, and invited other men to offer them up, in accordance with the lenient view of the Hillelites on the festival, as private sacrifices, as burnt or peace-offerings. He could also afford to bring a guilt-offering daily. This he sacrificed to God not in order to atone for any definite sin which he had unwittingly committed and of which he had later become conscious; for in such a case it would have been a proper sin- or a guilt-offering, whereas his was a conditional guilt-offering for a sin of which he was not sure at all. He felt the need of purging himself daily, by means of such a sacrifice, of sins possibly committed on the previous day. He evidently considered the moral weakness of man in general and his own in particular, and thought that he could not escape altogether a sin of some kind, either in his daily activities and his intercourse with his fellow-men, or in his conduct towards God. And as, in his opinion, his actions and his thoughts during the day must have occasioned sin, he felt it his duty to clear away his guilt and his burden daily before God.[2] As the note of a teacher, possibly R. Eliezer's, in the Mishnah indicates, Baba was one of a group of men who felt the responsibility of their daily sins; and as R. Eliezer stated that the sacrifice was called the guilt-offering of the pious, they themselves were called חסידים, and this epithet already was applied to them by their contemporaries.

Of course, it may be taken for granted that it was not merely the sprinkling of the blood by the priest and

[1] Baraitha Beṣah 20 a bottom; Tos. Ḥagig. II, 11; jer. II, 78 a. 50; Gitt. 57 a; Baba bath. 3 b ff.

[2] Did the sacrifices of the father for each of his sons, Job 1. 5. 'for Job said, It may be that my sons have sinned, and cursed God in their hearts', suggest it to Baba? But Job brought burnt offerings!

the other formal acts constituting the sacrifice that brought to Baba and the pious men who followed the same religious principles, alleviation and relief from their burden of daily sin; but, as may be for the present safely assumed, their feeling of true repentance, the accompanying confession of sin, and the prayer for forgiveness. Even immediately after the Day of Atonement Baba felt anxious, though on that day he could have had no transactions of any kind with his neighbours. In judging himself very strictly, and in his sensitiveness to the slightest moral or religious deviation, he may not have been sure as to whether he had not in conversation offended one of them; or whether perhaps his thoughts, his imperfect repentance, his possible lack of concentration at the public sacrifices, and his insufficient contrition at the high priest's confessions of sin had not incurred for him some moral sin. The Day of Atonement, as Baba's protestation suggests,[1] with its strict demands on the sensitive soul, may have roused in him even graver doubts of sin than an ordinary day; though, from the legal point of view and in their consideration of business as the main source of sin, the Shammaites could not see how their fellow scholar Baba could have on the Day of Atonement come near even the shadow of sin. As far as our information goes, such piety expressed in daily guilt-offerings has no parallel in anything reported of the Essenes, though it is possible that there were Essenes among the disciples of the Shammaites. It is a type of piety characterized by its over great anxiety about sin, not expected even in a scholar of the strict Shammaite school at the beginning of the first century; and there is no information as to the kind of sin the fear of which could have

[1] The form of oath המעון הזה was once used by R. Simeon b. Gamaliel I in Kerith. I, 7: When once a pair of pigeons cost two gold denars in Jerusalem, and such a price prevented women from bringing the sacrifices due after childbirth, R. Simeon b. Gamaliel said, By this Temple, I shall not rest this night, until they have gone down to two denars! The Essenes never swore, Josephus, *Wars*, II, 8. 6. 135; *Antiquit.*, XV, 10. 4. 371; Philo, Quod omnis probus, 12ff, II, 458.

oppressed the pious men, and about the social and religious conditions in Jerusalem that might have stimulated such a movement. It is hardly necessary to tell those who know anything of the history of the rabbinic law and institutions that it was not the law of levitical purity that was responsible for Baba's anxiety about sin. For, as his action on the Temple Mount shows, he was not a priest; and levitical purity was in his days not yet observed by non-priests, not even by his teacher Shammai who in the school dealt only academically with individual rules of such purity.

R. Eliezer's well-informed disciple, R. Jehudah b. Ilai, reports: 'The ancient pious men desired to bring a sin-offering, because God did not bring an offence into their hands; what did they do? They voluntarily made the vow of the Nazirite to God in order to become liable to bring a sin-offering. R. Simeon says, They did not vow to be Nazirites; but whoever desired to bring a burnt-offering or a peace-offering, or a thanks-offering with the four kinds of loaves belonging to it, brought voluntarily any of those, but they did not voluntarily make the vow of the Nazirite, because for doing so they would have been called sinners according to Num. 6. 11.'[1] These pious men were filled with the anxiety lest they might be committing sins and in need of atonement. The sin-offering prescribed in Lev. 4. 27 in the case of a transgression in error of a biblical prohibition required that the sinner should have

[1] Baraitha Nedar. 10 a; Tos. I,1: תניא רבי יהודה אומר חסידים הראשונים היו מתאוין להביא קרבן חטאת לפי שאין הק״בה מביא תקלה על ידיהם. מה היו עושין, עומדין ומתנדבין נזירות למקום כדי שיתחייבו קרבן חטאת למקום. רבי שמעון אומר לא נדרו בנזיר אלא הרוצה להביא עולה מתנדב ומביא שלמים מתנדב ומביא תודה וארבעה מיני לחמה מתנדב ומביא אבל בנזירות לא התנדבו כדי שלא יקראו חוטאין שנאמר וכפר עליו מאשר חטא על הנפש. In jer. Nedar. I, 36 d. 48: רבי שמעון אומר חוטאים היו שהיו נודרים בנזיר שנאמר וכפר עליו מאשר חטא על הנפש חטא זה על נפשו שמנע עצמו מן היין, R. Simeon did not deny the fact of the vow of the pious men, but called them sinners for it.

later become conscious of having unwittingly committed a definite offence; but the pious men who in their strict care and watchfulness naturally did their utmost to avoid such a violation of the law, could not satisfy that condition laid down for a sin-offering, and found no occasion for bringing such a sacrifice. Their desire for it suggests that, in their opinion, a sin-offering brought for one definite sin would, at the same time, atone for other offences which, on account of their uncertainty, had to remain without atonement by sacrifice. For that purpose they looked out for an act which implied no sin, but automatically provided an occasion for a sin-offering. While Baba b. Buta in the same anxiety resorted to a daily guilt-offering for a doubtful sin, the pious men either knew nothing of its admissibility or disapproved of it, or did not consider such a sacrifice of sufficient force for their need of atonement. The sin-offering prescribed in Num. 6. 14 for the Nazirite at the conclusion of his temporary vow was not brought for any definite breach of the law, but for an unknown, yet possible levitical defilement and for other offences against the rules of the vow, and could therefore include in its atonement other trespasses of the same uncertainty. As the temporary vow of the Nazirite extended only over thirty days,[1] the pious men could repeat the vow as often as they liked, bring the sin-offering every month, and thus satisfy their desire for regular atonement. Some scholars see in these Ḥasids Essenes, without even attempting to prove that the scruples and the anxiety about frequent, unconscious sins and the strong desire to bring sin-offerings, or the short Nazirite vow for the sake of the atoning sacrifice are anywhere even indicated or implied as peculiarities of the Essenes. In his

[1] Nazir, III, 2: וזו עדות העיד רבי פפיים על מי שנזר שתי נזירות שאם גלח את הראשונה יום שלשים מגלח את השנייה יום ששים ואם גלח ליום ששים חסר אחד יצא שיום שלשים עולה לו מן המנין; and the Shammaites in Nazir, III, 6: מי שנזר נזירות הרבה והשלים את נזירתו ואחר כך בא לארץ בית שמאי אומרים נזיר שלשים יום ובית הלל אומרים נזיר בתחלה, Josephus, *Wars*, II, 15. 1. 313.

endeavour to support somehow his preconceived idea of the identity of these Ḥasids with the Essenes, Geiger [1] had to remove from the report as an alleged misunderstanding of the author who read into the vow of the pious men a desire for atonement of a later period, the clear statement about their eagerness for sin-offerings. But Geiger not only ignored the old reference of R. Eliezer to the guilt-offerings of the Ḥasids, and the even earlier instance of the daily sacrifice of Baba b. Buta; but he also failed to adduce his evidence for his assumed later period, when a section of Jews, not named by him, had that desire for private atoning sacrifices. By such arbitrary treatment of early historical sources any preconceived view can, without any evidence or much argument, be proved. As to the date of these ancient pious men of Temple times, it may be noted that though R. Eliezer spoke of the guilt-offering of the חסידים, and his disciple R. Jehudah described the sin-offerings of the חסידים הראשונים, the same younger contemporaries of Shammai and Hillel were meant by both of them; the difference of more than forty years between the ages of the two reporters, and the consequent different distances from the incident described sufficiently account for R. Jehudah's additional word הראשונים.[2]

[1] *Jüd. Zeitschrift*, IX, 1871, 52.

[2] It is true, R. Jehudah used the same adjective הראשונים 'ancient', of a period not far from his own. R. Joḥanan in his name says in Berakh. 35 b, Come and see that the last (present) generations are not like the first: for the earlier generations deliberately brought their produce home in such a way as to make it liable to be tithed, whereas the last generations bring in their produce through the roofs and enclosures to make them exempt from tithes. In spite of the contrast in אחרונים, it would be difficult to define the date of הראשונים, were it not for the express statement about the incident that occasioned that comparison, in jer Ma'as. III, 50 c. 6: When once R. Jehudah b. Ilai saw Rabbi and R. José b. R. Jehudah bring in a basket of produce by the back of the garden, he said, Look, what difference there is between you and earlier men: R. Akiba bought three kinds of produce for a Perutah in order to tithe each kind, and you bring in your produce by the back of the garden! Consequently, R. Jehudah referred to his own teacher, R. Akiba, as הראשונים. Also his reference there to the earlier men who made the

3. In the early description of the popular Feast of Water-drawing, celebrated on the Temple Mount in the second night of Tabernacles, the pious men appear in very interesting circumstances. The Mishnah relates:[1] 'The pious men and the men of deed danced before them (the people assembled on the Temple Mount) with burning torches in their hands, and recited before them words of songs and praises'. The parallel Baraitha[2] has a fuller account: 'The

study of the Torah their regular duty and their ordinary work occasional, and found that both were well established, and to the present generation who make their ordinary work their regular duty and the study of the Torah occasional, and find that neither is well established, no doubt views in its first part the days of his teachers in Judaea. His fellow-student, R. José b. Dormaskith in Tos. Yaday. II, 16 reports, I was with the early scholars, זקנים הראשונים, when they came from Jamnia to Lydda, and I found R. Eliezer sitting in the shop of the bakers in Lydda; when he asked me what news there had been that day in the school, I related to him the subjects discussed, the arguments advanced, and the divisions taken. When I mentioned to him the Halakhah about the obligation of the Jews in Ammon and Moab to give the tithe for the poor in the year of rest, he said to me, Ignore your division, for I have a tradition to the same effect from R. Joḥanan b. Zakkai going back to Moses. Some of the details of the discussions referred to have been preserved in Yad. IV, 3, and they mention R. Tarfon, R. Eleazar b.'Azariah, and R. Ishmael, and also the division and R. Eliezer's conversation about it are stated there. (The parallel Baraitha in Ḥagig. 3 b does not mention the early scholars.) The whole incident happened before the year 120; and R. José whom we find later discussing difficult passages of the Bible with R. Jehudah (Sifré Deut. 1, 64 b. ff.; Midr. Tann. Deut. 1. 1, 3; Bacher, I, 390 ff.), described that occurrence, no doubt, in Galilee after 136. When he told his fellow-scholars in Usha of the incident with R. Eliezer, he referred to the members of the central school in Jamnia with whom he had travelled from Jamnia to Lydda (among whom was, no doubt, R. Tarfon who, after attending the discussions in Jamnia, was returning to his home in Lydda), as the early scholars. It appears that the bar-Kokhba-war and the horrors of the Hadrianic religious persecutions had, in the minds of the scholars affected, removed the generation immediately preceding into a great distanc. Cf. R. Jehudah in Gitt. 81 a.

[1] Sukk. V, 4: חסידים ואנשי מעשה היו מרקדים לפניהם באבוקות של אור שבידיהן ואומרים לפניהן דברי שירות ותשבחות; in the Cambridge Mishnah שירות is missing, see also Rabbinovicz.

[2] Tos. Sukk. IV, 2: חסידים ואנשי מעשה היו מרקדין לפניהם באבוקות ואומרין לפניהם דברי תושבחות, מה היו אומרים, אשרי מי שלא חטא ומי שחטא יימחל לו. יש מהן שהיו אומרים אשריך ילדותי שלא ביישת את זקנותי

pious men and the men of deed were dancing before them with torches, and said before them words of praises. What did they say? Happy is he who sinned not, and to him who sinned may it be forgiven! Some of them said, Happy art thou, my youth, that thou didst not put to shame my old age; they were the men of deed: others of them said, Happy art thou, mine old age, that thou wilt atone for my youth; they were the repentant'. Only a part of the account and in a different form has been preserved in the third version:[1] 'Of the pious men and the men of deed some said, Happy art thou, my youth, that thou didst not put to shame mine old age; these were the men of deed; others of them said, Happy art thou, mine old age, that thou hast atoned for my youth; these were the repentant; both groups said, Happy is he who sinned not, and to him who sinned, may it be forgiven'. In both, nearly identical versions of the Baraitha, the opening sentence mentions the pious men and the men of deed; the second part, however, which quotes their respective declarations of happiness, puts the repentant in the place of the pious men in one case. On the other hand, in the version of the Babylonian Talmud[2] the pious men and the men of deed are combined as the authors of one declaration, so that here three groups of distinguished men appear, no doubt, by a wrong distribution of their statements. As the reference to their old age indicates, all of them were advanced in years, or at least

אילו אנשי מעשה, ויש מהן אומרים אשריך זקנותי שתכפר על ילדותי אילו בעלי תשובה.

[1] jer. Sukk. V. 55 b. 68: החסידים ואנשי המעשה יש מהן שהיו אומרים אשרייך ילדותי שלא ביישת את זקנותי אילו אנשי מעשה ויש מהן אומרים אשרייך זקנותי שכיפרת על ילדותי אילו בעלי תשובה, אילו ואילו היו אומרים אשרי מי שלא חטא ומי שחטא יימחל לו.

[2] Sukk. 53 a top: תנו רבנן יש מהן אומרים אשרי ילדותינו שלא ביישה את זקנותינו אילו חסידים ואנשי מעשה ויש מהן אומרים אשרי זקנותינו שכפרה את ילדותינו אלו בעלי תשובה, אלו ואלו אומרים אשרי מי שלא חטא ומי שחטא ישוב וימחל לו.

elderly; some of them, as the atonement, the shaming and the repentance show, looked back upon their younger years as not free from some undefined blame.[1] Later they repented, changed their course, and their latter years atoned for the failings of their youth. The character of their present life and the attitude of their minds fill them with satisfaction, and it seems to be the ideal life to which, however, they attained only after a hard struggle, as indicated by the need of repentance. On the other hand, they pointed to their past and to the subsequent change of their actions without restraint or fear; evidently the fact of their repentance and their final peace of mind fill them with such happiness that the unsatisfactory past lost its sting. Others of their company on the Temple Mount had led already, when young, a life in agreement with their present ideal, and never swerved from that line of determined and consistent piety. Still they know that man is weak, and his going astray is the rule, therefore they declare him happy who did not sin; and they are not proud of their comparative freedom from error in their youth, and do not compare in self-contentment the actions of others with their own. They consider their present companions just as worthy as themselves; for their past mistakes have been wiped out by their true repentance and, in their conviction, also forgiven by God, as they abandoned the path of sin and since then have consistently walked in the ways of piety. How the men of deed who in the parallel sentences correspond with the repentant, should have meant such as followed the right line of conduct, is not at all clear, as the word מעשה would then have had the otherwise unknown meaning of firmly established moral and religious action of life.

4. The term is found again[2]: 'Since the death of R. Ḥaninah b. Dosa the men of deed ceased. R. Pinḥas

[1] Cf. Eccl. 11. 9: Rejoice, O young man, in thy youth; and let thy heart cheer thee in the days of thy youth, and walk in the ways of thy heart, and in the sight of thine eyes; and Sotah I, 4 הרבה ילדות עושה. It would suggest a free enjoyment of youth in pleasures of all kinds.

[2] Sotah, IX, 15: מ״שמת רבי חנינא בן דוסא בטלו אנשי מעשה

F

b. Yair said, ‘Since the destruction of the Temple the חברים and free men have been put to shame and have wrapped their heads, and the men of deed have been reduced, while the men of violence and of the tongue have grown powerful’.[1] And in the description of the sad years which will precede the coming of the Messiah[2] it says, ‘In the third year great famine, men, women, and little ones and the pious men and the men of deed die, and the Torah is forgotten by those who study it’. Rashi[3] explains the man of deed to be one relying on his worthiness (in the sight of God) and performing miracles as those in Ta‘an. 25 a ; Levy[4] as

[1] Bacher, II, 498, 2 explains חברים to be used as a contrast to עם הארץ. If he meant scholars, R. Pinḥas employed an unusual term which occurs, as far as I know, only in later sources, as in Midr. Psalm 1. 16 : הדור הוא תלמיד חכם בשעה שהוא מקבץ את החבירים ולא להחניפם אלא על דבר אמת ועונה צדק, Yalkut Deut. 797 : מ״של לחכם שהיה יו״ב בבית הכנסת ועוסק בצרכי צבור ולא היו החברים מביטים בו כיון ״נכנס לדרוש ודורש כענין התחילו מקלסין אותו ואומרים לו ודאי זו תורה ואלו דברים; Exod. r. 27. 9 : אם ערבת לרעך, אמר רבי נחמיה נאמרה על החברים, כל הימים שאדם חבר לא איכפת לו בציבור ואינו נענש עליו, נתמנה אדם בראש ונטל טלית לא יאמר לטובתי אני נזקק לא איכפת לי בציבור אלא כל טורח הציבור עליו, in the parallel Midr. Psalm 8. 3 : בתלמידי חכמים הכתוב מדבר. In Deut. r. 3. 3 two men forgot two measures of barley left with R. Pinḥas b. Yair who sowed the barley and kept the harvests for them ; after seven years אותן החברים came to claim their deposit. See also 2 ARN. 28, 29 b where R. Joḥanan b. Zakkai says to his disciples חבירינו למדו תורה, and 2 ARN. 8, 11 b R. Jehudah b. Ilai, when a bridal procession was passing by his school, called on his disciples חבירינו עמדו והתעסקו עם הכלה; ARN. 29. 45 a top, R. Yiṣḥak b. Pinḥas says : ואל תשתדל לראותו שב במקום חבירים. In jer. Berakh., I, 2 d. 34 R. Pinḥas in the name of R. Eleazar b. R. Menaḥem said, David placed a lyre and a harp above his head, and rose at midnight to play them, so that חבירי תורה might hear them ; and what did the חבירי תורה say? Since King David is engaged in the study of the Torah, how much more should we study. The parallel in Pesik. 62 b has חכמי ישראל. In jer. Bikk. III, 65 c. 48 ; Kidd. 33 b חבר is the title of a scholar of the second degree, but already qualified to be a member of the school. See also Bacher in *MGWJ.*, 43, 1899, 345 ff., 572 ; 2 ARN. 19. 21 a ; Ginzberg in *Students' Annual*, 1914, 139 ff.

[2] Baraitha Synh. 97 a. [3] Sotah, 49 a. [4] Neuhebr. *WB.*, III, 197 a.

men distinguished by rare virtues to whom on account of that miracles happened frequently; Löw,[1] Geiger,[2] J. Brüll,[3] Blau,[4] and Kohler[5] as miracle workers, Krochmal[6] as adherents of some esoteric religious teaching who, unlike the ancient pious men, did not devote themselves to contemplation only, but responded also to the practices of life; M. Friedländer[7] as practical men, Schorr[8] and Frankel[9] as miracle-working Essenes. The great difficulty in defining the meaning of אנשי מעשה could perhaps be reduced by establishing the possible significations of מעשה. As far as my memory serves me, the word standing by itself, without the addition of the essential qualifying noun נסים or a synonym of it, never denotes a miracle. How Rashi arrived at his explanation is clear from his reference to the miracles of R. Ḥaninah b. Dosa: as the latter was called a man of deed, and several of the most characteristic reports of his activities deal with miracles, his title must in his opinion have been derived from these. But is it not just as probable that other actions of his, though less fully and less prominently described, and of a totally different nature, were responsible for that designation? מעשה in 1 Sam. 8. 8, Jer. 7. 13 denotes a man's or a people's doings, whether good or bad; Hillel's doings were in the honour of God; 'Akabia b. Mahalalel said to his son,[10] 'Thy doings will bring thee near to the scholars, and thy doings will remove thee from them'. When once a heathen woman came to R. Eliezer and asked him to admit her into Judaism, he wanted first to ascertain her antecedents, and asked her to state in detail her past doings,[11] whether good or bad. In the schools where evil deeds were rare and would not have

[1] Ben Chananja, V, 1862, 281 b on Synh. VII, 11.
[2] *Urschrift*, 126.
[3] *Introduction into the Mishnah*, I, 61.
[4] *Zauberwesen*, 149. 5.
[5] *Jewish Encyclop.* V, 227 a.
[6] מורה, 144 a; Ben Chananja, II, 2.
[7] *Ben Dosza*, 24.
[8] החלוץ, VII, 57 ff., cf. Derenbourg, *Essai*, 460 ff.
[9] *Zeitschrift f. d. rel. Interessen*, III, 1846, 458; *MGWJ.* II, 1853, 70.
[10] 'Eduy. V, 7.
[11] Koh. r. 1. 8. 4: פרטי את מעשיך.

been tolerated, מעשה was applied only in the good sense; and it is of special interest for this inquiry that R. Ḥaninah b. Dosa himself[1] says, The learning of him will last whose deeds are greater than his learning. And its meaning is clear in R. Akiba's statement[2] about a scholar who was caught in so terrible a sea-storm that R. Akiba thought that he had perished; when he reappeared in Cappadocia, R. Akiba asked him, 'What deeds had you performed that you were so miraculously saved?'[3] He replied, On my way to the boat I met a poor man who asked me for help; when I gave him a loaf of bread he said, "As you by your gift have given me my life, may your life be given to you!" Here the deed is one of charity which is generally called מעשים טובים,[4] as in the sentence of R. Joḥanan b. Zakkai explaining the white garments and the oil in Eccl. 9. 8 to refer to the observance of the commandments, to good deeds and to the study of the Torah.[5] As the commandments are specially mentioned, the deeds refer to acts of kindness and of love to the fellow-man.

In the great dispute between the teachers assembled on a certain occasion before 135 in Lydda the subject of מעשה was fully considered. A Baraitha reports: 'When once R. Tarfon and the scholars were sitting in the upper room of the family of Nithzah in Lydda, the question was put to them as to whether the study of the Torah or the

[1] Aboth, III, 9.

[2] Koh. r. 11. 1; Yebam. 121 a; ARN. 3, 9 a. R. Akiba in Aboth III, 15 says, Everything is foreseen, yet freedom of choice is given, and the world is judged by grace, yet all is according to the number of deeds (see the commentaries).

[3] When several sons of קמחית had become high-priests in turn, the scholars asked her, מה מעשים טובים יש בידך, what good deeds hast thou (to have merited such a rare distinction)? She replied, I swear that the beams of my house never saw the hair of my head, nor the skirt of my frock, jer. Yoma I, 38 d. 11. In the parallel Baraitha Yoma 47 a the question of the scholars reads: What hast thou done to have merited this? In ARN. 35, 53 a: מה זכות היה בידך. Cf. Mekhil. 14. 13, 28 b.: מעשה הטוב.

[4] Cf. Aggad. Cant. 7. 14: בני אדם של מעשה ושל צדקה, Schechter, 92.

[5] Koh. r. 9. 8; Bacher, I, 36. 1, cf. 2 ARN. 26, 27 a; ARN. 16, 32 b.

practice of it was more important. : R. Tarfon declared the practice and R. Akiba the study more important, but in the end all present agreed that the study was more important, as it led to the practice of the Torah'.[1] The discussion and the arguments advanced show that מעשה, as also the word itself suggests, refers generally to the practice of the positive precepts in the Torah, as indeed the prohibitions require for their observance no action, but only refraining from action. But when the disciple of the scholars of Lydda, R. Jehudah b. Ilai, applied that rule in a practical instance, מעשה seemed to mean something else. When R. Jehudah saw either a funeral or a bridal procession pass by his school, he looked at his disciples and said, 'The deed has precedence before the study'.[2] The parallel account states: 'It is reported of R. Jehudah that he set aside the study of the Torah before a funeral or a bridal procession,[3] and he called on his disciples to interrupt the study of the Torah and to join in the bridal procession and to add to the joy of the bride.' R. Jehudah unmistakably quoted the rule not adopted in Lydda, but the case to which he applied it is nowhere prescribed in the Torah; it was one of the duties of lovingkindness which the rabbis impressed upon their disciples and upon the people as very important.

[1] Baraitha Kidd. 40 b; Cant. r. 2. 14. 5; Sifré Deut. 41, 79 b; jer. Ḥagig. I, 76 c. 46; Bacher I, 296. 3: וכבר היה רבי טרפון וזקנים מסובין בעליית בית נתזה בלוד נשאלה שאילה זו בפניהם תלמוד גדול או מעשה גדול, נענה רבי טרפון ואמר מעשה גדול נענה רבי עקיבא ואמר לימוד גדול נענו כולם ואמרו לימוד גדול שהלימוד מביא לידי מעשה. R. José the Galilean in b. and Sifré proved that the study was more important, since the law about the heave offering from dough in Num. 15. 18–21 was given forty years before it was practised, and the laws about the heave offerings and the tithes fifty-four years, &c. So R. Simeon b. Gamaliel II later expressed it in Aboth I, 17: לא המדרש עיקר אלא המעשה, not the interpretation of the Torah is the essential thing, but the practice of it. See also Sifra Lev. 18. 4, 85 d: תשמרו זו המשנה, ללכת בהם זו המעשה, תשמרו ללכת בהם לא המשנה נגוד אלא המעשה נגוד, see RABD's note.

[2] jer. Ḥagig. I, 76 c. 44.

[3] Baraitha Kethub. 17 a bottom; in ARN. 4, 9 b ff. two instances are reported in which R. Jehudah acted in the same way.

R. Jehudah did not hesitate as to his duty to interrupt his lesson and to take away his disciples from their work; and the master with his students joined in the joy of a bride who probably was a stranger to them. He followed in the performance of this duty his teacher R. Tarfon who once, when the procession of a poor bride passed by his school, took her to his house where his mother and his wife bathed, anointed, and adorned her, and then all of them danced before her, until she reached the house of her husband.[1] As R. Jehudah was most conservative in following his masters, it is very probable that already they had extended that rule to such duties of lovingkindness, and it may even in Lydda have been already included in the discussion of the teachers mentioned;[2] at least the Shammaite R. Tarfon applied it practically in that sense, and מעשה may have meant to him in the first instance such

[1] ARN. 41, 67 a.

[2] In Semaḥ. XI: אין מבטלין תלמוד תורה מפני המת והכלה, אבא שאול אומר המעשה קודם לתלמוד תורה, כך היה רבי יהודה עושה . . . ואמר המעשה קודם ללימוד, the first view does not permit the interruption of the study of the Torah for the sake of a funeral or a bridal procession. But already Brüll in his *Jahrbücher*, I, 43, note 94, suggested that the first word might be a mistake, as it is not found in the parallel Baraitha in Kethub. 17 a. In note 93 he points out that מעשה here, as it is evident from the context in all the reports, denotes especially the occupation with the charity of burial and similar acts as it was practised particularly by the חבורות, brotherhoods (see below). In favour of this explanation can be quoted two incidents of the second half of the third century in connexion with which the rule about the precedence of the practice is quoted. R. Abahu sent his son Ḥaninah to Tiberias to learn Torah, instead of which the son devoted himself there to the burial of the dead (גמל חסד, as the father's witty application of Exod. 14. 11 shows, meant burial). R. Abahu reminded him of the decision arrived at by the scholars in Lydda, that study was more important than practice. R. Ḥiyya b. Abba, R. Assi, and R. Ammi once came late to R. Eleazar's lecture, because they had been engaged in a deed of lovingkindness to a stranger, and R. Eleazar quoted to them the rule as applying to a special case, jer. Ḥagig. I, 76 c. 46–54. As the three scholars were all priests, גמל חסד cannot refer to burial, but, as very frequently, to the comforting of a mourner. In the parallel in jer. Pesaḥ., III, 30 b. 51 the rule is applied to other religious commandments.

deeds. In any case, the word does not mean a miracle, but the practice of religious duties, and frequently the practice of deeds of lovingkindness. R. Ḥaninah b. Dosa and other men of deed would accordingly have distinguished themselves by the most conscientious observance of the positive precepts of the Torah,[1] or by devoting themselves particularly to acts of loving-kindness; perhaps even with greater enthusiasm and more exclusively than R. Ḥaninah's contemporary, the Shammaite R. Tarfon and his disciple R. Jehudah b. Ilai.

Of the life of R. Ḥaninah b. Dosa several incidents have been preserved which should support or refute the explanation of מעשה just suggested. He lived in ʻArabh near Sepphoris where his early commencement of the Sabbath was noticed.[2]

[1] See Marmorstein, *Doctrine of Merits*, 10, 191.

[2] Jer. Berakh. IV, 7 c. 57: Ass drivers once came up from ʻArabh to Sepphoris and said that R. Ḥaninah b. Dosa had begun the Sabbath rest in his town. They reported it of him only; his fellow-citizens evidently did not follow his example, nor did the Jewish ass drivers see any objection to their driving their asses to Sepphoris after that act of R. Ḥaninah. It is an interesting coincidence that some information has been preserved about the observance of the Sabbath in ʻArabh, questions about which were submitted to R. Ḥaninah's friend, R. Joḥanan b. Zakkai. Mishnah Shabb. XVI, 7 reads: On Friday night a dish may be tilted over a lamp to prevent the beam from being set on fire, or over the excrements of a child, or over a scorpion so that it should not sting; R. Jehudah says, When once such a case came before R. Joḥanan b. Zakkai in ʻArabh, he said, I fear, the person has to bring a sin-offering. (Note the lamp on the Sabbath eve in the house of the Galilean Jew, as in R. Ḥaninah b. Dosa's house in Taʻan. 25 a, and the place of the lamp near the ceiling.) According to Baraitha Shabb. 121 b it was permitted to kill a scorpion on the Sabbath as a danger to life, and only the pious men would not allow it. That in ʻArabh even the ordinary man did not think of killing a scorpion, and R. Joḥanan did not advise him to do so, suggests that such permission was unknown or not approved of in ʻArabh at that time. In Shabb. XXII, 3 we read: If the plug of a cask has a hole, wax must not be put over it, as that would be an act like the application of a plaster; R. Jehudah said, When once such a case came before R. Joḥanan b. Zakkai in ʻArabh, he said, I fear, the person has to bring a sin-offering. The fact of the submission of the questions to the rabbi shows that the Jews of ʻArabh observed the Sabbath strictly. It is true that in jer. Shabb. XVI, 15 d. 59 R. Ulla states that during the eighteen years of R. Joḥanan b. Zakkai's stay in ʻArabh only those two questions were submitted to

When he once saw the people of his town taking gifts and offerings to Jerusalem and he himself had nothing to contribute, he went outside the town and found a stone which he planed and polished, and which he, with the help of five men, took up to Jerusalem. When here his assistants disappeared, before he had paid them their wages, he went to the authorities sitting in the chamber of hewn stones in the Temple to ask for advice.[1] Accordingly, he was already a man before the year 70; and, if Neḥunyah, the digger of pits, about the accident to whose daughter R. Ḥaninah was consulted,[2] was identical with the official of the Temple of that name and the same occupation,[3] R. Ḥaninah was already in Temple times a man whose advice was sought. He was very poor, as according to Rabh's remark which was, no doubt, based on earlier information, he lived the whole week on a kabh of carobs, the food of the poor,[4] and oppressive want of the necessaries of life prevailed in his household[5] even on the Sabbath. It is nowhere suggested that such poverty was of his own choice. His occupation seems to have been that of a stone mason, as he shaped and polished the stone of his gift to the Temple himself; and besides there is a reference to his rearing goats.[6] He was married, and had a daughter. R. Eleazar of Mode'im, a younger contemporary of his, in explaining the men of truth in Exod. 18. 21,[7] illustrated his words by adding: like R. Ḥaninah b. Dosa and his companions. His absolute truthfulness and reliability must have been known, at least among the scholars; for it was in his association

him and that on that account he exclaimed, Galilee, Galilee, thou hatest the Torah, thou shalt ultimately fall into the power of oppressors. He meant their attitude to the rabbinic interpretation of the law, of which they probably knew too little to have doubts and questions about details of the Sabbath observance and other matters.

[1] Koh. r. 1. 1; Cant. r. 1. 1. 4. [2] Baraitha Yebam. 121 b.

[3] Shekal., V, 1. [4] Ta'an. 24 b. [5] Ta'an. 25 a.

[6] Ta'an. 25 a; the prohibition against rearing sheep and goats was either not passed yet or did not yet apply to Galilee, as R. Jehudah b. Baba also disregarded it, Baba kam. 80 a; Tos. VIII, 13.

[7] Mekhil. 60 a; Mekhil. R. Simeon, 90.

with them that his personal qualities were revealed. His scrupulous honesty is illustrated by an interesting incident. When once a man left a few chickens in front of R. Ḥaninah's door, the latter took them in, stored their eggs for hatching, increased the number of the chickens, and exchanged them for a pair of goats which he later returned to the claimant of the fowls.[1] He was most scrupulous in tithing the produce used for his food;[2] even his ass refused to eat untithed fodder.[3] As he is invariably quoted with the title of Rabbi, he was a fully qualified scholar; who his teachers were is not known, but he himself had a school and disciples.[4] Apart from two sentences,[5] nothing has been preserved of his halakhic or haggadic teaching.

On his religious thought an incident throws some light.[6] Several inhabitants of his town were bitten by a snake; after killing it, R. Ḥaninah brought it to the school and said, 'My sons, it is not the serpent that kills, but sins kill.' He believed that God's providence extended to every individual, watched the deeds of every single person, and rewarded and punished already on earth; and when God considered the measure of the sins of a man to be full and

[1] Ta'an. 25 a; as Rabbinovicz and others have pointed out, this report of the Amora R. Pinḥas is a later insertion in the Talmud, but it may still have been taken from an early and authentic source. A similar story is told of R. Pinḥas b. Yair in jer. Dammai, I, 22 a. 5; Deut. r. 3. 3: When once two poor men deposited two measures of barley with R. Pinḥas, he sowed the barley and its successive harvests for seven years, so that, when the owners called for their deposit, camels and asses were required for the removal of their property. In the Midrash the account concludes with the same words as another story there about the honesty of Simeon b. Shetaḥ: from the honesty of man you can conclude the trustworthiness of God.

[2] Jer. Damm. I, 22 a. 40: When one Friday night, during his meal, the table began to contract, his wife accounted for it by her having borrowed spices from her neighbour and not having tithed them. When R. Ḥaninah had arranged for the rectification of the matter, the table rose again.

[3] ARN. 8, 19 b; in Shabb. 112 b Rabha b. Zimona remarks, Not like the ass of R. Ḥaninah b. Dosa and that of R. Pinḥas b. Yair. In Gen. r. 60. 8; Ḥull. 7 a ff. it is stated only of the ass of R. Pinḥas.

[4] Jer. Berakh. V, 9 a. 63.

[5] Aboth, III, 9, 10.

[6] Baraitha Berakh. 33 a.

him as deserving an untimely and violent end, He sent a serpent to carry out His decree of retribution. What he thought of the way in which God rewarded obedience and good deeds, is not stated clearly. If the legend about his wife's peculiar wish is even in part based on fact,[1] she and also he held the belief that the righteous after death enjoy in heaven meals at golden tables standing on three golden legs; an ideal which is also reflected by statements of R. Joḥanan b. Zakkai[2] and of other early teachers. When he prayed, his concentration and devotion were great; once, while praying, he was bitten by a snake, but did not interrupt his prayer. When the serpent was later found dead at the entrance to its den, people said, Woe to the man whom a serpent bites, but woe to the serpent that bit R. Ḥaninah b. Dosa. To his disciples' question, 'Master, hast thou not felt it?' he replied, I assure you, that as my heart was concentrated on the prayer, I felt it not.[3] Such devotion rested on true humility,[4] faith and trust in God,

[1] Ta'an. 25 a. [2] Ḥagig. 14 b.

[3] Jer. Berakh. V. 9 a. 56; his miraculous immunity, if it is not altogether legendary, and even more the statement that, when a serpent bit him, it expired, have parallels in Indian and other stories. It seems to be due to the application of some strong chemicals to the body.

[4] In ספר מעשיות. ed. Gaster, Ramsgate, 1896, 115 ff., the following story is given, no doubt taken, as others in the collection, from some earlier rabbinic source. When once R. Ḥaninah b. Dosa went to visit his master, he went early to the school and opened his discourse by saying, Receive everybody always with a friendly countenance. There came a hegemon, stood in the entrance of the school and asked, Which of you will carry me on his shoulder to his house and do for me all that I want? R. Ḥaninah b. Dosa rose and offered himself, took him upon his shoulder to his house, brought him water, sat down in the dust and asked the hegemon, Master, what is thy wish, and what will my master have for dinner? When he replied, Honey and nuts, Ḥaninah went one way and his wife another, and they brought the food. When the hegemon took the table and threw it to the ground, Ḥaninah asked, Master, kindly tell me what thy wish is. When he replied, Who will carry me to my house, Ḥaninah again offered himself. When he came out to the market of the town, he felt that the hegemon had dismounted; and he saw a flame rising to heaven and heard its voice say to him, Haninah, return, thou hast been tried and found perfect, we shall no longer trouble thee, for I heard it said about thee (Isa. 51. 16), And

and on complete self-surrender, and characterized his religious attitude to God. It would be interesting to know whether the prayer which he once recited in the open air was that prescribed by the scholars, as the context suggests, or the pouring out of his heart not restricted by time or place.

5. In Rabh's statement quoted above a heavenly voice called R. Ḥaninah the son of God, indicating his intimate relations to God the sources of which are, however, not recorded. As that voice expressed the public opinion of his merits, as in the case of Ḥoni, the circle drawer,[1] his contemporaries must have had a high opinion of his recognition by God. People sought his advice or his reassurance, when a sudden calamity befell an individual or the inhabitants of his town. And he must have readily shared the daily troubles and sorrows of his fellow-men; and that was another reason why they came to him, to have his sympathy in addition.[2] When the daughter of Neḥunyah, a digger of public pits, fell into a deep pit,[3] R. Ḥaninah was informed of the accident; in the first while he said, Peace, in the second while he said, Peace, and in the third while he said, She has come out. When they asked him how he knew it, whether he was a prophet, he answered that he was neither a prophet nor the son of a prophet, but that he had said to himself, Should the daughter of the righteous man perish by the very thing that is his occu-

I have put my words in thy mouth, and have covered thee in the shadow of mine hand. Ḥaninah's voluntary self-humiliation is similar to that of Hillel who ran out before a poor man in Jerusalem; here also Ḥaninah offers himself to do the duties of a slave of the hegemon and in addition to provide food for him. It would be interesting to know R. Ḥaninah's master and the place of his school where a Roman high official could so insolently demand such humiliating services of scholars in the school. As R. Ḥaninah lived in ʿArabh, his master may have taught in Sepphoris or Tiberias, the residence of Roman officials; but we know nothing of schools in Galilee before 70.

[1] Taʿan. III, 8.

[2] In the parallel account in jer. Shekal. V, 48d. 44 R. Pinḥas b. Yair went with the rest of the people to the house of the bereaved father to comfort him.

[3] Baraitha Yebam. 121b.

pation? He must have often thought about the ways of God's providence, especially when sudden accidents offered perplexing riddles to his religious mind. As his conviction about the deaths caused by serpents' bites showed us above, he had no doubt that this or any other calamity that threatened to destroy a young life was sent by God; on the other hand, God is not only just, but full of consideration in meting out punishment, and He would not use just a pit, the unselfish work of the pious father, as his instrument to end the life of his daughter. Such religious conviction about God's justice filled him with the strongest confidence about the fate of the girl. He did not pray for her rescue, at least nothing is said about it. While it is possible that in the intervals between his reassuring words he prayed, and the single exclamations of certainty were the outcome of his supplications, it seems more probable that he did not pray, as in his explanation of his prophetical powers he did not refer to any prayer. When a more general calamity visited his town, and a serpent injured several persons, some of the inhabitants informed R. Ḥaninah. Here again he did not intercede by prayer, but by action; for he put his heel upon the entrance to the serpent's den, and the beast, after biting him, expired. Whether it was such apparently supernatural intervention that the people expected of him, is not clear; but undoubtedly, when they came to him, they looked for either direct help or some directions about the removal of the trouble. Could his intervention be described as מעשה, and would he have been described for that as a man-of deed?

His prayer of intercession was considered not only by the ordinary man, but even by leading scholars of his time as effective. When his son was seriously ill, R. Joḥanan b. Zakkai asked him to pray for his recovery[1]: 'When R.

[1] Baraitha Berakh. 34 b bottom: אמר לו חנינא בני בקש עליו רחמים ויחיה, הניח ראשו בין ברכיו ובקש עליו רחמים וחיה. אמר רבן יוחנן בן זכאי אלמלא הטיח בן זכאי את ראשו בין ברכיו כל היום כולו לא היו משגיחים עליו.

Ḥaninah b. Dosa came to R. Joḥanan b. Zakkai to learn Torah from him, and the latter's son was taken ill, R. Joḥanan said to him, Ḥaninah, my son, pray for mercy for him, that he may recover. He put his head between his knees[1] and prayed for mercy for him, and he recovered. R. Joḥanan b. Zakkai then said, Even if the son of Zakkai had put his head between his knees for the whole day, God would not have heeded him. When his wife asked him, Is then Ḥaninah greater than thou, he said, No, but he appears to be like the slave before the king, and I appear to be like a high official before the king. When R. Gamaliel's son was taken ill, the patriarch sent two scholars to R. Ḥaninah b. Dosa to ask him to pray for mercy for his son. As soon as R. Ḥaninah had seen them, he went up to his upper room and prayed for mercy for the patient. On coming down he said to them, Go, for the fever has departed from him. When they asked him as to whether he was a prophet, he said, I am neither a prophet nor the son of a prophet, but I have the tradition that, when my prayer is fluent in my mouth, I know that it is acceptable, and when it is not fluent, it is rejected'.[2] The patient was not brought before him, nor was R. Ḥaninah invited to see him, so that no personal influence was to be exercised upon the child; it was exclusively the prayer of R. Ḥaninah that was expected to act. His own view of it is most interesting. Every illness is sent by God, and nobody knows His intentions as to its outcome; as He inflicted it, so He alone can remove it. Prayers for His compassion may have the effect that God in His mercy will allow the patient to recover; but as the father, R. Joḥanan b. Zakkai, a great man, distinguished by learning and piety, had no doubt prayed most devoutly and humbly for his son's

[1] R. Eliezer in Pesik. 192 a comments on 1 Reg. 18. 42, where Elijah prayed with his head between his knees; Bacher, I, 150. 4; 151. 1.

[2] The second incident is reported also in jer. Berakh. V, 9 d. 27, where R. Ḥaninah said, I trust that the son of R. Gamaliel has been relieved from his illness; see also Mishnah Berakh. V, 5.

recovery, and the illness still continued, has anybody's intercession for mercy any prospect of being accepted? Did God regard R. Ḥaninah more favourably? By applying for his prayer, R. Joḥanan openly admitted that in this instance his own supplication was not deemed by God worthy of acceptance; will such additional humility assist R. Ḥaninah's intervention? He did not, in modesty, refuse to intercede for R. Joḥanan's son; for it would be a sin, as Samuel, the prophet, when asked by the people of Israel to pray for them, said in 1 Sam. 12. 23, 'Moreover as for me, far be it from me that I should sin against the Lord in ceasing to pray for you'.[1] But his readiness to pray in the two instances might be interpreted as showing that he believed in his own power; to what extent? Did he presume that his great and true devotion and his concentration of mind could influence God? He does not seem to have held that opinion, as, in spite of all prayer, he said that he sometimes was not successful, as hesitation in his words indicated to him.[2] His fluency was sent to him by God, when He in His mercy was willing to grant recovery to the patient, as a reassuring sign and not as the means of His acceptance, as in the case of His refusal the

[1] Rabh in Berakh. 12 b, inferred from this verse that he who could pray for his neighbour and refused to do so, was called a sinner. Prayers for the recovery of others are mentioned in Num. 12. 13, Moses for Miriam, in Josephus, *Wars*, I, 3. 2, *Antiquit.*, XIII, 11. 1, Antigonos for his brother Aristobul, in *Antiquit.* XIX, 8. 2, the people for King Agrippa I. When the scholars visited R. Tarfon in his illness, his mother said to them, Pray for my son Tarfon, for he honours me very greatly, jer. Pe'ah, I, 15 c. 37; Pesik. r. 23, 123 a. The rule is applied to other occasions: R. Joshua b. Karḥa in Baba b. 91 b said that Maḥlon and Kilyon in Ruth 1. 5 were punished, because they failed to pray for their generation. When R. Meir visited the town of Mamla, inhabited by priests, and learned that they were all dying young, he was asked to pray for them, Gen. r. 59. 1. Abba Jehudah in Ḥolath Antiochia who supported the schools in Judaea, lost all his property; when he recovered it again and R. Eliezer, R. Joshua, and R. Akiba came to him to solicit help for the schools, he said to them, Your prayers have borne fruit, jer. Horay. III, 48 a. 51–9; Lev. r. 5. 4. See also Apoc. Bar. 2, 2; Pesik. 147 a, Midr. Tann. 26. 3, 172.

[2] He prayed, unlike Ḥannah in 1 Sam. 1. 13, not merely in his heart, but aloud.

hesitation of his prayer by God's will told R. Ḥaninah His decision; but not even his intercession had force to compel God to yield, as only the magicians believed to possess. On the other hand, R. Joḥanan b. Zakkai unreservedly admitted that the personality of R. Ḥaninah and his nearness to God were, for the successful submission to God of special requests, qualifications which the greatest scholar and the highest position in the school could not equal. R. Ḥaninah was in the position of the personal attendant of the king, who, though of a low rank, could, on account of his personal relations to his master, submit his request at any time, and plead for the life of one condemned to death, and feel justified in pressing his claim, in his expectation of seeing it speedily granted. R. Joḥanan was like the high official, kept at a distance from his king by the formalities of the court; and as he is not continually in his presence, he cannot hope to have his most urgent prayers for mercy for the life of one condemned to death considered and realized. The influence of R. Ḥaninah upon God is, in a popular form, described in an anonymous interpretation of 'the honourable man' in Is. 3. 3:[1] one for whose sake consideration is shown to his generation, as to R. Ḥaninah b. Dosa in heaven, and to R. Abahu by the Roman governor. According to Rabh's statement, a heavenly voice daily proclaimed, 'While the whole world is sustained for the sake of My son Ḥaninah, he himself is contented with

[1] Ḥagig. 14 a: ונשוא פנים זה שנושאין פנים לדורו בעבורו למעלה כגון רבי חנינא בן דוסא למטה כגון רבי אבהו בי קיסר. An anonymous story in Aramaic, in Pesaḥ. 112 b bottom, says: Originally, the female demon Agrath, daughter of Maḥlath, came every day; when once she met R. Ḥaninah b. Dosa, she told him, Had it not been announced in heaven, Take care of Ḥaninah and his learning, I should have brought you danger. He retorted, If I am considered in heaven, I decree that thou shalt never pass through inhabited land. But when she besought him to allow her some time, he granted her two nights in the week. The idea of limiting the activities of the evil spirits is found in Jubil. 10. 7–11, where Noah, with the consent of God, reduced the great number of the demons considerably, and at the request of their chief, Mastema, allowed them a tenth of their original number.

a kabh of carobs from one Friday to another'. So his merit was extended by God to all the inhabitants of his town or even his district; and his presence in his generation secured their sustenance for them, either by his mere living among them or by his providing by his prayers ample rain in its proper time and protection for the crops.[1] At the same time R. Ḥaninah and his family suffered want; and he, of his own accord, never tried to improve his own poor state by his prayer,[2] as though such use of it were unworthy, or poverty were one of the requirements of the life of a pious man.

6. A few words must be said about the miracles recorded as performed by R. Ḥaninah himself, and about others which happened to his wife; for they are, in every way, different from all that has so far been considered here of his activities. Once, on a Friday night, he noticed that his daughter looked sad; and she explained to her father that by mistake she had taken for the Sabbath lamp a vessel containing vinegar instead of one filled with oil. He said, My daughter, why are you troubled? He who said to the oil to burn will say to the vinegar that it should burn. A Baraitha adds: It burnt continually the whole day, so that they used its light for the blessing at the conclusion of the Sabbath.[3] The

[1] When R. Simeon b. Lakish in jer. Ma'as. sheni, V, 56 d. 7 Ḥull. 86 a said, Since certain Jews had come up to Palestine from Babylonia, and the flax was never smitten and the wine never turned sour, the scholars thought of the merits of R. Ḥiyya and his sons. Of much earlier times Sifra Lev. 26. 4, 110 d reports: In the days of Simeon b. Shetaḥ and Queen Salome the rain fell every Friday night, so that the wheat grew to the size of kidneys, the barley to that of olive stones, and the lentils to that of gold denars. So the piety of the two righteous personalities secured abundance of food for everybody. Cf. Sifré Deut. 11. 14. 42, 80 a.

[2] In Ta'an. 24 b it is reported that, when he was once on the road and it rained, he prayed, Master of the Universe, everybody is at ease, only Ḥaninah is in trouble; and the rain stopped. On reaching home he prayed, Master of the Universe, everybody is in trouble (owing to the drought), only Ḥaninah is at ease; and the rain fell again. The report is in many respects without a parallel.

[3] In Gaster's ס' מעשיות, No. 163, 116, his wife asked him on the Friday what food they would have for the Sabbath, and his daughter asked what they would light for the Sabbath; to his wife he replied, God will have

Sabbath had already begun, when R. Ḥaninah heard his daughter's account; the vessel could no longer be exchanged, and no other lamp must be lighted, but evidently the vessel filled with vinegar was burning. To R. Ḥaninah's mind oil was a liquid just as vinegar, and as such had no inherent quality to make it burn, it is God who by His will bestowed on it at the creation that special force; if He wills it, He can confer that power in the same way on any other liquid which in our experience does not at present possess it. R. Ḥaninah's words may have been meant as a declaration of God's might, possibly also as a wish; but his strong faith uttered them as a statement of assured certainty. Did he, according to the author of the report, in his own opinion possess the power of making God bring about the miracle? For it is God and not R. Ḥaninah who can change the nature of vinegar; and the miracle happened, because he expressed his certainty that God would act to that effect.[1] It should be noted that the report in its present form consists of two distinct parts, the first begins in Aramaic, but soon goes over into Hebrew, and finishes with R. Ḥaninah's statement; then a Baraitha relates the miracle. The same is noticeable in the next report. A female neighbour of R. Ḥaninah, while building her house, found that the beams were too short for it. When she came to him and told him of her trouble, he asked her for her name and, in addressing her by it,[2] said, Ibbu, Ibbu, may

mercy, and to his daughter he said, Light what is in that vessel. The wife made a fire in the empty oven and the latter was miraculously filled with bread; and when the daughter found that the vessel contained vinegar, R. Ḥaninah spoke the words quoted in the text. When the Sabbath approached, R. Ḥaninah sanctified the Sabbath by pronouncing the blessing over the bread, the daughter lighted the lamp, &c.

[1] A miracle happened in a different form to a Sabbath lamp in Gen. r. 60. 16: As long as our mother Sarah lived, the lamp was burning from one Friday night to the other, but after her death the lamp failed; when Rebekkah came into the tent, the lamp's strength returned. In Pesikta r. 23, 117 b R. Eleazar b. Jeremiah (in Gen. r. 11. 2 R. Eleazar, see Theodor) reports, I once lighted the lamp on a Friday evening, and it burnt till Sabbath night, and I found it then still full of oil, nothing was missing.

[2] It was according to the evidence in Rabbinovicz איבו, not איכו.

thy beams extend! (A Baraitha continues: they extended, so that they projected one cubit on each side; some say, they added parts).[1] Another Baraitha proceeds: 'Pelimo says, I saw that house, and its beams were projecting a cubit on each side, and I was told that it was the house which R. Ḥaninah had covered with beams by his prayer.' The author of the last part who was a contemporary of R. Jehudah I,[2] specially mentions that R. Ḥaninah's prayer brought about the miracle. But he does not say what occasion there was for such an intervention, whether it was the extreme poverty of a helpless widow or some other grave trouble from which R. Ḥaninah in his compassion thought it his duty to liberate her; for that he should have invoked God's miracles for anybody and at any time, is hardly credible. The fragmentary nature of the three statements put next to each other is probably responsible for the incompleteness of connexion. The first part in Aramaic ends with R. Ḥaninah's wish to the woman for which he, as magicians would, required her name.

In another Aramaic account, mentioned before, the wife of R. Ḥaninah was once tired of her abject poverty, and she induced him to pray to God for material assistance;[3] and in answer to it God sent him the golden leg of a table. Soon after he saw in a dream, how all the righteous men in heaven were eating at tables having three legs, while his table had only two legs. When he told his wife of his dream, she induced him to pray to God that the golden leg be taken back; and so it happened. A Baraitha continues: 'The second miracle was greater than the first (for they had a tradition that God gave, but did not take back).' For a righteous man should not ask for material help, as his reward is awaiting him in heaven, and this should not be reduced by the granting of requests on earth. His wife, ashamed of her poverty, used every Friday to light a fire

[1] The part in brackets is absent in the Munich MS. and other texts.

[2] Menaḥ. 37 a and Baraitha Berakh. 48 b bottom.

[3] In some texts (see Rabbinovicz) she induced him to pray for an instalment of his future reward in the world to come. See Yelamd. Exod. 11 b.

in her oven, to produce the impression upon her neighbours that she was making preparations for the Sabbath. When once a wicked neighbour who knew her poverty saw the smoke rise from R. Ḥaninah's house, she knocked at the door to see what was going on there. The poor wife of R. Ḥaninah in her shame withdrew into a corner; but meanwhile a miracle happened: the oven was filled with bread and the kneading trough with dough. When the inquisitive neighbour called out, 'Bring a shovel, for thy bread is getting burnt', the poor woman replied, 'For that purpose have I come here.' A Baraitha continues: 'Also she went in to fetch a baker's shovel, for she was used to miracles.' The whole account is in Aramaic, except the Baraitha; and this seems to differ from the main story in which the miracle happened only to silence the wicked, unwelcome visitor, and to protect the pious woman from being put to shame. In the Baraitha R. Ḥaninah's wife is described as having before experienced several miracles, and therefore justified in expecting another; her husband had no share in all this. The exaggeration is too great even for the house of R. Ḥaninah; and there is no doubt that the strange stories all belong to one class of later expansions of the originally plain accounts. Their date seems to be that of the Tanna Pelimo who, as shown above, quoted his having seen the wonderful house that had been covered with beams by R. Ḥaninah's prayer. Unfortunately the information extant does not enable us to trace the gradual growth of the legends from the year 100 to 200; but it is most instructive to note that the Palestinian Talmud has preserved no account of any of the miracles,[1]

[1] Except the one about R. Ḥaninah's table giving way at his meal on a Friday night, because his wife had forgotten to tithe the spices which she had borrowed from a neighbour for the preparation of that meal, jer. Damm. I, 22 a. 40. Line 43 reads: When once R. Tarfon was having his meal, a piece of bread fell from his hand; when asked what it meant, he said, I borrowed an axe and prepared my levitically pure food with it. In comparing the two incidents we see clearly that the occurrence at R. Ḥaninah's table was similar to that of R. Tarfon, and not a miracle.

though Pelimo was a Palestinian Tanna. The interest of the Babylonian teachers in those stories was greater; and just as Rabh's statement about R. Ḥaninah was preserved in the Babylonian Talmud, so also the legendary Baraithas about him were repeated in the schools in Babylonia. Gradually they were told in Aramaic, and only one fragment of the original Baraitha was quoted as evidence in Hebrew, a method frequently to be observed in accounts cited in the Talmud. The uncertainty of the tradition as to whether the incident happened to R. Ḥaninah or to R. Pinḥas b. Yair concerns only the sober, historical accounts preserved also in Palestinian sources; and it must have begun fairly late, as the name of R. Pinḥas b. Ḥama, a Galilean teacher of the first half of the fourth century, in connexion with the account of R. Ḥaninah's scrupulous honesty seems to suggest.

R. Ḥaninah b. Dosa has been declared by those scholars who identify the Ḥasids with the Essenes, to have been a Ḥasid, though the early accounts all designate him only as a man of deed, and distinguish him clearly from the Ḥasids.[1] But how many of the numerous details of his

[1] Tos. Sotah, XV, 5: משמת רבי חנינא בן דוסא בטלו אנשי מעשה, משמת אבה יוסי בן קיטנית בטלה חסידות; Baraitha Sotah 49 b bottom: משמת רבי חנינא בן דוסא בטלו אנשי מעשה, משמת אבא יוסי בן קטנותא בטלו חסידים; jer. IX, 24 c. 25: משמת רבי חנינא בן דוסא פסקו אנשי המעשה. משמת רבי יוסי חסידא ורבי יוסי קטנותא פסקו אנשי חסידות. Weiss, *Zur Geschichte der jüd. Tradition*, I, 109, calls R. Ḥaninah, a contemporary of R. Joḥanan b. Zakkai and R. Gamaliel II, one of the ancient pious men. His source for that statement is Berakh, V, 1: The ancient pious men waited a while before reciting the prayer, in order to direct their hearts to their Father in heaven; אפילו המלך שואל בשלומו לא ישיבנו ואפילו נחש כרוך על עקבו לא יפסיק, even if the king greets him, he must not answer (during prayer), and even if a serpent is wound round his heel, he must not interrupt. Already the subjects and the suffixes referring to them in the singular make it clear that the sentence does not continue the previous statement about the pious men in the plural. In addition, the first sentence reports a fact of the past, while the second gives directions about the conduct of a man engaged in prayer, so that a connexion between the two is not possible. Weiss, of course,

life and his activities agree with the picture drawn by the various writers of antiquity of the Essenes? Philo[1] says, 'Among all men they alone are without money and without possessions, but nevertheless they are the richest of all, because to have few wants and live frugally they regard as riches.' Not even this statement fits R. Ḥaninah who was living with his family not frugally, but in real, oppressive poverty that transcended everything reported of the Essenes. His truthfulness and honesty could be quoted as Essenic, if anything special concerning those virtues were known of the Essenes that was not equally strongly emphasized by the rabbis. The most characteristic facts, his prayers for the sick and his strictness in tithing, have no parallels in Philo or Josephus. Nor is anything reported similar to the advice and help which individuals or a community in distress sought of him; as even Hippolytus' interesting sentence about the Essenes, 'Special zeal they manifest in offering sympathy and succour to those in distress', does not suggest anything like R. Ḥaninah's attitude, when the daughter of Neḥunyah, the digger of pits, fell into a pit, or when several persons were bitten by a serpent. The gift of prophecy which Josephus proves in several instances as most remarkable in some Essenes who imparted the art of prediction to their disciples, is not to be found in R. Ḥaninah who, unlike those Essenes, emphatically declined

saw the difficulty, but assumed that originally also the second sentence was an account of the habits of the pious men, but the redactor of the Mishnah changed it into a rule. Now, as the second part is illustrated by R. Ḥaninah b. Dosa's conduct in Tos. Berakh. III, 20; jer. V, 9a. 56, he belonged, in the opinion of Weiss, and Kohler in *Jew. Enc.*, V, 225 b top, to the ancient Ḥasids. It is true that the parallel Baraitha Berakh. 32 b bottom reports the same incident of a חסיד; but what happened in the Babylonian schools is clear, and known from other instances: in the place of the name originally mentioned, and still preserved in the Baraitha in jer. and Tos., but lost in those schools, the word חסיד was put. A simple analysis of the Mishnah and a comparison with the Baraithas preserved which formed its sources show convincingly that the redactor of the Mishnah never intended any connexion between the two sentences. Cf. Kohler in Neumark's *Journal*, I, 1919, 31.

[1] *De vita contempl.*, ed. Conybeare, 53, 206; Kohler in *Jew. Encl.*, V, 227a. ff.

to be considered a prophet. When Josephus referred to the morning prayer of the Essenes, he would not have missed the opportunity to refer to the devotion which is specially mentioned about the ancient pious men and R. Ḥaninah, had the Essenes in this respect surpassed the Pharisee teachers. On the other hand, there is no trace of R. Ḥaninah's observance of levitical purity, as he not only mixed, as far as one can see, freely with the inhabitants of his town who visited him, but even took a dead serpent to the school, and ignored the immediate defilement; no immersions or frequent purifications of his are mentioned. He was a rabbi and teacher, while no reference is made to such among the Essenes. It is true, the rabbinic reports considered are not sufficient to provide parallels to many of the characteristic features of Essenism; but they contain sufficient material for the establishment of several essential differences between R. Ḥaninah and the Essenes. On the other hand, he certainly exhibited in his attitude towards his fellow-men the love and sympathy of the Ḥasid, and his humility and deliberate self-abasement were those of Hillel; so that his description as a man of deed seems to have viewed his acts of love, and not miracles. As no trade nor any regular daily work seems to have claimed his time and his attention, it is probable that he devoted his life to the service of his fellow-men, and that all his energies and the activities of those who bore the same title were given to deeds of loving-kindness.[1]

7. The men of deed and the pious men, as we have seen, took part together in the popular Feast of Water-drawing held in the second night of Tabernacles on the Temple Mount; this was certainly not due to their alleged Essenism, unless the whole, still enigmatic feast could be proved an Essenic creation and institution.[2] But again we find

[1] See also Schlatter, *Jochanan b. Zakkai*, 58 ff.

[2] That the pious men of both groups danced before the assembled people with burning torches in their hands was certainly not peculiar to them as Essenes, as R. Simeon b. Gamaliel I who is well-known by his

Hillel on a similar occasion teaching in a like manner; and as the pious men spoke about a sinless life, sin, repentance, and forgiveness, he referred to the relation between God and man as affecting conduct and religion. As his sentences very probably reflect the same spirit as theirs, they deserve, for the sake of the pious men, a few words of explanation. Hillel, the old, said,[1] 'To the place which my heart loveth, my feet carry me; (God says), If thou comest to My house, I shall come to thy house, but if thou comest not to My house, I shall not come to thy house, as it says in Exod. 20. 24, In every place where I cause My name to be mentioned, I will come to thee and bless thee.' The parallel Baraitha expressly states the occasion: 'It is reported of Hillel, the old, that when he rejoiced at the joy of the Water-drawing, he said this, (God says), If I am here, all is here, but if I am not here, who is here?[2] He also said, To the place which I love my feet carry me. (God says), If thou comest to My house, &c.[3] When Hillel, the old, saw the people observe the feast in a lighthearted mood, he said to them, Though we are here, who is here? (we count for nothing), for does God need our praises? Is it not written, Dan. 7. 10, Thousand thousands ministered unto Him, and ten thousand times ten thousand stood before Him? When he saw them observe the feast properly, he said, If we were not here, who would be here? For though praises are offered to Him, Israel's praises are more pleasing to Him than all the rest, according to 2 Sam. 23. 1; Ps. 22. 4.'[4]

activities during the last war against the Romans in 66–70, and who with R. Joḥanan b. Zakkai was at the head of the Beth-din in Jerusalem, is reported to have exhibited similar clever tricks of a juggler on the Temple Mount, Tos. Sukk. IV, 4; jer. V, 55 c. 1; Baraitha b. 53 a.

1 Tos. Sukk. IV, 3; in Mekhil. 20. 24, 73 b R. Eliezer b. Jacob appears as the author; evidently he was mentioned only as the tradent in the name of Hillel, and the latter fell out; Bacher, I, 5.

2 See, however, the different interpretation of the Tosafoth.

3 Sukk. 53 a; ARN. 12, 28 a.

4 Jer. Sukk. V, 55 b. 72; in a shorter form in 2 ARN. 27, 28 a: מעשה בהלל הזקן שהיה יושב על בית השואבה ובני אדם עומדים ומתפללים, ראה אותם שגבה לבם אמר להם יודעים אתם שאנו ושבחינו כלום והלא יש

Hillel tried to impress it upon the large and merry crowd on the Temple Mount that neither their great numbers nor their festive joy in themselves counted anything as a manifestation of worship, unless God was present, that is, unless the purity of their sentiments and their devotion in joy brought to them God's acceptance and His presence in their midst. Like David, Hillel loved the Temple as God's habitation, and that is why he came there; his visit to the Temple Mount on the festival of pilgrimage was not mere obedience to duty, but the genuine desire of his heart to appear before God. God again wished the Jew to visit His Temple, it was not indifferent to Him; and, in Hillel's view, in order to induce them to come to His house, God made His visit to the house of the individual Jew conditional on the latter's appearance in the Temple. As the continuation shows, Hillel did not mean merely the physical visit on the Temple Mount, but a true and humble worship of God. Considering the views of Professor Bousset and of other prejudiced historians of Jewish religious thought about the alleged Palestinian-Jewish conception of the transcendence of God, it is important to learn incidentally that, in Hillel's opinion to which he gave public and popular expression, God visited the house of every obedient Jew.

Just as the pious men of both groups, so Hillel, a teacher of religious conduct like them, availed himself of the opportunity and taught the people, assembled for the merry feast on the Temple Mount, in plain and intelligible language an essential truth about the relation between God and man. As it was for the people a feast of unrestrained joy, and, as the references to the praise of God indicate, a special occasion, perhaps due to the completed ingathering of all fruit, for worshipping Him, it was liable to stimulate self-satisfaction. And the sight of the great masses may have excited pride and levity which would degrade the purer

לפניו אלף אלפים ורבי רבבות של מלאכי השרת שיעבדו אותו . . . כיון שראה אותם שנשבר לבם אמר להם . . .

feelings of the worshipper, and make his praise and prayer worthless before God, if not sinful. Only if they are, amid the joy of the day, offered with dignity and from a humble heart, will God accept them as the joyful tribute of homage of his people Israel, even in preference to the glorification by His ministering angels. Thus Hillel tried to subdue the overjoyous mood which threatened to degenerate into conceit, as unsuitable for the Temple Mount. Was it perhaps also intended to neutralize the employment by the pious men of dances and of the exhibition of the feats of jugglers for winning the confidence and the attention of the people? The fact that his great-grandson, R. Simeon b. Gamaliel, displayed the same feats would be strong evidence against such intentions of Hillel. Just as in his teaching, so also in the few words of the pious men there is no trace of mysticism of any kind, no names of God or of angels, no esoteric thought of any description, no word or idea beyond the simple principles of the school, nothing to justify the identification of the pious men with mystics or with the Essenes. If, in spite of the total absence of anything characteristic of the latter, they were Essenes, they successfully concealed their identity on the occasion of their visit to the Temple Mount at the Feast of Water-drawing. It is true, there is equally nothing in the account about their conduct on the Temple Mount to explain their designation as pious men and men of deed. But this observation alone should warn every student of history that even apparently unusual and specially striking expressions of conduct are not necessarily characteristic of the person's general religious attitude or of the religious sect to which he otherwise belonged. To declare such traits, without further evidence, as characteristic of Essenism, will not satisfy the accepted standards of scientific methods of research. As to the date of these pious men, it lies within the time extending from Hillel to R. Simeon b. Gamaliel I, which, according to a statement of an early Baraitha,[1] covered the whole century before the

[1] Baraitha Shabb. 15a bottom.

destruction of the Temple. The fact that Hillel, like the pious men, addressed the people at the Feast of Water-drawing on the Temple Mount, would suggest that they were contemporaries; and so the pious men would be identical with those who, like Baba b. Buta, the disciple of Shammai, brought daily sacrifices of atonement or undertook frequently the vow of the Nazirite so as to be able to bring a sin-offering. On the other hand, it is probable that the custom of Hillel and of the pious men of addressing the people was continued by their successors, though there has been no information preserved that R. Gamaliel I or R. Simeon b. Gamaliel I ever did so. And as the latter did on the occasion of the Feast of Water-drawing exhibit feats of jugglery, and all our information about the details of the celebration of that feast refers to the last years of the Temple, the dancing of the pious men with burning torches and the feats of R. Simeon b. Gamaliel I may have belonged to the same time, between the years 50 and 67.

8. We hear again of the ancient pious men in connexion with their prayers:[1] 'Before reciting the prayer, the ancient pious men waited a while, in order to direct their hearts to their Father in heaven'. It should be noted first that God to whom they addressed their prayers was to them their Father in heaven, as to R. Joḥanan b. Zakkai in several of his statements,[2] and to many scholars after him. And it is significant that this their conception of God was present in their minds just during their prayers, when it must have determined the sentiment with which they approached Him in their daily devotions. In those moments He was to them not God the Almighty whose greatness overawed His creature, nor God the Creator and Master of all beings to whom the frail mortal and helpless worm from the dust

[1] Berakh. V, 1: חסידים הראשונים היו שוהים שעה אחת ומתפללים כדי שיכוונו את לבם לאביהם שבשמים; some texts of the Mishnah have instead of the last two words למקום, see Rabbinovicz.

[2] Mekhil. 20. 25, 74 a; Mekhil. R. Simeon, 116; Tos. Baba kam. VII, 6, 7; jer. Ḥagig. II, 77 a. 66; Tos. II, 1.

appeals for mercy, nor God the king of the Universe from whose rule man cannot hide or escape; but the Father to whom the son without fear or trembling, but in trust and attachment addresses himself. This was not exceptional nor peculiar to this instance of the pious men; it was the general rule with the rabbis, though it is not only not readily recognized, but even deliberately minimized and obscured by certain historians of Jewish-religious thought. Again, the ancient pious men, like any rabbi, considered the concentration of the mind towards God an essential preparation for prayer. The term כוון את לבו is to be found in numerous sentences and rules of the rabbis of succeeding generations, and we met it in R. Ḥaninah b. Dosa's words about his prayer;[1] but the reference to the pious men is evidently the earliest, as it most probably belongs to the beginning of the first century. The exceptionally high degree of devotion, however, which they demanded of themselves could, as a rule, not be attained amid the distractions of human work and thought, nor by a momentary and quick collection and concentration of the mind. They required some time for the transition from ordinary thought to devotion in prayer.[2] Here again Geiger[3] sees in the pious men Essenes, without however stating his reasons for his assumption, just as little as those scholars[4] who take every Ḥasid to have been an Essene. As to the probable date of these pious men, their designation as חסידים הראשונים points to R. Jehudah b. Ilai

[1] Jer. Berakh. V, 9 a. 64: לבי מתכוין בתפלה.

[2] The explanatory Baraitha in Berakh. 32 b bottom which seems a relatively late comment, took שעה to mean an hour, multiplied it by nine for the three daily prayers, each requiring a certain time for concentration, the prayer itself, and for the transition from devotion to common thought, and so obtained nine hours required for prayers daily, and then asked, when the pious men found the time for work and study. Incidentally, we learn that the original report on which the Baraitha was based had stated that the pious men waited a while also after their prayers, before proceeding to their occupation.

[3] *Jüd. Zeitschrift*, IX, 1871, 51.

[4] Löw in *Ben Chananja*, V, 100 a; Kohler in *MGWJ.* 37, 1893, 494; *J. Q. R.*, V, 1893, 403; Neumark's *Journal*, I, 1899, 30 ff..

as the author of the statement used by the redactor of the Mishnah, and to the beginning of the first century as the date of the pious men.

Again, in connexion with the old custom of comforting the mourners, an early Baraitha relates: 'Associations, חבורות in Jerusalem visited the houses of mourning, or places where wedding feasts or circumcisions took place, or a temporary grave from which the bones of a dead person were collected for their final interment. Whenever two such functions were held at the same time, the members of the associations gave the preference to the joyous occasions; but the ancient pious men preferred visiting the house of the mourner, for it is said in Eccl. 7. 2, 'It is better to go to the house of mourning than to go to the house of feasting: for that is the end of all men, and the living will lay it to his heart'.[1] The custom of visiting and comforting mourners is biblical, and was general in Jerusalem also before 70, as R. Eleazar b. R. Ṣadok related from his own observation,[2] how on the Feast of Tabernacles the men of Jerusalem, with the obligatory palm-branch in their hands, visited the sick and the mourners. The visiting of the sick is expressly reported of scholars in Jerusalem: 'When Abba Saul b. Batnith was ill, our teachers went to see him'[3]; and also the fact that the Shammaites prohibited the visiting of the sick and the comforting of mourners on the Sabbath,[4] shows that both customs were practised by those whose actions those scholars could influence. And though Abba Saul is

[1] Semaḥ. XII: אבל חסידים הראשונים היו מקדימין לבית האבל מלבית המשתה שנאמר טוב ללכת אל בית אבל מלכת אל בית המשתה . . .
The same report is given by R. Eleazar b. R. Ṣadok in Tos. Megil. IV, 15, but, in the place of the ancient pious, R. Ishmael, a younger contemporary of R. Eleazar b. R. Ṣadok is mentioned.

[2] Baraitha Sukk. 41 b bottom; Tos II, 10; in jer. III, 54 a. 46 the words לנחם אבלים seem to have fallen out.

[3] Jer. Beṣah, III, 62 b. 19: פעם אחת חלה ונכנסו רבותינו לבקרו, אמר לון אתון חמון הדא ימינא דהוות מכילא בקושטא.

[4] Shabb. 12 a bottom.

on account of his title considered an Essene by Dr. Kohler,[1] his visitors during his illness are expressly described as 'our teachers'. Many years before that the disciples visited their master Hillel,[2] and his disciple R. Joḥanan b. Zakkai was visited by his disciples.[3] Only a few years after 70, we see the teachers visit R. Tarfon, when he was ill,[4] and R. Eliezer;[5] R. Ḥaninah b. Teradyon visited R. José b. Kisma.[6] And when one of R. Akiba's disciples was, during his illness, not visited by the scholars, the master visited him, and, seeing the effect of his call upon the patient, publicly taught, 'He who does not visit a sick person is sinning as though he shed blood'.[7] And when R. Ishmael lost two sons, R. Tarfon, R. José the Galilean, R. Eleazar b. 'Azariah, and R. Akiba went to comfort him.[8] Consequently, it was not a custom peculiar to the Ḥasids; apart from the fact that none of the existing reports about the Essenes ever hints that these specially cultivated such visitation.[9] The dogmatic statements of Dr. Kohler[10] in no way contribute to the elucidation of the actual conditions and facts; for he says: 'The systematic charity (of the Jews) is undoubtedly a creation of the Chasid-brotherhoods or Essenes who devoted their whole lives to such activity of love, ARN. III, 17, VIII, 36 ff.; Moëd kat. 27 b; Semaḥ. XII. They then also traced such activity of love to Abraham, Job, and Daniel, nay even to Malkiṣedek.' It is difficult to understand how the word 'undoubtedly' escaped from the pen of that scholar, considering that there is no evidence of any kind to substantiate the sweeping assertion that the Ḥasids had anything whatever to do with the institution of systematic charity; especially as in the only passage, Semaḥ. XII, as already Geiger pointed

[1] *J. Q. R.*, XIII, 1901, 572 ff.; see my *'Am-ha'areṣ*, 209, note ff.
[2] Jer. Nedar. V, 39 b. 42.
[3] Berakh. 28 b.
[4] Jer. Pe'ah, I, 15 c. 37; Pesik. r. 23, 123 a.
[5] Synh. 101 a. 68 a; jer. Shabb. II, 5 b. 67; Mekhil. 20. 23, 73 a; Berakh. 28 b.
[6] 'Abod. z. 18 a.
[7] Nedar. 40 a top.
[8] Moëd kat. 28 b, Baraitha.
[9] Geiger, *Urschrift*, 123 ff, 126.
[10] Berliner's *Festschrift*, 199 ff. Cf. Mekhil. Exod. 13, 19, 24 a.

out, the associations that were engaged in work of loving-kindness are distinguished from the ancient Ḥasids. And is even the slightest detail known about the members of the associations that shared the grief and the joy of others? And who were the pious men who, according to the concluding part of the verse adduced, for educational purposes placed the visit to the mourner higher than that to the house of joy? And what do the passages referred to by Dr. Kohler prove? A Ḥasid who used to help the poor, once journeyed in a terrible storm by sea; R. Akiba feared that he had been drowned, but God saved the man for his charity.[1] This then is the evidence for the assumed connexion between the Ḥasids and charity! But by comparing the Baraitha in Yebam. 121a that formed the direct or indirect source of the collector of ARN. for that story we find that he or his immediate source turned the learned disciple of R. Akiba, R. Meir, into an anonymous Ḥasid. As was pointed out above,[2] this is one of the numerous instances in which a later narrator substituted for the express name of a person or for an unnamed man[3] a Ḥasid, meaning thereby a person distinguished by the one virtue that constituted the point of the incident related, in this instance charity. The same applies to the Ḥasids in the other passage[4] who went to ransom some captive girls and who, in their strictness of morality, watched over the purity of the maidens.[5] It is true that already the Baraitha[6] reports that incident of a Ḥasid; but that it was originally a scholar, probably even mentioned by name, who ransomed and protected the girl, is evident from a comparison of the details of the statement with another Baraitha immediately following about R. Joshua b. Ḥananiah's political mission to a matrona. In both accounts the acting person was one accompanied by his disciples, in both he lectured to them after the incident, and in both he had a purifying

[1] ARN. 3, 9a.
[2] p. 41.
[3] מעשה באיש אחד.
[4] ARN. 8, 19a.
[5] See *R. É. J.*, 42, 1901, 220 ff., 223.
[6] Shabb. 127b.

immersion before the lesson; so that the man in the first report was of the same position as R. Joshua, a scholar whose name was soon lost.[1]

R. Jehudah b. Ilai has a further report about the ancient pious men: they were visited by a disease of the bowels (diarrhoea)[2] for about twenty days before their death, in order that it should purge everything, so that they might come pure to the world to come, as it says in Prov. 27. 21, The refining pot is for silver, and the furnace for gold, and a man is tried by his praise.[3] As diarrhoea purges the body only, it is not certain whether the visitation inflicted upon the pious men was to effect merely physical, or also moral cleansing. As on the other hand, R. Jehudah expressly stated that the object of the illness was to bring the pious men to heaven זכאין, and this word invariably designates moral purity, innocence; and as the body does not after death go to heaven (if this is meant, and not the time after the resurrection), it seems fairly certain that the purging did not refer to the body. The word מרק, however, is used in both senses. R. Johanan says, On account of a tooth or an eye which is only one part of the body, a slave becomes free, Exod. 21. 26, 27: how much more should a man become free through visitations that cleanse the whole body; R. Simeon b. Lakish says, Visitations purge all sins of man.[4] The first is physical, the second moral. R. Yannai demanded a clean body for the use of the Tefillin; he himself put them on three days after his illness, to indicate

[1] A rich man of Kabul in Galilee, Pesik. 169 b; Lev. r. 20. 3; Kohel. r. 2. 2. 4, is styled in Tanḥ. שמיני 2; B. 3 a Ḥasid. R. Pinḥas again puts in a Ḥasid in Pesik. rab. 23, 119 a in a passage which in Gen. r. 11. 4 reports the same of an unnamed man.

[2] Cf. Shabb. 11 a; Sirach, 25. 13, 19, Schechter in *J. Q. R.*, III, 1891, 697 ff.; Mekhil. 18. 27, 60 b, bottom.

[3] Semaḥ. III, end: אמר רבי יהודה חסידים הראשונים היו מתייסרין בחולי מעיים בעשרים יום קודם מיתתן כדי למרק את הכל כדי שיבאו זכאין לעתיד לבא שנאמר מצרף לכסף וכור לזהב ואיש לפי מהללו. In the parallel in Gen. r. 62. 2: ten to twenty days, to indicate that illness purges. See D. Luria's note on the last passage, and Tosaf. Shabb. 118 b.

[4] Berakh. 5 a bottom.

that illness purged, as it says in Psalm 103. 3, Who forgiveth all thine iniquity, who healeth all thy diseases.[1] The account began with physical purging and finished up with the removal of sin, as in the rabbi's mind the two were closely connected. The same variation is met also in Tannaitic statements. R. Jonathan says, Moses in Exod. 24. 16 had to wait on Mount Sinai six days for God's revelation, in order that the food and the drink in his body be purged and he become like the ministering angels.[2] Here the physical meaning is clear. On the other hand, in R. Ishmael's well-known sentence about the various means and occasions of atonement, מרק is, as in the case of the pious men, connected with suffering and followed by death, both to atone for a grave sin.[3] So that the idea underlying seems to have been that God sent a severe illness upon the pious men to purge them by suffering of their few sins, so that their souls should arrive in heaven free from sin. So R. José b. Ḥalaftha expressed the wish to share the lot of those who died of diarrhoea;[4] and a Baraitha[5] says, It is a good sign for a man that he dies of diarrhoea, since most of the righteous men die of that disease. It is an application of the great idea expressed later by R. Akiba, One should rejoice more at suffering than at good fortune: for if one enjoys happiness throughout life, the sins which one commits are not simply forgiven to one, as only

[1] Jer. Berakh. II, 4 c. 6.

[2] Baraitha Yoma, 4 b top; ARN. I, 1 a; Bacher, *Tannaiten*, II, 363.

[3] Yoma, 86 a and parallels; Bacher, I, 250. 3: ... עבר על כריתות ומיתות בית דין ועשה תשובה ויום הכפורים תולין וייסורין ממרקין שנאמר ופקדתי בשבט פשעם ובנגעים עונם, אבל מי שיש חילול השם בידו אין לו כח בתשובה לתלות ולא ביום הכפורים לכפר ולא ביסורין למרק אלא כולן תולין ומיתה ממרקת שנאמר ונגלה באזני ה׳ צבאות אם יכפר העון הזה לכם עד תמותון; jer. VIII, 45 c. 7: ... אבל מי שנתחלל בו שם שמים אין כח לא בתשובה לתלות ולא ביום הכפורים לכפר ולא בייסורין למרק אלא תשובה ויום הכפורים מכפרין שליש והייסורין מכפרין שליש והמיתה ממרקת בייסורין ...

[4] Shabb. 118 b.

[5] Kethub. 103 b.

suffering brings one forgiveness.[1] When R. Eliezer fell ill, and all his former disciples stood round his bed mourning, R. Akiba was calm and composed; for, so he said to his colleagues, when I saw my teacher enjoy a materially undisturbed life, I thought, perhaps, God forbid, he has received his reward here on earth (and punishment awaits him after death); but now that I see him suffer, I am glad.[2] Another account of R. Eliezer's last illness relates there that, while R. Joshua, R. Tarfon, and R. Eleazar b. ʿAzariah bewailed the impending loss, R. Akiba said to R. Eliezer, חביבין יסורין, 'beloved is suffering', because it brings about repentance. Already R. Akiba's master, Naḥum of Gimzō, when suffering terribly from the effects of leprosy, taught his disciple not to complain of suffering, not to raise any questions and doubts about it, but to welcome it.[3] R. Eleazar b. R. Ṣadok taught that God sends suffering upon the righteous in this world, so that they may inherit the world to come;[4] the latter term denoting, as the context shows, the life after death.

And such was already the idea of the pious men at the beginning of the first century, who, as R. Jehudah b. Ilai's report indicates, were conscious of not being entirely free from sin, as there is no human being totally sinless (Eccl. 7. 20). For, in his statement about the suffering of the pious men, R. Jehudah did not give his own interpretation of the effects of their illness, but merely recorded the views of the pious men about God's providence and His object in meting out physical suffering. God watches the individual actions and the whole life of every human being separately, notes among others the approaching end of a pious man, reviews the sum total of his deeds, and apportions bliss to his soul. But, when He finds that a few errors

1 Mekhil. 20. 23, 72 b; Sifré Deut. 6. 5. 32, 73 b top.

2 Synh. 101 a bottom, Halévy, דורות הראשונים Ie, 149 a.

3 Jer. Shekal. V, 49 b. 19; b. Ta'an. 21 a; cf. R. Akiba in Semaḥ. VIII; Bacher, I, 320 ff.

4 Kidd. 40 b; ARN. 39, 60 a.

and wrong actions of the righteous may impair and reduce the future happiness of his soul, God in His love for the pious reminds him by the suffering inflicted on him of his few transgressions, and thus leads him to repentance of them, and purges all his sins. There is in God's arrangements a close connexion between visitation as a punishment on earth and sin; and when God, by an illness of about twenty days' duration, has removed the few stains from the soul of the righteous, He rewards it in heaven for his consistent obedience to His will. All this was the generally accepted doctrine of the rabbis of the first century, and there is in the belief of the pious men nothing to suggest that they were in this respect anything but Pharisees; as J. Léhmann[1] already rightly emphasized that not a single fact reported about the ancient pious men in rabbinic literature agreed with the details given by Josephus about the Essenes. If Baba b. Buta, the contemporary of Herod,[2] might be taken as a typical Ḥasid, he was certainly not an Essene. For he was a man of wealth, just as another Ḥasid who owned cattle and land, which decidedly appears to be opposed to Essenic principles; he was a disciple in the school of Shammai whose teachings he followed, zealous for God's Temple, altar, and sacrifices, and brought daily a guilt-offering for doubtful sins. The Ḥasids were married, and had children. If they formed in Jerusalem and elsewhere associations of their own, as they appeared as a body of two groups on the Temple Mount at the Feast of Water-drawing, and recruited their adherents from among the pious and the repentant; and if they engaged in regular deeds of loving-kindness: no distinctly Essenic trait of character or action can be detected in all that. Only in one respect do they seem in their religious practice more active and even more zealous than the Pharisee teachers of their time: in frequent sacrifices of atonement. Apart from their exaggerated fear of sin committed and their desire for frequent atonement, their contemporary Hillel was like

[1] *R. É. J.*, 30, 1895, 185. [2] Baba b. 3 b ff.

them a Ḥasid. Though modern scholars have come to admit that, in spite of Josephus' ambiguous assertion, the Essenes did not refrain from offering sacrifices,[1] the unparalleled zeal of the Ḥasids in their frequent offerings of atonement is certainly not Essenic.[2]

9. Several Tannaitic statements refer to זקנים הראשונים, the ancient scholars, mainly in connexion with rules of levitical purity. And as Frankel, Weiss, and Kohler identify them with the ancient pious men, it will be necessary to analyse at least one of the traditions, to ascertain the exact date of the reference, and to show how hasty the interpretation and how flimsy the evidence, and how little justification there is for the way in which some scholars use sound halakhic information to support their preconceived ideas. In a Baraitha R. Eleazar (b. Shammu'a) of the school of Usha (136–160) reports the stages of the development of a strictly levitical rule, and mentions as the representatives of the first stage the ancient scholars:[3] 'R. Eleazar said, Some of the ancient scholars said, Half a kabh of human bones and half a log of human blood have defiling force for everything, but a quarter of a kabh of bones and a quarter of a log of blood have not such defiling force for everything; others of the ancient scholars said, Also a quarter of a kabh

[1] Geiger, *Jüd. ZS.*, IX, 1871, 34; Kohler in *Jew. Encyclop.*, V, 228 b; Leszynsky, *Sadduzäer*, 150. 1.

[2] Weiss, *Zur Geschichte*, I, 110, who places the ancient pious men at the beginning of the Maccabean rising, points out that they could not have been Essenes on account of their numerous sacrifices, and that they were not an organized sect, but individual pious men of an extreme strictness. The incident at the Feast of Water-drawing he places after the defeat of the Syrians by the Maccabees, and refers it to such as had sinned during the Hellenistic movement and were now repentant.

[3] Nazir, 53 a; Tos. V, 1, and Ahil. IV, 13; jer. Nazir, VII, 56 c. 30: תא שמע שמאי אומר עצם אחד מן שדרה או מן גולגולת, אמר רבי אלעזר זקנים הראשונים מקצתן היו אומרים חצי קב עצמות וחצי לוג דם לכל, רובע עצמות ורביעית דם לא לכל, ומקצתן היו אומרים אף רובע עצמות ורביעית דם לכל, בית דין של אחריהם אמרו חצי קב עצמות וחצי לוג דם לכל, רובע עצמות ורביעית דם לתרומה וקדשים אבל לא לנזיר ועושה פסח.

of bones and a quarter of a log of blood have such defiling force. A later Beth-din (authority) said, Half a kabh of bones and half a log of blood have defiling force for everything; but a quarter of a kabh of bones and a quarter of a log of blood have defiling force only for the priestly heave-offering and for sacrifices, but not for the Nazirite and a person about to offer the Passover sacrifice'. Who the two groups of ancient scholars were, is not indicated, and can only be established by inference.

The earliest authorities that, in the records preserved, dealt with the defiling minimum of human bones were the two schools of the Shammaites and the Hillelites. 'The Shammaites say, The quarter of a kabh of bones must be made up of several bones, of two or three (at least); the Hillelites say, It must be made up of the body, either of the greater part of the structure (skeleton) or the greater number of the bones; Shammai said, Even a bone of the spine or the skull'.[1] As their dispute mentions no distinction between the various things to which the defilement might apply, it seems that Shammai and the two schools knew only the quarter of a kabh as the minimum measure of bones defiling in all possible cases and degrees. And as R. Joshua tried to reconcile the divergent views of the two schools without introducing any qualification as to the application of that measure, he agreed with them on that point; as he also on another occasion stated that the requirement of the greater part of the structure or a quarter of a kabh of bones applied to the human corpse.[2] Also

[1] Baraitha Nazir, 52 b; 'Eduy. I, 7; Tos. Ahil. III, 5: תניא בית שמאי אומרים רובע עצמות מן העצמים או משנים או משלשה ובית הלל אומרים רובע מן הגויה מרוב הבנין או מרוב המנין. אמר רבי יהושע יכולני לעשות דברי בית שמאי ודברי בית הלל כאחד . . . שמאי אומר אפילו עצם מן השדרה או מן הגולגולת.

[2] 'Eduy. VI, end; Nazir, 51 b: אמרו לו לרבי יהושע מה ראית לטהר בשניהם, אמר להם לא אם אמרתם במת שיש בו רוב ורובע ורקב תאמרו בחי שאין בו רוב ורובע ורקב; the same without the name of the author in Tos. 'Eduy. II, 10: השיבו את רבי נחוניא שלש תשובות, לא אם אמרת במת שיש בו רוב רובע רקב . . .

R. Akiba who allowed the minimum measure of bones to be made up by bones from two corpses, as also his opponents name as that measure without any qualification a quarter of a kabh.[1] With this view, shared by all the scholars just enumerated, agrees the opinion of one group of the ancient scholars who say that a quarter of a kabh of bones and a quarter of a log of blood have defiling force for everything.[2] As to the date of these teachers, they could be either earlier than the two schools of the Shammaites and Hillelites, or identical with them, or later than those. But as the two schools and also Shammai agreed on the minimum measure required, and there is quoted neither a contemporary nor an earlier scholar who would have differed from that accepted rule, it is most improbable that Shammai's teachers, Shema'yah and Abtalyon, if they knew the problem at all, held a different opinion. On the other hand, the agreement between the two schools continued in the schools of Jamnia and Lydda, as R. Joshua and his opponent, and R. Akiba and his opponents were all unanimous on the quarter of a kabh of bones. And so we are forced to look for the origin of the controversy between the two groups of the ancient scholars about the absolute or relative defiling force of a quarter of a kabh of bones in the school of R. Akiba at the earliest; and as there exist two versions of his opinion on this point, a contemporary of his may have raised the problem, and forced him, in his later years, to qualify his original view. If the inference from the existing information about the minimum measure of bones is correct, the dispute between the two groups of the

[1] Ohal. II, 6; Tos. 'Eduy. I, 7: השדרה והגולגולת משני מתים ורביעית דם משני מתים ורובע עצמות משני מתים ואבר מן המת משני מתים ואבר מן החי משני אנשים רבי עקיבא מטמא וחכמים מטהרין. As to the parallel Baraitha Nazir, 52 a bottom, where R. Akiba requires for the same defilement half a kabh, instead of a quarter of a kabh, of bones, see further.

[2] In Tos. and jer. this view is quoted in the first place, not, as in b., in the second.

ancient scholars about the minimum measure of blood should lead to the same conclusion.

Unfortunately no statement of the view of the two schools on that subject has been preserved, and in itself the rule is very difficult. For Num. 19, the biblical source of all the laws on the defiling force of the corpse and its parts, refers to blood neither under the defilement in the tent in vv. 14, 15, nor even under the defilement by touch in v. 16 where the bone is expressly mentioned. And still, when there appears to have been a dispute about the defiling force of blood altogether,[1] it was only as far as its biblical derivation was concerned, the defiling force of it being accepted by all the teachers. The earliest report about the question states, 'R. Akiba said, I once argued before R. Eliezer, Since a bone of the size of a grain of barley, which does not defile a man in the tent, still defiles, by being touched or carried, the Nazirite so that he has to cut his hair: how much more should a quarter of a log of

[1] Sifré Num. 19. 11. 125, 44 b: בנפש אדם להוציא את דמו דברי רבי ישמעאל, רבי עקיבא אומר לכל נפש אדם להביא את דמו, R. Ishmael excludes it from the words בנפש אדם in Num. 19. 13, which refer to defilement by touching the corpse; R. Akiba includes it on the generalizing word לכל (different in Ḥull. 72 a). Zuckermandel in *MGWJ.*, 22, 1873, 157, rightly, but without adducing any evidence, notes that in this dispute not the law itself is in question, but only its biblical source. In Ohal. II, 2 an anonymous teacher holds that a quarter of a log of blood from a corpse, and also a mixture of blood part of which came from the body when still alive, and the rest from the same body, when already dead, are defiling; R. Akiba extends the rule to blood of the same kind even when it came from two bodies. In Ohal. III, 5 R. Akiba and R. Ishmael differ about the measures of the two parts of the mixed blood: איזהו דם תבוסה, המת שיצא ממנו שמינית בחייו ושמינית במותו דברי רבי עקיבא, רבי ישמעאל אומר רביעית בחייו ורביעית במותו, R. Ishmael holding that the resulting mixture should be two quarters of a log of blood. This shows that he accepted the defiling force of blood; but it is not certain from the dispute whether he also agreed as to a quarter of a log of blood as the minimum measure in normal cases, or whether he required half a log. It seems that the word נפש in נפש אדם Num. 19. 11, 13 suggested the extension of the law of defilement to blood, since in Lev. 17. 11: כי נפש הבשר בדם הוא the נפש is declared to be in the blood, Sifré zuta Num. 19. 11, 136. 3 Horovitz.

blood which does defile a man in the tent, defile, by being touched or carried, the Nazirite so that he should have to cut his hair. R. Eliezer objected, What is this, Akiba, we cannot argue here *a minori ad majus.* When I submitted the argument to R. Joshua, he said, You are right, but the scholars have thus enunciated the rule'.[1] R. Akiba takes it for granted that a quarter of a log of blood has in the tent the same high grade of defiling force as a corpse. R. Eliezer and R. Joshua, his masters, raise no objection to that premise, but only to his inference from it, so that evidently he had, as their disciple, learned that rule from them; though no source is indicated from which the strict rule was derived.[2] But whether earlier scholars had already extended to blood the defiling force of a corpse, and had fixed a quarter of a log as sufficient for that, is nowhere stated. As R. Akiba, like his teacher R. Joshua, consistently represented the view of the Hillelites as against the Shammaites, and R. Eliezer was a champion of the latter, the agreement of the three would suggest that the two schools before them were of one and the same opinion. And the fact that R. Akiba put side by side, without the registration of another view, the quarter of a kabh of bones and the quarter of a log of blood, also suggests that they were unopposed measures of an earlier date of the two schools. When, therefore, one group of the ancient scholars taught that a quarter of a log of blood would defile everything, they agreed with R. Eliezer, R. Joshua, and R. Akiba; and as up to their time no divergent opinion had existed, the dispute between them and the other

[1] Nazir, VII, 4: אמר רבי עקיבא דנתי לפני רבי אליעזר מה אם עצם כשעורה שאינו מטמא אדם באהל הנזיר מגלח על מגעו ועל משאו, רביעית דם שמטמא אדם באהל אינו דין שיהא הנזיר מגלח על מגעה ועל משאה, אמר לי מה זה עקיבא אין דנין כאן מקל וחומר, וכשבאתי והרציתי דברים לפני רבי יהושע אמר לי יפה אמרת אלא כן אמרו הלכה. In Sifré zuta Num. 6. 12, 41 R. Joshua said: רואה אני להקל ולהחמיר אבל מה אעשה שגזרו חכמים על חצי לוג.

[2] See Baraitha Nazir 57 a top, and cf. Sifré zuta Num. 19. 11, 136, note 3 bottom.

group of the ancient scholars must be of a later date than R. Akiba's argument before R. Eliezer and R. Joshua which he submitted to them, when he was still their disciple in Lydda. This date of the dispute about the measure of blood is the same as that obtained for the measure of bones. Now, of R. Akiba's disciples R. José b. Ḥalaftha still adhered, without any qualification, to the measure approved of by his master;[1] similarly two other disciples, R. Jehudah and R. Simeon, give varying traditions about R. Akiba's dispute with one of his colleagues about a quarter of a log of blood which came from two corpses,[2] and neither suggests any limitation as to the measure. And the same two disciples define the mixture of blood part of which came from the body when still alive, and the remaining part from the same body after death, and the measure of the blood in their rule is, as in R. Akiba's, a quarter of a log.[3] This would show conclusively that R. Akiba at the time, when R. José, R. Jehudah, and R. Simeon were his disciples, still taught that a quarter of a log of blood defiled everything like a corpse.

10. But different seems to have been the attitude of the greatest of R. Akiba's disciples, of R. Meir.[4] 'R. Eleazar said, When I went to 'Ardiskos, I found R. Meir and

[1] Tos. Kelim, 1. I. 3: רבי יוסי אומר זובו של זב ורוקו ושכבת זרעו ומימי רגליו ורביעית מן המת, see the wording in the ordinary editions.

[2] Tos. Ahil. III, 1.

[3] Tos. Ahil. IV, 11; Mishnah, III, 5; Sifré zuta Num. 19. 11, 137.

[4] Tos. Nazir, V, 1; b. 56 b; Mishnah, VII, 4: אמר רבי אלעזר כשהלכתי לערדסקום מצאתי את רבי מאיר ויהודה בן פתירה שהם יושבים ודנים בהלכה, יהודה בן פתירה אומר רביעית דם אין נזיר מגלח עליה ואין חייבין עליה על ביאת מקדש, אמר לו רבי מאיר ותהא זאת קלה מן השרץ, שרץ הקל חייבין עליו על ביאת המקדש רביעית דם שחמורה אינו דין שיהו חייבין עליה על ביאת המקדש, שתק רבי יהודה בן פתירה, נמתי לו מאיר אל תבוז לו בקי הוא (אתה) ביהושע בן ממיל, אמר לו הן ובעל הלכות היה, נמתי לו בלשון הזה אמר לי משום רבי יהושע כל טומאה מן המת שהנזיר מגלח עליה חייבין עליה על ביאת המקדש וכל טומאה מן המת שאין הנזיר מגלח עליה אין חייבין עליה על ביאת המקדש.

Jehudah b. Pethera sitting and discussing a rule; Jehudah b. Pethera said, The Nazirite, when defiled by a quarter of a log of blood, need not cut his hair, and if a man defiled by a quarter of a log of blood enter the Temple, he is not guilty. To this R. Meir remarked, Should that defilement be less grave than that by a dead insect? Since one defiled by a dead insect, which is a lighter defilement, by entering the Temple incurs guilt, how much more should one defiled by a quarter of a log of blood, which is a graver defilement, be guilty. Jehudah b. Pethera answered nothing'. Here we see the defiling strength of a quarter of a log of blood disputed for the first time, and a declaration that that measure of blood is too weak to defile a Nazirite, or to make a man guilty, when he enters the Temple after that defilement. R. Meir did not dispute the first part of the rule stated by Jehudah b. Pethera; and when he raised an objection against the second, he was reminded by R. Eleazar that R. Joshua b. Ḥananiah had declared the two parts of the rule interdependent. From whom Jehudah b. Pethera learned the altered rule, cannot be traced, as nothing is known about his teachers; but R. Meir who had nothing to say against the first part and therefore agreed with Jehudah b. Pethera on that point, must have heard of it before. And as his master R. Akiba had taught his disciples the old rule, was perhaps the other teacher of R. Meir, R. Ishmael,[1] responsible for the new formulation of it, who, in connexion with the measure of the component parts of the mixture of blood,[2] required half a log? If there were any probability in this suggestion, the early scholars who disputed about the minimum of blood to defile the Nazirite, would have been R. Akiba and R. Ishmael, though for the corresponding measure of bones no contemporary of R. Akiba who would have differed about that from him, could so far be found.[3] The scholars of

[1] Jer. Sotah, II, 18 a. 75 ff.; b. 'Erub. 13 a.

[2] דם תבוסה, Ohal. III, 5, above, p. 118, 1.

[3] That the original minimum was a quarter of a log, is evident from

R. Meir's time adopted his view, and it was incorporated

all the passages quoted; also the report of R. Eleazar, as preserved in jer. Nazir and Tos., puts first that group of the ancient scholars that held that view. As to the wording of R. Eleazar's report, it is clear that the first view consisted only of the words: אמר רבי אלעזר בראשונה היו זקנים חלוקים מקצתן אומרים רביעית דם ורובע עצמות ומקצתן אומרים חצי קב עצמות וחצי לוג דם, as Tos. and jer. have it, containing only the respective measures in dispute, as it was only Jehudah b. Pethera who the first time mentioned the distinction between the defilement of the Nazir and the Temple on the one hand, and that of other things or persons not named on the other. As R. Meir in the end agreed with him, the Mishnah Nazir, VII, 2 codified his view: . . . על אלו טומאות הנזיר מגלח ועל חצי קב עצמות ועל חצי לוג דם . . . (3) ורביעית דם . . . ורובע עצמות . . . אין הנזיר מגלח; as also Symmachos, his disciple, in Baraitha Nazir, 49 b says that R. Meir taught him that Mishnah of which, it is true, he only quotes the beginning. Accordingly, the conclusion of R. Eleazar's report in Tos. Nazir, V, 1: בית דין של אחריהם אמרו רביעית דם ורובע עצמות לתרומות ולקדשים חצי קב עצמות וחצי לוג דם לנזיר ולמקדש, that a later authority held that a quarter of a log of blood and a quarter of a kabh of bones had defiling force for the priestly heave-offering and sacrifices, but that only half a log of blood and half a kabh of bones could defile the Nazirite and a man for entering the Temple, refers to the adoption of Jehudah b. Pethera's and R. Meir's view by the school of Usha of which R. Meir was a member. (In b. לתרומה וקדשים אבל לא לנזיר ועושה פסח instead of the general prohibition from visiting the Temple the special instance of one is selected who has to enter the Temple to do his duty and bring the Passover sacrifice; see the commentators.) The version of R. Eleazar's report in jer. Nazir is altogether incomplete: תני אמר רבי שמעון בן אלעזר בראשונה היו בתי דינין חלוקין מקצתן אומרים רביעית דם רובע עצמות מקצתן אומרים חצי לוג דם חצי קב עצמות לנזירות ולטומאת מקדש וקדשיו. רבי יעקב בר אידי בשם רבי שמעון מדרש אמרוה מפי חגי זכריה ומלאכי. The reference to the final decision is missing; on the other hand, the four words from לנזירות are certainly out of place, as no corresponding details were stated in the first part. As the statement of the Amora R. Jacob b. Iddi agrees with that in b., and refers to the final decision, it is evident that, owing to a homoioteleuton, a whole part has fallen out in j., and the sentence must have read: בית דין של אחריהם אמרו רביעית דם רובע עצמות לתרומה וקדשים חצי לוג דם חצי קב עצמות לנזירות ולטומאת מקדש וקדשיו. Rashi on R. Jacob b. Iddi in Nazir, 53 a has: לומר שעיקר הוא שהוא מפי שמעיה ואבטליון ואית דאמרי שאמרו מפי חגי זכריה ומלאכי, and presupposes in the text of the Talmud, beside the reference to the tradition of the last

by the redactor of the Mishnah as the accepted rule.[1] The difficulty however remains, how R. Eleazar who himself was a colleague of R. Meir in the school of Usha, could have spoken of the scholars of his own time as בית דין של אחריהם, when he himself had participated in the final decision, and he himself reported how he had heard Jehudah b. Pethera and R. Meir discuss the whole question, when all was still undecided.

First it must be pointed out that in R. Eleazar's report about his visit to 'Ardiskos where he heard that discussion, the relation of R. Eleazar to R. Meir is not at all clear: did he go there to meet him as his equal, and was it a visit of respect paid to a scholar who happened to be in the neighbourhood, or was he a regular visitor to that place, and was the meeting accidental? From the not quite clear wording of the report it is not even evident, whether R. Eleazar in the discussion spoke to R. Meir, as he seems to have addressed himself to Jehudah b. Pethera who was younger than R. Meir, and spoke to the latter as a disciple.[2] In addition, other accounts of R. Meir's stay in 'Ardiskos introduce another teacher who reported R. Meir's decisions in that place. 'R. Simeon b. Eleazar says, Once we were sitting before R. Meir in the school of 'Ardiskos, when a man said to him', &c.[3] It was R. Meir's well-known disciple, R. Simeon b. Eleazar, who, as in the previous report Jehudah b. Pethera, sat, with other disciples, before his master, when in 'Ardiskos. 'R. Simeon b. Eleazar reports, When an old man in 'Ardiskos, for purposes of exact tithing, weighed his basket first full and afterwards empty, R. Meir praised him'.[4] This seems to make it most pro-

prophets, another which mentioned in the first place a tradition of Shema'yah and Abtalyon.

[1] Nazir, VII, 2; Ohal. II, 1, 2.

[2] b. היה יושב ודן לפני רבי מאיר בהלכה, see Rashi and Tosafoth.

[3] Tos. 'Erub. IX, 4; in the parallel Baraitha 'Erub. 29 a bottom: Once R. Meir was in 'Ardiskos for the Sabbath; jer. III, 20 c. 60: R. Jehudah says, Once R. Meir was in 'Ardiskos for the Sabbath.

[4] Tos. Terum. III. 4.

bable that also in the report about the discussion between Jehudah b. Pethera and R. Meir in 'Ardiskos not R. Eleazar, but R. Simeon b. Eleazar came to that place to meet his master and, as in the other instances, heard a statement of his in the school. But, if this is correct, it follows also that the final decision about the rule, discussed in 'Ardiskos and reported by R. Eleazar in connexion with the dispute between the early scholars about the defiling force of blood and bones, was related not by R. Eleazar but by R. Simeon b. Eleazar. In fact, in jer. this very name is given; and though this part of the wording of the account is not at all free from doubt, it is certain that the name is correct.[1] But there is no doubt whatever that the ancient scholars whom Frankel, Weiss, and Kohler identified with the ancient Ḥasids, and whom they placed in the early years of the Maccabean movement, were rabbis, at the earliest, of the beginning of the second century; exactly as the ancient scholars referred to by R. José b. Dormaskith[2] were members of the school in Jamnia.

Of an earlier date were the ancient scholars mentioned in connexion with another point of levitical purity. The account reads, 'And the woman that is sick in her separation, Lev. 15. 33, the ancient scholars said, She should not paint her eyelids, nor rouge her face, nor adorn herself with a coloured dress; until R. Akiba came and taught that, if you insist on that, you make her look ugly in the sight of her husband, and he will divorce her'.[3] These ancient scholars lived before R. Akiba; but how long before cannot be deter-

[1] See the different arguments of Zuckermandel in *MGWJ.*, 22, 1873, 153–163.

[2] Tos. Yad. II, 16, above p. 78, note 2.

[3] Baraitha Shabb. 64 b; jer. Gitt. IX, 50 d. 42; Sifra Lev. 15. 33, 79 c: תניא והדוה בנדתה, זקנים הראשונים אמרו שלא תכחול ולא תפקים ולא תתקשט בבגדי צבעונין, עד שבא רבי עקיבא ולימד אם כן אתה מגנה על בעלה ונמצא בעלה מגרשה, אלא מה תלמוד לומר והדוה בנדתה בנדתה תהא עד שתבא במים. In Sifra: the matter will lead to ill-feeling, and the husband will desire to divorce her. Neither Sifra nor jer. has the coloured dress.

mined.[1] Their strictness in the separation of the menstruous wife is the same as reported by R. Simeon b. Eleazar of some unnamed early authority; he said,[2] 'How far levitical purity spread in Israel! The early (scholars) did not prescribe that a levitically pure person must not eat with a menstruous woman, for the early (men) did not eat with menstruous women; but they said, A man who has a running issue shall not eat with a woman who has a running issue, because it offers an occasion for sin'. As the Shammaites[3] prohibited a man who observed the law of levitical purity on his food, but who had a running issue, from eating with a man who did not observe the law of levitical purity and who had a running issue, while the Hillelites permitted it, it is most probable that the early scholars just mentioned were the Shammaites. Apart from this, R. Akiba opposed and displaced from practice other strict rules of the Shammaites which were in vogue in his time;[4] so that it follows with great probability from his opposition in this case that the authors of the earlier rule were the Shammaites. In any case, there is no occasion for seeing in the ancient elders any but scholars of the school of the Shammaites between 70 and 100.[5] But it is hardly

[1] Frankel, *Hodegetica*, 41; I. Halevy, דורות הראשונים, I c, 285 a.

[2] Tos. Shabb. I, 14: אמר רבי שמעון בן אלעזר עד היכן פרצה טהרה בישראל, לא הורו הראשונים לומר לא יאכל טהור עם הנידה שהראשונים לא היו אוכלין עם הנידות אלא אמרו לא יאכל הזב עם הזבה מפני הרגל עבירה; in jer. I, 3 b. 73 and b. 13 a הראשונים is missing.

[3] Baraitha jer. Shabb. I, 3 c. 3; Tos. I, 15; b. 13 a: תני בית שמאי אומרים לא יאכל זב פרוש עם זב עם הארץ ובית הלל מתירין.

[4] Tos. Pesaḥ. I, 7; b. 21 a; Tos. Moëd kat. II, 10; Nedar. IX, 6; Tos. V, 1; cp. Nedar. III, 2; Ma'as. sheni, V, 8; II, 4; 'Eduy. I, 8.

[5] In the rule of the ancient scholars about levitical purity quoted by R. José in Tos. Ahil. IV, 6, there is no indication whatever of a date, except the Greek word קטפרס which may have been substituted later for a Hebrew word; but R. José's tradition would probably not take us beyond the Shammaites. The same applies probably to the argument of the ancient scholars about the levitical defilement in Lev. 5. 2 in Sifra 22 d bottom, as it is not clear whether R. Akiba's different interpretation had theirs in view.

necessary to add that in all these passages no reference to Essenes was intended; for the strict separation of the menstruous woman is, as far as our information goes, nowhere stated or even suggested as a peculiarity of the Essenes, as little as the strict observance of the points of levitical purity discussed above. Beyond dogmatic assertions neither Frankel, nor Weiss, nor Kohler have adduced the slightest evidence of a scientific character to prove the identity of the ancient scholars with the Essenes.

Naturally, there must have been many points of strict religious observance common to the rabbis and the Essenes; but this very fact should be sufficient warning to scholars against the favourite inference from a peculiar observance or practice of any man in rabbinic literature who cannot otherwise be classified, that he was an Essene. Let this warning, in conclusion, be illustrated by a reference to a non-legal instance taken from Josephus. He reports[1] that Sameas and Pollion refused to take the oath of fealty to Herod, just as did the Essenes. The reason of the latter was their principle, never to swear, for in their opinion it was worse than perjury.[2] And what was the reason of the Pharisee teachers? Instead of admitting that in matters of oaths these observed the same principle as the Essenes, Dr. Kohler[3] says, 'Whether Sameas and Pollio, the leaders of the Academy, who also refused to take an oath, belonged to the Essenes, is not clear'. The question and the doubt have no foundation whatsoever. For Josephus reports *first* that the Pharisees refused to take the oath, the Essenes followed only in the second place; and then he expressly states in the account itself[4] that not only the two leaders, but also their followers and their disciples—note the two groups in his words—were asked by Herod and refused to

[1] *Antiquit.* XV, 10. 4. 370.

[2] Josephus, *Wars*, II, 8. 6. 135; Philo, Quod omnis probus 12, II, 458.

[3] *Jew. Encycl.* V, 224 b.

[4] Herod *συνέπειθεν δὲ καὶ τοὺς περὶ Πολλίωνα τὸν Φαρισαῖον καὶ Σαμαίαν καὶ τῶν ἐκείνοις συνδιατριβόντων τοὺς πλείστους ὀμνύειν.*

take the oath; and thirdly, Pollion at least is described as a Pharisee by the adjective 'the Pharisee' which probably referred also to Sameas.[1] The Essenes only adopted the Pharisee principle; any other explanation, at least in this instance, is unnatural and inadmissible. Had our literature preserved more information of that kind about rules of action and religious doctrines and practices common to both sections of Palestinian Jews, scholars would have been more cautious in their unjustified reference of rabbinic material to the Essenes. And even the prophetic gift or the training in prophesying of which Josephus is speaking as frequently and as emphatically as possible,[2] he reports once of the Pharisees[3] who prophesied to Pheroras and his wife and their descendants that they would rule over Judaea, and to the eunuch Bagoas that he would be called father and benefactor.[4] The Pharisees were believed to know the future by the appearance of God (in a dream). Unless we assume that Nicolas of Damascus, the author of Herod's biography, copied by Josephus often verbally, mistook the Essenes for Pharisees, but intended here Essenes as prophets, we shall have to concede the prophetic gift of an entirely different kind to some Pharisee teachers of Hillel's time,[5] and not infer from the attribution of that capacity to a man whose religious position is otherwise unknown, that he was an Essene.

[1] In *Antiquit.* XVII, 2. 4. 42 Josephus gives as their number more than six thousand, and expressly states that they were Pharisees; as Dr. Kohler himself admits in adding that they were scarcely different from those elsewhere called Essenes.

[2] *Antiquit* XIII, 11. 2. 311, XV, 10. 5. 373, XVII, 13. 3. 346; *Wars*, I, 3. 5. 78, II, 7. 3. 113, II, 8. 12. 159.

[3] *Antiquit.* XVII, 2. 4. 43.

[4] See Schürer, *Geschichte*, II[4], 599.

[5] Josephus speaks of his own capacity as an interpreter of dreams, *Wars*, III, 8. 3. 351, ; his prophecy of Vespasian's emperorship, *Wars*, III, 8. 9; Sueton., *Vesp.* 5; *Dio Cassius*, 66; Schürer, I, 76; and the interpretation of the portenta in *Wars*, VI, 5. 3. 291.

III

THE PIOUS MEN IN THE PSALMS OF SOLOMON

THE eighteen psalms which form this collection and are known as Psalms of Solomon, have been preserved in Greek, but are assumed to have originally been composed in Hebrew by one or several Pharisees in Jerusalem between the years 70 and 40 B.C.E. They express the religious views and sentiments of a section of Jews in Jerusalem who called themselves or were termed *ὅσιοι*, by which word LXX renders חסיד in the biblical Psalms.[1] From the numerous references to the pious men in the Psalms of Solomon Wellhausen and Ryle-James[2] reconstructed the character of the piety of the Judaean Pharisee of the year 50 B.C.E.; and without entering more deeply into the spirit of his special type in these poems, they declared that he closely approached the type drawn in the New Testament. As the commentators agree that these pious, righteous, God-fearing men were evidently not Essenes, they could very well have been the immediate predecessors and teachers, and in many instances even the fathers, of the pious men in the time of Hillel, discussed in the preceding chapter, if only the type of their piety proves to be the same. It is true, these psalms deal with the conquest of Jerusalem by Pompey and the slaughter of many thousands of Jews; a catastrophe which by its suddenness and greatness brought out certain features of the religious character of the pious, made manifest by terror, submission, resignation, and faith, and consequently different from the traits of piety preserved in rabbinic literature. The fear of the approaching Roman

[1] Wellhausen, *Pharisäer und Sadducäer*, 116, and other commentators.

[2] *Psalms of the Pharisees*, by H. E. Ryle and M. R. James, Cambridge, 1891.

army, the siege and the conquest of the city, the desecration of the Temple, the overthrow of the Sadducean king Aristobul II, the destruction of rulers and warriors, and the suffering of the whole population, including the pious, form the subjects of the author's religious meditations. They afford him the opportunity for expressing his feelings about God's justice and its execution, about sin and atonement, the love of God and patient submission, and various other religious problems of life. Naturally, it was a one-sided, though varied experience; but its instructive details constitute important evidence of the religious attitude of the pious men in Jerusalem, especially as they offer a few characteristic points identical with the rabbinic data about the pious, and supplement our knowledge about them to a considerable extent. And as the psalms represent non-rabbinic literature, they enable us to test some of the results of the preceding chapters.

1. An incident in the author's private life, in no way connected with his relations to his neighbour, allows an insight into his thoughts about a terrifying dream which stirred his fears and his hopes, his religious belief, and his faith in God. (6. 6),[1] 'He ariseth from his sleep, and blesseth the name of the Lord: (7) when his heart is at peace, he singeth to the name of his God, and he entreateth the Lord for all his house. (8) And the Lord heareth the prayer of every one that feareth God, and every request of the soul that hopeth for Him doth the Lord accomplish. (9) Blessed is the Lord, who showeth mercy to those who love Him in sincerity.' As he is referring to his own dream, he describes in those lines his own mental and religious attitude as of one who fears God, loves Him sincerely, and trusts in Him. No explanation of these qualities is given, nor is the way indicated in which they were realized in his actions and his life. But they are familiar as characteristic of the pious man in the biblical

[1] The translation of Prof. B. Gray in Charles, *The Apocrypha and Pseudepigrapha*, 1913, vol. II.

Psalms; and already his stress on the sincere love of God proves him a truly religious man who is attached to his God. As he does not boast of those his qualities, and in the whole psalm never even refers to himself directly, he does not seem to have belonged to the self-righteous. He shared the belief of his time and of his class that evil dreams foretold trouble. But (4) 'at what he sees in his bad dreams, his soul shall not be troubled; (5) when (in his dream) he passes through rivers and the tossing of the seas, he shall not be dismayed'. He differed from some of his neighbours by the firmness of his heart which rested on his faith; and this prompted him, immediately on rising from his disturbed sleep, to bless and praise God, and to pray to Him to obviate the trouble indicated by the dream, and to grant him and his house mercy. He felt reassured that God had listened to his prayer, and will fulfil his request. And such certainty he did not derive from the great number of 'works' performed in accordance with the law, nor did he present those to God as a bill of claims, nor accompany it by an insistent demand for the equivalent reward; but all he expected in his firm reliance was that God would show 'mercy' to those who love Him sincerely. It is true, Wellhausen interprets mercy to be merely another word for reward; but such assertions may be ignored. The psalmist's true piety is evident from his plain words, and need fear no comparison.[1] The opening lines contain further information about his faith: (1) 'Happy is the man whose heart is fixed to call upon the name of the Lord; (2) when he remembereth the name of the Lord, he will be saved. (3) His ways are made even by the Lord, and the works of his hands are preserved by the Lord his God'. It is not given to the worldly man, when his mind is anxious, to be ready for prayer; for God is not his first thought. But He is near to the soul of the pious man, and he traces his weal and his woe so naturally to God that, on rising from his

[1] The parts of his prayer deserve attention: first he blessed God, then he sang praise to Him, and last came the personal request.

disquieting dream, he at once turns to Him for protection. Such a prayer is wholly dissociated from any artificial preparations with which some scholars, without any justification, credit the Pharisee; it is the natural, spontaneous outpouring of his religious feeling. Such a man is happy, for his heart is ever ready for invoking the help of God which, in his conviction, will soon be granted.[1] God removes the trouble indicated by the dream, smoothes the path of the pious man, and preserves his work undisturbed.[2] In calling Him *his* God, he expresses his close and intimate attachment to Him.

2. Trouble and distress of another kind stirred up and revealed other sentiments of our author. (5. 7) 'O God, when we are in distress, we call upon Thee for help, and Thou dost not turn back our petition, for Thou art our God. (8) Cause not Thy hand to be heavy upon us, lest through necessity we sin. (9) Even though Thou restore us not, we will not keep away; but unto Thee will we come.' Though the biblical Psalms may have suggested to the writer the expression, the urgency of the prayer and the assurance of God's hearing on his own behalf and on that of his fellow-sufferers, which found such words, were his own. Some trouble was weighing upon them; he knows that it is due to the hand of God. It had continued for some time, and there seemed to be no prospect of relief; but the repeated disappointment not only did not turn away the pious men from God, but attached them to Him all the more closely, and our author, their spokesman, prayed again. For he was firmly convinced that God alone was sending all the distress, and that He alone could, and certainly would, remove it. To press his urgent call for relief, he reminded God that the sustained suffering might break the strained faith of the heart, which was only human, and lead him thereby to sin. As to the nature of

[1] See Hebrew Psalm 18. 4.

[2] The same in 10. 3: For He maketh straight the ways of the righteous, and doth not pervert (them) by His chastening.

such sin, Ryle-James refer to Prov. 30. 8, Feed me with the food that is needful for me, . . . lest I be poor, and steal, and use profanely the name of my God; and to Isa. 8. 21, It shall come to pass that, when they shall be hungry, they shall fret themselves, and curse by their king and their God. Though the two commentators continuously point to the dependence of our author on the Bible; and though the two parallels adduced fully cover the case; and though it is borne out by v. 19, 'If a man abound overmuch, he sinneth', which is identical with the continuation of Prov. 30. 9, Ryle-James are not satisfied with their natural explanation. Urged on by some instinct to search for hidden meanings, they suggest a forced, impossible alternative: 'The prayer . . . contains a hidden allusion to the laws of cleanliness in matters of food, concerning which the Pharisees were minutely particular. In times of scarcity, the difficulty of keeping to the letter the rules which regulated their food, became increasingly formidable; and the liability to sin, i.e. to transgression of the law, was proportionately aggravated.' The learned authors' information about Jewish life under the legislation of the Pharisees is but pure imagination; for the law assumed by them, as far as I know, never existed, and unless they quote in full, and give the date and place of their source, their statement is void of all force. Were they speaking of *priests* of the first century B.C.E. and of *priestly* food of a sacred character, the bare possibility of the existence of such a rule could be granted; but where is a trace to be found of its observance in those days by a non-priest? Even a full century after the Psalms of Solomon (and levitical law did develop in a century), few priests, and non-priestly scholars only in exceptional cases, still handled their food in accordance with the rules of levitical purity, and such scholars are enumerated by name in the Mishnah.[1] 'José b. Joëzer was a pious man among the priests, and his mantle was impure for sacrificial meat;

[1] Ḥagig. II, 7.

Joḥanan b. Gudgeda (the Levite) ate his food throughout his life in the purity of sacrificial meat, and his mantle was impure for the ashes of the red heifer.' Both lived in the last decades of the second Temple in Jerusalem.[1] After the destruction of the Temple R. Gamaliel II and Akylas the proselyte are reported to have kept their food in levitical purity;[2] and even priests were either ignorant of those rules,[3] or did not observe them.[4]

And as a closer parallel to the conduct of the Pharisee assumed by Ryle-James, the following incident may be quoted. 'R. Eleazar b. R. Sadok said, When I learned Torah with R. Joḥanan of Ḥauran, I noticed in a year of drought that he was eating dry bread with salt (nothing with it). When I told my father of it, he sent olives to him through me; but when R. Joḥanan saw that they were wet, he said to me that he did not like olives. When I reported it to my father, he said, Tell him that the cask (from which the olives were taken) had a hole (in its bottom) and only the lees stopped it (that is why the olives were in the juice and wet, and still not fit for receiving defilement from the touch of an unobservant person).[5] Here we have, on the one hand, R. Ṣadok the priest keeping his olives in a way that prevented their possible defilement; on the other hand, a scholar in Jerusalem of whose priestly descent we are not informed, refuses to eat olives which might possibly have been touched by a levitically unobservant person. Though R. Ṣadok was a priest, the scholar did not trust him, because he belonged to the school of Shammai which on this point was exceptionally lenient, as it held that the juice of fruit did not make the fruit liable to receive defilement;

[1] See above, 34 ff.

[2] Tos. Ḥagig. III, 2, 3.

[3] See the noble priest above, p. 35.

[4] R. Gamaliel the old gave his daughter to Simeon b. Nethan'el the priest for a wife, and stipulated with his son-in-law that she should not have to prepare levitically pure food for her husband. To this report R. Simeon b. Gamaliel II remarked, There was no need for that stipulation, as an observant person is not forced to prepare levitically pure food for a non-observant person, Tos. 'Abod. zar. III, 10.

[5] Baraitha Yebam. 15 b top; Tos. Sukk. II, 3.

but in fact R. Sadok followed the stricter view of the Hillelites. The incident probably occurred during the famine in 48,[1] when R. Eleazar b. R. Ṣadok was a boy. The point of levitical purity in question was based on a dispute between the two schools to whom the development of the rules of levitical purity was mainly due.[2] It is instructive to see how the Pharisee behaved in a famine, 'when the difficulty of keeping to the letter the rules which regulated their food, became increasingly formidable'; there was on his part not a moment's hesitation to decline the gift, though it was not even actually defiled, but only liable to receive possible defilement. To my knowledge, this incident of the year 48 C.E. is the earliest reference to such observance. But Ryle-James, in proceeding from the New Testament, easily bridged the interval of 100 years, and saw no difficulty in applying conditions which in themselves cannot be proved as having ever obtained in any part of Palestine in the first century, to a date 100 years earlier, when rabbinic levitical legislation was in its infancy.[3] The author of the Psalms of Solomon did not think and could not have thought of such a sin; he was rather afraid that in his suffering he might succumb to his human weakness and give up his trust in God.

The psalmist proceeds (5. 10), 'For if I hunger, unto Thee will I cry, O God; and Thou wilt give to me. (11) Birds and fish dost Thou nourish, in that Thou givest rain to the steppes that green grass may spring up, to prepare fodder in the steppe for every living thing; (12) and if they hunger, unto Thee do they lift up their face. (13) Kings and rulers and peoples Thou dost nourish, O God; and who is the help of the poor and needy, if not Thou, O Lord?

[1] Josephus, *Antiquit.* XX, 5. 2. 101; 2. 6. 51; III, 15. 3. 320; Schürer, *Geschichte*, I³, 567. 8.

[2] 'Eduy. IV, 6; Tos. II, 2; Schwarz, *Die Erleichterungen der Schammaiten*, 49. The account of Tos. adds, It teaches you that the teacher ate his ordinary food in levitical purity. This is important, as it draws attention to the fact as not frequent.

[3] Shabb. 15 a; jer. I, 3 d. 43–7; Weiss, *Zur Geschichte*, I, 105, 143 ff.

(14) And Thou wilt hearken—for who is good and gentle but Thou?—making glad the soul of the humble by opening Thine hand in mercy!' He then describes the difference between the hesitating help of a friend and God's ample gift in loving-kindness, and proceeds, (16) 'And he whose hope is on Thee shall have no lack of gifts. (17) Upon the whole earth is Thy mercy, O Lord, in goodness. (18) Happy is he whom God remembereth in (granting to him) a due sufficiency; (19) if a man abound overmuch, he sinneth. (20) Sufficient are moderate means with righteousness, and hereby the blessing of the Lord (becomes) abundance with righteousness. (21) They that fear the Lord rejoice in good (gifts), and Thy goodness is upon Israel in Thy kingdom. Blessed is the glory of the Lord, for He is our king.' The writer of these lines was poor, and starved during a famine; he feared God and was humble.[1] He believed that God's providence extended to the needs of every individual, whether high or low; all food was granted by Him and provided according to His will. He watches the doings of every being, and neither good nor evil escapes His attention (9. 5, 6). Therefore our writer prays to God for food, but not for abundance, for it would lead to self-sufficiency and arrogance; only a moderate provision, as in Prov. 30. 8, with righteousness is a blessing. The meaning of righteousness here is evident from the sin resulting from poverty as also from abundance: in one case it tends to cursing God, in the other to forgetting Him; to avoid in the first instance those two sins constitutes righteousness. But it undoubtedly meant more than that, and included obedience to the will of God expressed in the Torah; for not to forget God (Deut. 8. 11) meant not only gratitude, but the recognition of Him as the giver of everything, and submission to His commandments. The first step towards righteousness was the avoidance of sins, as the Pharisee knew human nature and its struggle with

[1] It seems that here, as in the biblical Psalms, עני and ענו were used side by side.

weakness; and the rest led to positive duties which were not, as the commentators would like us to believe, in the first instance legal, but, as will be shown later, chiefly moral and religious. But even the legal side of righteousness, not to steal, and not to curse God, should not be belittled, as without it no foundation for honesty and religion could be laid.

The introduction to the cry of distress is not less instructive. (5. 1), 'O Lord God, I will praise Thy name with joy, in the midst of them that know Thy righteous judgments. (2) For Thou art good and merciful, the refuge of the poor; (3) when I cry to Thee, do not silently disregard me. (4) For no man taketh spoil from a mighty man; (5) who, then, can take aught of all that Thou hast made, except Thou Thyself givest? (6) For man and his portion (lie) before Thee in the balance; he cannot add to, so as to enlarge, what has been prescribed by Thee.' Here again the author declares his belief in the providence of God that measures out the portion of food to every individual; and he adds the negative formulation of the same idea that no man can increase his share. This certainly goes too far, as it discourages man from bending his energy to the hard task; and perhaps it only intended to say that in those days of famine and want nobody could obtain more food, unless God of His own will provided such. And still he feels confident that his repeated prayer will be accepted, and as his opening line, so the conclusion of the psalm breathes joy and triumph. The words of the last verse, 'And Thy goodness is upon Israel in Thy kingdom. Blessed is the glory of the Lord, for He is our king,' are most impressive, though their meaning is not quite clear. Ryle-James interpret God's kingdom as being identical with Israel; but where is Israel ever so called? Their alternative explanation: 'in Thy reign', seems more natural. But just as 'He is our king' must have been intended as the climax of the poet's repeated certainty of God's help, and meant: He is our protector, He *will* help us, so also 'in Thy kingdom' means: in Thy capacity of our king, our saviour (17. 1).[1] In his certainty that God will supply food, the poet opens this psalm with the praise of God to be recited in the assembly of those who in the past had many an opportunity of witnessing God's merciful decisions, first to visit the pious, but in the end to relieve him from distress. This established way of God in dealing with those who are attached to Him, our author will also this time describe in the assembly to those who are his fellows in conviction and in suffering.[2]

3. The judgments of God which the righteous experiences in his own vicissitudes, reveal to him his sins, and to God his attitude to his trials. (3. 3) 'The righteous remember the Lord at all times, with thanksgiving and declaration of the righteousness of the Lord's judgments. (4) The righteous despiseth not the chastening of the Lord; his will is always before the Lord. (5) The righteous stumbleth and holdeth the Lord righteous: he falleth and looketh out for what God will do to him; he seeketh out whence his deliverance will come.' Misfortunes of various degrees, represented as stumbling and falling,[3] befell the pious, who saw in them God's visiting hand; and though he suffers, and perhaps cannot find in his past actions the reason for it, he declares the chastening inflicted on him by God as just,[4] and thanks Him for it. He does not call it undeserved and unjust, and does not criticize it,[5] and his willingness to submit to it is noticed by God.[6] Such

[1] In the conclusion of the first of the Eighteen Benedictions of the daily prayer God is called מלך עוזר ומושיע ומגן, where the epithets describe Him not as the Master of the Universe, but as the helping, saving, and protecting king of His people, 1 Sam. 8. 20; 12. 12, and below in Ḥoni's prayer, p. 220.

[2] Cf. Hebr. Psalm 31. 24.

[3] Hebr. Psalm 37. 24; Prov. 24. 16.

[4] It is the rabbinic מצדיק עליו את הדין; the parallelism in v. 5 requires and looks out for further visitation, and then perhaps ומצפה מאין יבא עזרו.

[5] Ryle-James rightly point to Prov. 3. 11; Job 5. 17.

[6] That is, according to the parallelism, the sense of *ἡ εὐδοκία αὐτοῦ διὰ παντὸς ἔναντι Κυρίου* = ורצונו תמיד לפני ה׳.

firmness in adversity is in itself a gift from God, the deliverer (7). When the righteous, by his own exertions, successfully struggled against temptation, it was God that gave him the moral strength for the fight.[1] Is not all this clear evidence of the poet's genuine piety? And as he is termed here four times, therefore evidently with delibera-tion, the righteous man, is it not clear that what constituted a righteous man's religious character was true fear of God, full trust in Him, patient and ready acceptance of visita-tion, and submission even with gratitude to it? He reminds us of the often quoted statement: [2] 'To such as are humiliated, but humiliate not, hear themselves reviled, but reply not, do all from love, and rejoice at their suffering, Judges 5. 31 applies, Those who love Him are as the sun, when he goeth forth in his might.' Such stress on the religious character of the pious will not appear superfluous, considering the interpretation put upon the continuation. (7 b) 'There lodgeth not in the house of the righteous sin upon sin. (8) The righteous continually searcheth his house, to remove utterly (all) iniquity (done) by him in error. (9) He maketh atonement for (sins of) ignorance by fasting and afflicting his soul, (10) and the Lord counteth guiltless every pious man and his house.' Having recognized that suffering comes from God, and that He metes it out in justice, the righteous man tells himself that it is a just punishment for sins committed. On the other hand, he is conscious of no deliberate sin, as he has ever been on his guard against any intentional trans-gression; he therefore concludes that the cause of his suffering must be some offence committed unwittingly. So his search turns not only in distress, but continually and without hesitation, to his house, to remove therefrom all iniquity done in error.

Why just to his house and not to himself? Ryle-James

[1] Line 7 a does not belong to the following paragraph, but is the con-cluding part of the preceding.

[2] Baraitha Shabb. 88 b.

assert[1] that the righteousness of the poet was fulfilled especially in such deeds as carried out the rules, or avoided the violation of the ceremonial law, 3. 8–10, 5. 20. There is, however, not only no express mention of ceremonial sins, but not even the remotest suggestion of such. The author unmistakably used here Job 11. 14, If iniquity be in thine hand put it far away, and let not unrighteousness dwell in thy tents. And just as this verse does, he is referring to actions clearly defined by the terms און and עולה, to sins against the fellow-man's property, to the acquisition of goods by dishonest means, be it theft, robbery, deceit, or the unlawful retention of a deposit or a pledge. That is why the house of the righteous is twice mentioned in connexion with the sin in question: he searches his house carefully and thoroughly for any goods of his neighbour that may not have come there legitimately. If he discovers there anything of such an origin, he removes it, that is, restores it to its rightful owner, for he makes scrupulous honesty the strict rule of his dealings. Having thus rectified his error by restitution, he follows it up by genuine repentance for his mistake and by self-humiliation expressed by fasting. Such voluntary fasts of repentance were known to Sirach,[2] the Testaments,[3] and to the rabbis of the first and second centuries;[4] it is not one of the alleged frequent fasts of the Pharisees, but one of true

[1] p. xlix. [2] 34 (31). 25, 26. [3] Testam. Simeon, 3. 4.

[4] R. Joshua b. Ḥananiah fasted for many years, because he had in a halakhic discussion made an offensive remark about the school of the Shammaites, Baraitha Ḥagig. 22 b. His contemporary and friend, R. Tarfon, fasted to the end of his life, because once, when the guards of the fields had taken him for a thief of fruit and beaten him, he mentioned his name to them, and thereby saved his life, jer. Shebi'ith, IV, 35 b. 17 ff.; in the parallel in Nedar. 62 a he merely grieved to the end of his life. R. Simeon b. Yoḥai fasted many a day for having made a slighting remark about his teacher after his death, Baraitha Nazir, 52 b. R. Eleazar b. 'Azariah fasted, because his cow was, against the adopted law, driven out on the Sabbath with a leather-strap between her horns, jer. Shabb. V, 7 c. 30. R. Eliezer b. Hyrkanos said that Reuben had fasted in repentance for his sin, Sifré Deut. 31, 72 b; Midr. Tann. Deut. 6. 4, 24; Pesik. 159 a; Pesik. r. 199 a; Midr. Prov. 1. 12.

contrition.[1] The oral tradition of the Pharisees instituted days of joy in commemoration of great and happy events, and included them in the Scroll of non-fast days; but, to my knowledge, it decreed no fixed fast days either in Judaea or Galilee, either in the days of Jesus or in the sad times of the Psalms of Solomon, and, as far as I know, no such fast days are recorded in rabbinic literature. It would be interesting to learn whence, if not by hasty inference from the New Testament, Ryle-James derived their remarkably definite information.[2] Again, by a change in the punctuation and by the transposition of a word, Ryle-James found in *ἐν παραπτώματι αὐτοῦ* a reference to an atoning trespass-offering by which, in accordance with Lev. 5. 1 ff., the transgressor would have brought offerings for sins of which he had been guilty through ignorance. But apart from their misunderstanding of the nature of the sin involved, the manuscript reads,[3] *τοῦ ἐξᾶραι ἀδικίαν ἐν παραπτώματι αὐτοῦ,* to remove utterly (all) iniquity (done) by him in error.[4] There is no trace here of an atonement by the sacrifice prescribed in Lev. 5. 21–6 in a case of misappropriation by the embezzlement of a deposit, a pledge or a thing found, or by robbery, or by deceit, when the denial is followed by a false oath; and it is noteworthy that the author of these psalms never refers to a sacrifice of atonement or any other sacrifice.

In trying to account for the destruction of the sinners in the recent catastrophe by their transgressions, the psalmist says, (1. 7) 'Their sins were in secret, and even I had no knowledge (of them). (8) Their transgressions (went) beyond those of the heathen before them; they utterly polluted the holy things of the Lord'. The context shows that the defilement of which the author is speaking, refers

[1] F. Perles, *Zur Erklärung der Psalmen Salomo's* (reprint from *Oriental. Literaturzeitung*, V, 1902), on 3. 8, p. 21 suggests as the original Hebrew בצום ועִנוי נפש.

[2] About the old fast-day of Abh 9th, see 'Erub. 41 a bottom.

[3] Gebhardt, *Die Psalmen Salomo's*, 99, 75.

[4] Παράπτωμα is used also in 13. 4, 9, but not for a sacrifice.

to actions comparable with those of the Canaanites, meaning clearly the kind of immorality described in 8. 10–14, where also the list concludes, 'They left no sin undone, wherein they surpassed not the heathen'. Such defilements may to modern distinctions appear to be ceremonial; to the Jew they were grave offences against his religion, because they were sins against the holiness of God, against human natural feeling, and man's higher instincts. Similarly in (2. 3), 'Because the sons of Jerusalem had defiled the holy things of the Lord, had profaned with iniquities the offerings of God', the profanation was caused by iniquities; consequently, the parallel defilement was brought about in the same way, not by ceremonial impurity. Ryle-James rightly point to Ezek. 5. 11, 'Because thou hast defiled My sanctuary with all thy detestable things and with all thine abominations'; but the parallel extends not only to the meaning of the single word τὰ ἅγια, 'sanctuary', but to the whole verse which unmistakably influenced the poet, as also Ezek. 23. 38, 'They have defiled My sanctuary in the same day (by adultery and idolatry)'. Not levitical laws relating to the priests are meant, but, as in the prophet, immorality. So our author says (2. 11), 'For no man upon it (the earth) had done what they did'. For levitical defilement even of the holy things such language is too strong; and he expressly mentions (13) harlots and the unnatural intercourse of the daughters of Jerusalem, and he again terms such doings iniquities (14). So (8. 24), 'He led away their sons and daughters, whom they had begotten in defilement'. Ryle-James remark, ἐν βεβηλώσει seems to mean here 'in the time when they disregarded all laws of ceremonial uncleanness'. But the parallel (2. 14) reads, 'And the daughters of Jerusalem βέβηλοι, were defiled in accordance with Thy judgement, (15) because they had defiled themselves, ἐμίαινον ἑαυτὰς, with unnatural intercourse'; here certainly not ceremonial uncleanness, but immorality, is termed defilement. (8. 25) 'They did according to their uncleanness, even as their fathers (had done): (26) they defiled Jerusalem and the things that had been hallowed to the name of God'. Ryle-James say, 'Priests who were neglectful of the levitical ceremonial'. But how was Jerusalem defiled thereby? Or is this merely poetical exaggeration? The land of Canaan was defiled by incest, bestiality, and immoral idolatry, Lev. 18. 25–28, as bloodshed would defile the land of Israel, Num. 35. 33, 34; and as Jer. 13. 27 said to Jerusalem, 'I have seen thine adulteries and thy neighings, the lewdness of thy harlotry, and thine abominations on the hills in the field. Woe unto thee, O Jerusalem! thou wilt not be made clean! When shall it ever be?' Within the list of stern reproaches of heathen immorality the only ceremonial point is (8. 13), 'They trode the altar of the Lord, (coming straight) from all manner of uncleanness; and with menstrual blood they defiled the sacrifices, as (though these were) common flesh. (14) They left no sin undone, wherein they surpassed not the heathen'. According to the context those priests plundered the property of the Temple for their adultery and their unnatural mingling, and coming from such moral uncleanness they ascended the altar of God and officiated. And when eating at home of the sacrifices which they received as their dues, with their wives and children, they treated the sacred portions with indifference, as though they were common flesh.[1] Perhaps a parallel in Testament Levi 14. 5 will make this interpretation more certain: 'The offerings of the Lord ye shall rob, and from His portion shall ye steal choice portions, eating (them) contemptuously with harlots. (6) And out of covetousness ye shall teach the commandments of the Lord, wedded women shall ye pollute, and the virgins of Jerusalem shall ye defile; and with harlots and adulteresses shall ye be joined, &c. (8) For ye shall contemn the holy things with jests and laughter'. The reference to the menstrual blood in connexion with the sacrifices only serves to illustrate the terrible irreverence of the priests toward everything holy. And even here the ceremonial defilement is quoted only as relating to the priests,

[1] Epistle of Jeremy, v. 29.

the Temple and its sacrifices; outside those it did not apply to anything, not even yet to the priestly heave-offering, the Terumah.

In any case, there is no trace in 3. 8–10 of any levitical defilement as suggested, without the slightest justification, by Ryle-James. And it may, at the same time, be stated that the common mistaken assumption of modern Christian historians of rabbinic Judaism that the contraction of a levitical defilement implied a sin, is totally foreign to rabbinic law, especially with reference to Temple times. Not even if the high-priest accidentally contracted the gravest defilement from a human corpse, did he incur the slightest sin, unless he, in his defiled state, entered the Temple or handled holy things.[1] And when Ryle-James with particular insistence point several times to the alleged countless methods of purification multiplied by tradition; and when they assert, without adducing any evidence, that the Sadducees were on that point not as scrupulous as the Pharisees,[2] I confess that any early information in the existing Jewish literature to support the statements just quoted is not accessible, and unknown to me. It is true, the righteous in 3. 8–10 is extremely watchful not to commit a sin; but his anxiety did not concern levitical purity or the ceremonial law, but, as stated before, a possible misappropriation of any goods belonging to a fellow-man. This is a principle worthy of the highest recognition, as, far from leading to a perversion of the noblest ethics, it inculcated the duty of extreme honesty in business dealings. In the absence of an earlier instance, an incident may be mentioned that occurred in Jerusalem in the last years of the Temple.[3] R. Eleazar b. R. Ṣadok and Abba Saul

[1] On the Day of Atonement, when the high-priest had to take part in the sacrificial service and to enter the Holy of Holies, an accidental defilement was unwelcome to him, as it prevented him from officiating, Josephus, *Antiquit.*, XVII, 6. 4. 166; Tos. Yoma, I, 4; jer. II. 38 d. 2; b. 12 b about the self-defilement of Matthia b. Theophilos by pollution, of Simeon b. Kamhith by spittle in Tos. Yoma, IV, 20; jer. I, 38 d. 8; b. 47 a; cf. also Tos. Nid. V, 3; b. 33 b.

[2] p. xlv, xlvii.

[3] Jer. Beṣah, III, 62 b. 13; b. 29 a bottom; Tos. III, 8; Mishnah, III. 8.

b. Batnith who were grocers in Jerusalem, filled their measures on the day before the festival, and gave them to their customers on the festival; according to R. Ḥaninah b. 'Akabyah they did the same also on the intermediary days of the festival for the sake of exact measuring. From the drops which remained in the measures, one of them collected three hundred casks of oil, and his companion three hundred casks of wine. These they brought to the treasurer of the Temple who, however, informed them that it was not their duty to hand over the oil and the wine to the Temple. But when they still refused to keep the liquids as not belonging to them, the treasurer of the Temple said, As you impose upon yourselves such strictness, let the equivalent of the oil and the wine be used for public purposes. When Abba Saul fell ill and the teachers visited him, he said to them, Look at this my right hand that measured honestly! As one of the two scrupulous men, R. Eleazar b. R. Ṣadok, was, as his title shows, a scholar and not an Essene, probably also his companion who bore the title Abba, was not an Essene, especially as there is no proof of any force that Abba denoted an Essene.[1] In any case, the scholar was most particular in his measuring of oil to his customers, and would not keep for himself the accumulated drops as not belonging to him; and so Abba Saul on his death-bed felt reassured that he had observed during his life at least this one duty of scrupulous honesty.[2] It is a curious coincidence that, like the author of the Psalms of Solomon, Abba Saul b. Batnith denounced the violence, avarice, injustice, and favouritism of the high priestly families of his own times.[3]

[1] Kohler in *J. Q. R.*, XIII, 1901, 567–80, above, pp. 34, 108.

[2] Another instance of the most scrupulous honesty was that of Abba Ḥilkiah, the grandson of Ḥoni the circle-drawer, in Ta'an. 23 a, b. According to a report preserved in Aramaic, he did not turn his face to the two teachers sent to him by the authorities to ask him to pray for rain, because he was working as a hired labourer in the field, and would not waste time by returning their greeting, see *R. É. J.*, 48, 1904, 275.

[3] Tos. Menaḥ. 13. 21; b. Pesaḥ. 57 a, Baraitha.

4. The righteous man who in a similar way removed from his house all that had been acquired in error and was not his property, atoned for his sin of ignorance by humbling himself and by fasting, and prayed for forgiveness. (3. 9) 'And the Lord counteth guiltless every pious man and his house.' His sin still exists, even after such atonement on his part, until God purifies him of his guilt. This grace of His forgiveness is expressed in Lev. 4. 20–5. 26 by ונסלח לו, here by καθαρίζω, probably corresponding with טהר or נִקָּה. So also in 9. 12, 'He cleanseth from sins a soul when it maketh confession, when it maketh acknowledgement,' where it is the great act of the admission of sin that obtains for man God's forgiveness. Also in 10. 1, 'Happy is the man whom the Lord remembereth with reproving, and whom He restraineth from the way of evil with strokes, that he may be cleansed from sin, that it may not be multiplied. (2) He that maketh ready his back for strokes shall be cleansed, for the Lord is good for them that endure chastening.' As above, also here chastening is inflicted for sin; it is, however, not implied that thereby alone God cleanses the guilt, as only submission to the chastisement obtains God's grace. On the other hand, (13. 9) 'the Lord spareth His pious ones, and blotteth out their errors by His chastening,' the latter alone may be regarded by God as sufficient. The great stress which, for the removal of sin, the author lays on repentance and atonement appears again. (9. 11) 'Unto whom art Thou good, O God, except to them that call upon the Lord? (12) He cleanseth from sins a soul when it maketh confession, when it maketh acknowledgement; (13) for shame is upon us and upon our faces on account of all these things. (14) And to whom doth He forgive sins, except to them that have sinned? (15) Thou blessest the righteous, and dost not reprove them for the sins that they have committed; and Thy goodness is upon them that sin, when they repent.' First the admission of the sin, and then repentance are necessary for obtaining God's forgive-

ness and His mercy. The wording of the confession given here and moulded on biblical patterns, expresses the shame which the sinner feels in having to admit that sin is a grave offence against God, that could have been avoided; on the other hand, forgiveness exists only for the sinner who, if repentant, has almost a claim to it. Expecting his repentance, God does not really punish the pious for his sin of ignorance, and even rewards him for his contrition. The author means by this real and not outward piety of which there is no trace in the whole book, nor of the exhibition of the religious attitude which some theologians call Jewish-legalistic. It is true, Ryle-James have detected in 7. 8 a reference to the yoke alleged to have been laid by the Scribes and Pharisees upon the Jewish people. There the poet prays to God that, if the well-deserved punishment must be inflicted, He should rather send it in the form of a pestilence than in that of a foreign nation; for God is merciful, whereas the nations would consume Israel. (7, 5) 'While Thy name dwelleth in our midst, we shall find mercy; (6) and the nations shall not prevail against us. For Thou art our shield, (7) and when we call upon Thee, Thou hearkeneth to us; (8) for Thou wilt pity the seed of Israel for ever and Thou wilt not reject (them): but we (shall be) under Thy yoke for ever, and (under) the rod of Thy chastening. (9) Thou wilt establish us in the time that Thou helpest us, showing mercy to the house of Jacob on the day wherein Thou didst promise (to help them).' The whole chapter deals with one single idea, chastisement, and contrasts that inflicted directly by God with that imposed by the Roman conqueror. As in 2 Sam. 24. 13, there is no escape here from the alternative, and 9 b describes the affliction by God preferred by the psalmist. Already the parallelism in 8 b is sufficient to establish punishment as the meaning of God's yoke; for the rod of chastening is actually found in parallelism with yoke in Isa. 9. 3 where the defeat of the Assyrian conqueror and tyrant is described thus: 'For Thou hast broken the yoke of his burden and the staff of his shoulder, the rod of his oppressor.' And also in Isa. 10. 24: 'Be not afraid of Asshur, though he smite thee with the rod, and lift up his staff against thee', for which the parallel in v. 27 has the burden and the yoke. In addition, yoke is actually used in Isa. 47. 6 in connexion with the harsh treatment of the Judaeans in the Babylonian captivity, 'Thou didst show them no mercy; upon the aged hast thou very heavily laid thy yoke'. As it expresses there the heavy and hard labour aggravated by the severity of punishment, so here it means: we prefer to be under God's burden, rod, and yoke, and suffer His visitation rather than be under the cruel rule of the Romans.

The object of the chastisement of the righteous by God is stated to be, to cleanse him from the few sins which he committed, and to prevent him from multiplying them (10. 1). He must at all times expect suffering, and be ever ready to receive more, and endure chastening without murmuring. (3) 'For He maketh straight the ways of the righteous, and doth not pervert (them) by His chastening. (4) And the mercy of the Lord (is) upon them that love Him in truth, and the Lord remembereth His servants in mercy . . . (6) Just and kind is our Lord in His judgements for ever, and Israel shall praise the name of the Lord in gladness. (7) And the pious shall give thanks in the assembly of the people, and on the poor shall God have mercy in the gladness (?) of Israel; (8) for good and merciful is God for ever, and the assemblies of Israel shall glorify the name of the Lord.' The righteous who not only submit without complaint to the affliction sent by God, but are ready for more to come, are described as those who love God in truth, as His servants, the pious and the poor, clearly defining the character of those who in the terrible calamity of their time proved their love of God by their stoic attitude to suffering. But the central idea of the author is more fully elaborated in the short psalm, and the various effects of affliction upon the religious mind of the pious are considered from several points of view. God's mercy and goodness, and His kindness in executing strict justice are repeatedly emphasized; when He punishes the righteous, He does not pervert the ways of his life by too heavy chastening, nor make it so miserable as to lead him, as in the case of Job, to sin. While suffering or after passing through affliction, the pious give thanks[1] to God in the assembly of the people, and the assemblies of Israel glorify Him. The people are those who shared the religious views of the pious, and assembled either on the Temple Mount or in one of the gates of the city to hear, as in Ps. 107. 32, the public recognition of God's help afforded to the pious men. The assemblies of Israel may have been private meetings of their adherents to whom they explained the ways of God as revealed in the experiences of the hard tried righteous, and whom they confirmed in their faith and their hopes and convictions as to the ultimate triumph of their cause. They derived their expectations from the repeated assurances given by God to the obedient in the Torah, and from the way in which God visits the pious for their sins of error.

This idea is the subject also of 13. 1 ff. where the poet states how God saved him and his fellows from the sword that passed through the land, and from famine, and from the death of sinners. (4) 'The righteous was troubled on account of his errors, lest he should be taken away along with the sinners; (5) for terrible is the overthrow of the sinner; but not one of all those things touched the righteous. (6) For not alike are the chastening of the righteous (for sins done) in ignorance, and the overthrow of the sinners. (7) Secretly (?) is the righteous chastened, lest the sinner rejoice over the righteous. (8) For He correcteth the righteous as a beloved son, and his chastisement is that of a first-born. (9) For the Lord spareth His pious ones, and blotteth out their errors by His chastening'. After a long siege Jerusalem was taken by the blood-thirsty army of Pompey; while thousands of Jews were cut down by

[1] If the original was Hebrew, יודו meant declare and acknowledge.

the Romans, the righteous did not, as some Christian theologians and historians would make us believe of the Pharisees, rely on his righteousness, nor expect in return for his numerous deeds an equivalent amount of protection. Just the reverse is stated here: he trembles lest he be carried off with the sinners on account of his lesser sins of error; though he is not actually conscious of any, and they were of a minor character, in judging them and himself most strictly he considers them as sufficiently weighty and certain to cause his death. When he suffered along with sinners, he did not for a single moment protest his innocence to God, as Job had done, and therefore think himself as suffering undeserved affliction; but on the contrary, he expressed gratitude to Him for his special protection in saving him from utter destruction. His suffering differed only in degree and by its privacy from that of the sinners. Thus his justification of his sore trials by his sins, and his whole religious attitude to his suffering, mark a considerable advance beyond Job. This difference finds fitting expression more than a century later in the statement of R. Joḥanan b. Zakkai that Job had served God only from fear, while the true service of Him should be from love.[1] In our psalm it is expressly stated that in his true love of God the pious patiently submitted to all the trials to which He subjected him, and even justified Him and His justice by his errors unknown to himself. As to the reward of the righteous the author says, (9 b) 'For the life of the righteous shall be for ever; (10) but sinners shall be taken away into destruction, and their memorial shall be found no more. (11) But upon the pious is the mercy of the Lord, and upon them that fear Him His mercy'. The words 'for ever' in v. 9 sound at first sight strange, and were by Ryle-James referred to the life after death. But the contrast between the visitation of the sinner and that of the righteous merely suggests that the pious is not carried away into destruction, as in vv. 3 b–5, and is not forgotten

[1] Sotah, V, 5.

by the next generation; so that 'for ever' seems only to mean: prolonged life and continued protection to the end of his life.[1] And even the more definite terms in the parallel (9. 9) appear to signify the same: 'He that doeth righteousness layeth up life for himself with the Lord; and he that doeth wrongly forfeits his life to destruction; (10) for the judgements of the Lord are (given) in righteousness to (every) man and (his) house'. Here the just judgment of God, as also the whole context shows, clearly refers to the Roman slaughter in Jerusalem, and the destruction, as elsewhere in numerous passages of these psalms, is that of the sinners by Pompey; and the contrast meant for the pious their escape from the terrible slaughter and their survival for several years after the catastrophe. Consequently, there is no reference here to life after death as the reward of the righteous.

5. A pious man, whether the same person as in the psalms considered so far or another, reviewed in chapter 16 a recent phase of his life, when on account of his association with sinners he nearly forgot God and was, within a little, carried off in their destruction. Again the sins of the pious, the merciful reminder by God, the thanks and the prayer of the righteous reveal some characteristic features of their piety and some of their ideals. (16. 1) 'When my soul slumbered (being afar) from the Lord, I had all but slipped down to the pit, when (I was) far from God, (2) my soul had been wellnigh poured out unto death, nigh unto the gates of Sheol with the sinner, (3) when my soul departed from the Lord God of Israel,—had not the Lord helped me with His everlasting mercy. (4) He pricked me, as a horse is pricked, that I might serve Him, my saviour and helper at all times saved me. (5) I will give thanks unto Thee, O God, for Thou hast helped me to (my) salvation; and hast not counted me with sinners to (my) destruction.' He was in the company of sinners, and through that, so he feels, he temporarily turned away

[1] Cf. Hebr. Psalm 37. 9, 10.

his thoughts from God: but He, while destroying his companions, merely grazed him with the grave danger, and not merely saved his physical life, but restored his soul to salvation.[1] (6) 'Remove not Thy mercy from me, O God, nor Thy memorial from my heart until I die. (7) Rule me, O God, (keeping me back) from wicked sin, and from every wicked woman that causeth the simple to stumble. (8) And let not the beauty of a lawless woman beguile me, nor any one that is subject to (?) unprofitable sin.' Here his sin is fairly clearly stated: the sinners with whom he associated brought him into the company of women, perhaps of their families, to induce him to marry one of them. From the injurious influence that seemed to continue even after his separation from the sinners, it appears that he was attached to one of those women: so that he can be saved only if God helps him to keep the thought of Him in his heart. (9) 'Establish the works of my hands before Thee, and preserve my goings in the remembrance of Thee. (10) Protect my tongue and my lips with words of truth; anger and unreasoning wrath put far from me. (11) Murmuring, and impatience in affliction, remove far from me, when, if I sin, Thou chasteneth me that I may return (unto Thee). (12) But with goodwill and cheerfulness support my soul: when Thou strengthenest my soul, what is given (to me) will be sufficient for me. (13) For if Thou givest not strength, who can endure chastisement with poverty? (14) When a man is rebuked by means of his corruption, Thy testing (of him) is in his flesh and in the affliction of poverty. (15) If the righteous endureth in all these (trials), he shall receive mercy from the Lord.' When God chastizes the pious for his sin, or in order to pull him back from sin, he does not pray for the removal of his suffering by God; but whereas the righteous of other psalms bore the trials patiently and in his love of God submitted to them, and felt reassured that his firm endurance

[1] Israel, as Ryle-James note, means not the whole people, but only its pious section.

would obtain for him God's mercy, in this psalm he bears his affliction impatiently and murmurs. Like Job, he is full of anger, and words of wrath, unworthy of the righteous, escaped from his lips. His soul is deficient in moral strength, and his prayer for patience and cheerfulness betrays the unsatisfactory state of his mind. His doings and his life are endangered by his conduct, because in his sufferings of poverty and physical pain he did not remember God. He could bear poverty calmly, if only God granted him the strength to stand illness. His prayer reflects not only the frank admission of his sin and of his relative moral weakness, but also the ideals of the pious which we found similarly stated in other psalms.

The religious and moral character of the righteous is again reflected in 14. 1, 'Faithful is the Lord to them that love Him in truth, to them that endure His chastening, to them that walk in the righteousness of His commandments,[1] in the law which He commanded us that we might live. (2) The pious of the Lord shall live by it for ever; the Paradise of the Lord, the trees of life, are his pious ones. (3) Their planting is rooted for ever; they shall not be plucked up all the days of heaven: for the portion and the inheritance of God is Israel. (4) But not so are the sinners and transgressors. . . (6) but the pious of the Lord shall inherit life in gladness.' The description of the pious as those that love God in truth and bear His trials patiently was analysed before. New is here the statement that they walk in the righteousness of His commandments by which life is obtained. Of course, nobody had the slightest doubt that the pious observed the enactments of the Torah; and as that was understood, no special and

[1] The meaning of the phrase is not clear, but it is certainly not the righteousness consisting in the observance of the enactments of the law. As it is intended as a praise of the Torah, as in Hebr. Psalm 19.10, 'The ordinances of the Lord are true and righteous altogether', and 119. 144, 'The righteousness of Thy testimonies is everlasting', it means the perfectness of the laws. To obey them is one of the ways of loving God, Deut. 10. 12, 13.

emphatic reference to it by the poet was necessary, nor expected. Did he mention it only to contrast with it the disobedience of the sinners? The meaning of his words is clear: God gave Israel the Torah to show them the way to life, to the prolongation of life. The pious man acts in accordance with its commandments, and thereby will live long, while the sinners are carried off before their time. Ryle-James see also here eternal life, as it is referred to in the question of the young Pharisee in Mark 10. 17, 'What shall I do to inherit eternal life?' and in 'the day of mercy' they see the resurrection in the messianic kingdom. For this interpretation they find a support in 3. 13, 'The destruction of the sinner is for ever, (14) and he shall not be remembered, when the righteous is visited. (15) This is the portion of sinners for ever. (16) But they that fear the Lord shall rise to life eternal, and their life (shall be) in the light of the Lord, and shall come to an end no more.' But let us clearly realize the situation from which these sentences arose. God's chastening had fallen upon both, the sinners and the righteous, but, as several passages state, with this difference: the sinner was completely crushed, and disappeared for ever, while the pious was sparingly hit, and, as he hoped, only temporarily. (15. 13) 'And sinners shall perish for ever in the day of the Lord's judgement, (14) when God visiteth the earth with His judgement. (15) But they that fear the Lord shall find mercy therein, and shall live by the compassion of their God; but sinners shall perish for ever.' God will not allow him to suffer long, but visit, remember him again, while the sinner is destroyed for ever, and is never again remembered by God. 'When the righteous is visited' would be a strange expression for the resurrection, or for the bliss of the soul in the presence of God. Not one single word in the poem suggests that the pious died, and that the change promised would only come after his death. (3. 13) 'But the sinner falleth . . . and riseth no more. (16) But they that fear the Lord rise to life eternal, and . . . shall come to an end no more.'[1] God visits in either of two ways, either by judgment, that is punishment, or with His mercy, to help those who, by His decree, temporarily suffer for their sins of ignorance, and will be lifted out of their affliction by Him. The righteous continues to live in happiness in the presence of God in Jerusalem for many years after the sudden end of the sinner.[2] This does not mean to say that the pious men of Jerusalem in the year 63 B.C.E. did not believe in a life after death or in the resurrection of the body. Daniel 12. 2, 3 is sufficient evidence for it. But the strikingly different fate of the sinners and of the righteous in the catastrophe under Pompey riveted the attention of the poet to the complete destruction of the lawless men and to the miraculous survival of the pious, and to his hope for a speedy recovery from the sudden, but still sufficiently heavy punishment. And, as he was thus absorbed by the recognition of God's punishing justice, in confession of sin, in thanks for his rescue, and in prayer for help, he had no

[1] Cf. Hebr. Psalm 37. 27: 'Depart from evil, and do good; and dwell for *evermore.* (28) For the Lord loveth justice, and forsaketh not His saints; they are preserved *for ever*; but the seed of the wicked shall be cut off. (29) The righteous shall inherit the land, and dwell therein *for ever.* Deut. 15. 17: And he shall be thy bondman *for ever.*'

[2] This Pharisee, unlike that drawn from imagination and prejudice by Wellhausen, Schürer, Bousset, and other theological historians of Judaism, did not work for reward, as no such idea is to be found in the whole book, nor did that thought obsess his religious mind. When Wellhausen, *Pharisäer*, 119, says that the poet did not refer to a mathematical compensation for his deeds, because he was dealing not with an individual, but with the whole community, he did not prove his case as to the reward of the individual. In Chapter 1 the poet introduces the city of Jerusalem or the nation speaking as a person of its own perfect righteousness as proved by its wealth and the multitude of its children. As the writer does not combat the force of the proof, it would seem that he agreed with it. But as he was poor, we should have expected him either to pray for wealth to prove him righteous, or to show that worldly possessions were no proof of a man's righteousness. As he never refers to wealth except in Chapter 1, where he in fact shows that the wealthy Sadducees were sinners, it is clear that property and treasures were no evidence of a man's piety to him.

thought left for the reward of the righteous in the distant future, in heaven.

6. Righteousness is referred to in 9. 5 in a very instructive way: 'For from Thy knowledge none that doeth unjustly is hidden, (6) and the righteous deeds of the pious ones (are) before Thee, O Lord; (7) our works are subject to our own choice and power to do right or wrong in the works of our hands; . . . (9) He that doeth righteousness layeth up life for himself with the Lord; and he that doeth wrongly forfeits his life to destruction.' The author is speaking of actions which are either good or bad; as the latter, like stealing, robbery, cheating, lying, are transgressions of biblical prohibitions, good deeds carry out one or several of the numerous positive commandments of the Torah. And the only pertinent question is, whether by the righteous deeds the writer referred indiscriminately to all of those positive duties, or had a special class of good actions in mind. The comment of Ryle-James on this is: 'To the Jewish mind the acts included would be of two kinds principally: (a) ceremonial observances, (b) works of mercy. . . . The general conclusion of the foregoing is that we seem to be justified in attaching the special meaning of works of mercy to *δικαιοσύναι* in this passage.' For one not trained in that peculiar method of interpretation it is difficult to understand how the righteous deeds of the pious which are set over against the *ἄδικα* of the sinners could have a meaning so different in idea and compass from *ἄδικα*. One would think that as these denoted every kind of wrong, so *αἱ δικαιοσύναι* meant every kind of proper actions. LXX renders Gen. 15. 6, 'And he believed in the Lord; and He counted it to him for righteousness', by *καὶ ἐλογίσθη αὐτῷ εἰς δικαιοσύνην*, and undoubtedly the translators thought neither of a ceremonial observance nor of an act of charity. In the similar application of the Hebrew צדקה and of the Greek translation of Psalm 106. 30, 'Then stood up Phineḥas and wrought judgement,...(31) and that was counted unto him for righteousness unto all genera-

tions for ever', there can be no doubt about its meaning. Nor were in Deut. 6. 25, 'And it shall be righteousness unto us, if we observe to do all this commandment', where LXX has ἐλεημοσύνη, as has been observed by scholars, charity or ceremonial acts intended by that strange Greek word. The nine cases in which LXX has the plural form of the word δικαιοσύνη, are in no way more instructive for the present purpose than the Hebrew צדקות which, when referring to God's righteous deeds, can undoubtedly include neither ceremonial nor charitable works. And when Psalm 11. 7 says, 'For the Lord is righteous, He loveth righteousness', the juxtaposition of the adjective and the noun, formed from the same root and describing God's character and man's deeds, makes the meaning of צדקות and δικαιοσύναι clear, at least to this extent that it cannot refer even in the case of man to ceremonial works and to charity. The same applies to Ezek. 18. 24; 33. 13 where the tradition hesitates between the plural and the singular form, but where the prophet must have used 'righteous deeds' in the same sense as repeatedly in the rest of the chapter, and that was, as will be shown presently, neither charity nor ceremonial observances.

As that chapter in Ezekiel is frequently referred to as the earliest legalistic and Pharisean exposition of righteousness, a few words on its spirit will not be superfluous. In four paragraphs Ezek. 18. 5–21 deals with the right acts of the good man and the sins of the sinner. The shortest is vv. 21, 22: והרשע כי ישוב מכל חטאתיו אשר עשה ושמר את כל חקותי ועשה משפט וצדקה חיה יחיה לא ימות. (22) כל פשעיו אשר עשה לא יזכרו לו בצדקתו אשר עשה יחיה. The repentance of the sinner is expressed by his observance of God's statutes and by his practice of equity and justice, and both are summed up in בצדקתו אשר עשה. The only doubt that could arise is, whether ועשה משפט וצדקה is an explanation of ושמר את כל חקותי or not. But v. 19 says of the righteous son of the sinner: והבן משפט וצדקה עשה את כל חקותי שמר ויעשה אותם, and not only the inversion of the parts, but also the two verbs שמר ויעשה אותם referring to חקותי are in favour of distinguishing between the statutes and the rules of equity. And with reference to the same righteous son of the sinner, v. 17 says: משפטי עשה בחקותי הלך where משפטי stands for משפט וצדקה, and בחקותי is, by having its own verb, clearly separated from it. The three or two nouns with their respective verbs sum up very briefly the abstention from the sins, and the practising of the right actions, enumerated in vv. 15–17: 'That hath not eaten upon the mountains, neither hath lifted up his eyes to the idols of the house of Israel, hath not defiled his neighbour's wife, (16) neither hath wronged any, hath not taken aught to pledge, neither hath taken by robbery, but hath given his bread to the hungry, and hath covered the naked with a garment, (17) that hath withdrawn his hand from the poor, that hath not received interest nor increase, hath executed Mine ordinances, hath walked in My statutes.' The parallel left in vv. 5–9 is even more explicit. 'But if a man be just, and do that which is lawful and right, (6) and hath not eaten upon the mountains, neither hath lifted up his eyes to the idols of the house of Israel, neither hath defiled his neighbour's wife, neither hath come near to a woman in her impurity; (7) and hath not wronged any, but hath restored his pledge for a debt, hath taken nought by robbery, hath given his bread to the hungry, and hath covered the naked with a garment; (8) he that hath not given forth upon interest, neither hath taken any increase, that hath withdrawn his hand from iniquity, hath executed true justice between man and man, (9) hath walked in My statutes, and hath kept Mine ordinances, to deal truly; he is just.' Apart from the introductory line, every group contains the same division of the duties enumerated into חקותי and משפט וצדקה; and it seems that the obligations termed חקות are of a nature different from that of those contained in משפט וצדקה.[1] Now

[1] Cf. Lev. 25. 18; 18. 4, 26; Exod. 15. 26, and especially Lev. 18. 30: לבלתי עשות מחקות התועבות אשר נעשו לפניכם ולא תטמאו בהם, about peculiar forms of idolatrous worship and of immorality.

it is a striking fact that in the list in vv. 6–8 the prophet most clearly grouped his roll of duties, in so far as v. 8 deals exclusively with the relations between a man and his fellows, whereas v. 7 exclusively refers to so-called ceremonial laws.[1] Would it not be natural that משפט וצדקה should refer to vv. 7, 8, and חקותי to v. 6? But צדיק and צדקה are also used as the comprehensive terms for both groups of laws together; and there is no justification for Smend's remark[2] that the standard of morality set by the moral-social duties that are more numerous than the rest in Ezek. 18, is not sufficiently high. All that one could safely say is that modern social life has not succeeded yet in realizing the prophet's postulates of righteousness.

Wellhausen[3] says about the Jewish righteousness of the Psalms of Solomon: 'As the New Testament shows and Josephus repeats many times, righteousness is on the one hand the goal of the whole of Jewry,[4] on the other hand the special cue of the Pharisees, as the same sources, especially Matt. 5 and *Antiquit.*, XIII, 10. 5 prove. When Hyrkanos saw that the Pharisees were in a good mood, he told them that, as they knew, he endeavoured to be righteous and to do everything to please God and them; and he asked them, if he should deviate from the righteous

[1] The first two prohibitions refer to two forms of idolatry, the fourth to the intercourse with menstruous women, and the third to adultery expressed in a peculiar way. The parallels in vv. 11, 15 do not mention No. 4, and consequently put No. 3 next to the two forms of idolatry. Does not all this suggest that the defilement of the neighbour's wife took place in connexion with some idolatrous worship of Astarte, as also in Ezek. 22. 9: 'And in thee they have eaten upon the mountains; in the midst of thee they have committed lewdness. (10) In thee have they uncovered their father's nakedness; in thee have they humbled her that was unclean in her impurity. (11) And one hath committed abomination with his neighbour's wife; and another hath lewdly defiled his daughter-in-law; and another in thee hath humbled his sister, his father's daughter.' Here it is my impression that all the cases of immorality and incest belonged to the cult of Astarte, as in the earlier Canaanite-Phoenician service in Hos. 4. 13, 18; Amos 2. 7, and later in the Psalms of Solomon 8. 9, 10.

[2] Commentary on Ezekiel, p. 117.

[3] *Pharisäer*, 17 ff.

[4] *Antiquit.* XVI, 2. 4; 5. 4; 6. 8.

way, to bring him back to it. Then a certain Eleazar answered him, 'If thou really wishest to be righteous, do this', &c. Now, it must have been clear to Wellhausen that, in order to please God, even the ordinary Jew had to live according to His will and to observe the commandments of the Torah, as far as and when they applied to him, and in order to please the Pharisees, he had to fulfil the very same enactments according to their interpretation. To observe one of those commandments and, at the same time, to neglect another, could not obtain God's pleasure for him; so that to be righteous or to walk in the right way [1] unmistakably comprised not a selection of a certain group of duties, say of the ceremonial rules, but the fulfilment of all the laws of the Torah applying to the individual concerned. Hyrkanos consequently must have known about himself that he had always lived and acted in accordance with the law; and that was confirmed by the fact that his opponent had to single out the violation of a rule on his part for which not the high-priest, but the alleged captivity of his mother was responsible. That Hyrkanos could have pleased God by his observance of the ceremonial laws only, nobody would suggest; for even only as the ruler of his people he had according to Deut. 17. 19 to possess a copy of the Torah, and to read in it throughout his life, 'that he may learn to fear the Lord his God, to keep all the words of this Torah and these statutes, to do them'. Consequently, 'righteous' in Hyrkanos' case described him as obeying the Torah, therefore as religiously and morally blameless, good, pious. So when Josephus [2] says of Onias whose prayer for rain in the days of Aristobul II and Hyrkanos II was accepted by God: *δίκαιος ἀνὴρ καὶ θεοφιλής*, a righteous man and loved by God, he undoubtedly wanted to describe his piety as great, so as to justify the special distinction bestowed on him by God.

[1] The translation of *τῆς ὁδοῦ τῆς δικαίας* cannot be: righteous way, but, as the identical rendering in LXX of דרך ישר, the right and proper way.

[2] *Antiquit.*, XIV, 2. 1. 22; cf. *Assumptio Mosis*, 7. 3.

Of Sameas he says[1]: a righteous man and on account of that fearless; of Herod's father, Antipater,[2] that he was distinguished by righteousness and piety, and of his own father Matthias[3] that he was not only distinguished by noble descent, but was praised for his righteousness. In all these instances there is not the slightest doubt that the general piety of the men enumerated was meant.[4] And of the Essenes he reports,[5] 'They teach the immortality of the soul, and that the reward of righteousness is worth fighting for'; especially worthy of praise is their righteousness, *τὸ δίκαιον*, as an example of which he quotes their community of property and their organization.

As the dictionaries tell us, *δικαιοσύνη* is the way in which the *δίκαιος* acts, and this is a person who acts in accordance with the established custom, one who fulfils his duties towards God and men. In that sense Josephus uses it[6]: 'Herod wished to be honoured, but the Jewish people was averse from all such things on account of its law, *καὶ συνείθισται τὸ δίκαιον ἀντὶ τοῦ πρὸς δόξαν ἠγαπηκέναι*, and was accustomed to esteem more highly the religious (requirement) than outward honour, . . . and they were not in a position to flatter the king's vanity either by statues or by temples or by other similar things.' Here *τὸ δίκαιον* is an attitude in keeping with the law that prohibited the things stated later. In his description of the Pharisees[7] Josephus says that according to their principles *τὸ μὲν πράττειν τὰ δίκαια καὶ μὴ κατὰ τὸ πλεῖστον ἐπὶ τοῖς ἀνθρώποις κεῖσθαι*, to do or not to do the right things depended to a great extent on man himself.[8] In comparing Philo's picture of

[1] *Antiquit.*, XIV, 9. 4. 172.
[2] Ibid., 11. 4. 283.
[3] *Vita*, 2. 7.
[4] Of Ezra in *Antiquit.*, XI, 5. 3. 139.
[5] *Antiquit.*, XVIII, 1. 5. 18, 20.
[6] Ibid., XVI, 5. 4. 158.
[7] *Wars*, II, 8. 14. 163.
[8] Wellhausen, *Pharisäer*, 22; Bousset, *Religion*², p. 435, in his usual style remarks: 'Sie mussten der Ueberzeugung sein, dass der Gerechtigkeit — schon der Name provociert auf das Gottesurtheil — endlich auch zu Rechte werde verholfen werden.' But he failed to adduce one single passage to prove that righteousness even in its root referred to the judgment of God. Josephus certainly measured it by the Jewish law and

the Essenes,[1] we find that they were instructed in holiness, piety, and righteousness; and the author explains that among the numerous laws of the Torah that are expounded by the Jews generally in their meetings on the Sabbath, there are two chief principles, one referring to the Godhead and dealing with piety and holiness, the other relating to men, and its contents are love of man and righteousness.[2] Here δικαοσύνη is expressly defined as referring only to the duties of man to his fellow. And in the account of Hippolytus[3] about the oath taken by the Essenes on their admission into the brotherhood we read: They swear to fear God and to practise righteousness towards men, and to do wrong in no way to anybody, nor to hate anybody who did them wrong, not even an enemy, but to pray for them. As in Philo's report, so here the duties are divided into two groups, one toward God, the other to men, righteousness meaning not merely strict justice, but including the higher duties of fairness and loving-kindness. Josephus also supplies several instances of that denotation of the word. In his account of King David's grave sin[4] he states: ὄντι φύσει δικαίῳ καὶ θεοσεβεῖ καὶ τοὺς πατρίους νόμους

custom; and though the Torah is the embodiment of God's will, he did not mean to say that the Pharisee weighed every action of his by what God would say to it. It is true, in *Antiquit.*, VI, 7. 4. 147 he freely renders 1 Sam. 15. 22 by these words: God delights not in sacrifices, but in good and righteous men; good and righteous, however, are those who obey the will and the orders of God, and who consider good and laudable only what God Himself commanded to do. Though here the text of the Bible influenced Josephus, we have a welcome definition of a righteous man; one that obeys the commandments of God. See also 1 Macc. 2. 29, where the strictly observant, pious men are described as seeking righteousness and justice.

[1] Quod omn. prob. liber, 13. 83, II, 458: ὁσιότητα καὶ δικαιοσύνην; of the treasurer of the Temple who trusted Crassus, *Antiquit.*, XIV, 7. 1. 106 says: ἀγαθὸς γὰρ ἦν καὶ δίκαιος.

[2] *De Septen.*, II, 282 = *De spec. leg.*, II, 63; the saintliness of the Essenes, ὁσιότης, is referred to by Philo several times (Schürer, *Geschichte*, II[4], 654. 3).

[3] *Refutatio haeres.* IX, 23; Kohler in *Jew. Encycl.*, V, 228 ff. and in Hermann Cohen's *Festschrift*, *Judaica*, p. 476.

[4] *Antiquit.*, VII, 7. 1. 130.

ἰσχυρῶς φυλάσσοντι, 'he was by nature righteous and God-fearing, and kept the ancient laws zealously'. The same terms are applied to King Hezekiah: φύσις δ' ἦν αὐτῷ χρηστὴ καὶ δικαία καὶ θεοσεβής.[1] The distinction between righteous and God-fearing at once suggests that the first meant the king's conduct towards men, as the commandments of the Torah which he conscientiously obeyed, deal with the duties to both God and men. At the dedication of the Temple King Solomon prayed to God[2] that He might keep their minds pure from all wickedness ἐν δικαιοσύνῃ καὶ θρησκείᾳ, in righteousness and the fear of God, and in the practice of the laws which He had given them through Moses for all times. Then the king warned the people that, as they had obtained their well-being δι' εὐσέβειαν καὶ δικαιοσύνην, they could preserve it only by the same means. King Jehoshaphat ruled δικαιοσύνῃ καὶ τῇ πρὸς τὸ θεῖον εὐσεβείᾳ.[3] Menaḥem the Essene,[4] in predicting to the boy Herod his future greatness, warned him, εἰ καὶ δικαιοσύνην ἀγαπήσειας καὶ πρὸς τὸν θεὸν εὐσέβειαν ἐπιείκειαν δὲ πρὸς τοὺς πολίτας, if only he would love righteousness, and piety towards God and gentleness towards the citizens.[5] In a speech put into the mouth of Nikolaos of Damascus and addressed to Marcus Agrippa in defence of the observance of the Sabbath by the Jews of Asia Minor, Josephus says:[6] Ἐθῶν τε τῶν ἡμετέρων ἀπάνθρωπον μὲν οὐδέν ἐστιν, εὐσεβῆ δὲ πάντα καὶ τῇ σωζούσῃ δικαιοσύνῃ συγκαθωσιωμένα· καὶ οὔτε ἀποκρυπτόμεθα τὰ παραγγέλματα, οἷς χρώμεθα πρὸς τὸν βίον ὑπομνήμασιν τῆς εὐσεβείας καὶ τῶν ἀνθρωπίνων ἐπιτηδευμάτων; he divides the Jewish laws into two classes, one, εὐσέβεια, referring to the honouring of God, the other, δικαιοσύνη, to the conduct towards men.[7] And just as

[1] *Antiquit.*, IX, 13. 1. 260.

[2] *Antiquit.*, VIII, 4. 4. 120; cf. IX, 10. 4. 222.

[3] *Antiquit.*, IX, 1. 4. 16. [4] *Antiquit.*, XV, 10. 5. 375.

[5] In the next sentence he varies the expression: λήθην δ' εὐσεβείας ἕξεις καὶ τοῦ δικαίου, the last word being identical with δικαιοσύνη.

[6] *Antiquit.*, XVI, 2. 4. 42.

[7] Aristobul, the Jewish-Hellenistic philosopher, describes the contents

explicit is that distinction in his statement[1] that, while the customs (of worship) of one and the same nation vary in almost every town, *τὸ δίκαιον* is recognized as most useful by both, Greeks and barbarians; our laws have the greatest sense of *τὸ δίκαιον*, so that, if we only keep them properly, we must be kind and friendly to all men. Here Josephus explains as clearly as possible that *τὸ δίκαιον* is the proper conduct, prescribed by our law, towards the fellow-man.[2] John the Baptist[3] taught the Jews *καὶ τῇ πρὸς ἀλλήλους δικαιοσύνῃ καὶ πρὸς τὸν θεὸν εὐσεβείᾳ χρωμένους βαπτισμῷ συνιέναι*, to practise two things, righteousness towards one another, and piety towards God,[4] clearly stating that the proper and perfect conduct towards the neighbour, as he understood it, was *δικαιοσύνη*, as that towards God *εὐσέβεια*, exactly as in the passages quoted from Philo and Josephus.[5]

of the Jewish law book in the same way, Eusebius, *Praepar. evang.*, XIII, 12. 666 d; Bernays, *Ueber das Phokylideische Gedicht*, XXXIII, 1; *Gesamm. Abhandlungen*, I, 248.

[1] *Antiquit.*, XVI, 6. 8. 176.

[2] Cf. *Contra Apion.*, I, 12. 60: We most of all things strive to educate our children to keep the laws and the ancient piety. The last word, though God is not added, undoubtedly means the same as above, as the parallel in I. 22. 212 has it: the observance of the laws and piety towards God. Montgomery in *J. Q. R.*, XI, 1921, 297. 26 adopts the view of Schlatter in his 'Wie sprach Josephus von Gott?' in *Beiträge zur Förderung christl. Theologie*, 1910, part I, 76, and Brüne, *Flavius Josephus*, 98, that *εὐσέβεια* meant the practice of the cult. See *Antiquit.*, XIV, 4. 3. 65.

[3] *Antiquit.*, XVIII, 5. 2. 117.

[4] Cf. Matt. 21. 32: For John came unto you in the way of righteousness, and ye believed him not; see G. Klein, *Der älteste christl. Katechismus*, 142 ff., 162; Abrahams, *Studies in Pharisaism*, I, 30.

[5] In Matt. 5. 20 Jesus says, For I say unto you, That except your righteousness shall exceed that of the scribes and Pharisees, ye shall not enter the kingdom of heaven. He illustrates his meaning by 'Thou shalt not commit murder' (21), extending it to one who is angry with his brother and calls him names (22), and warning him to be first reconciled to his brother and then offer a sacrifice (23, 24), and to agree with his adversary, while with him on the way (25, 26). The second illustration is, Thou shalt not commit adultery (27); and he extends the prohibition to lust by looks (28), and warns the tempted rather to pluck out his eye and cut off his right hand (29, 30), and about divorce (31, 32). The third illustration is, Thou shalt not swear falsely (33), and not swear at all (34–7); the fourth is, Eye for Eye (38), with the extension, not to resist

And so also the Psalms of Solomon which term the pious the fearers and lovers of God and also the righteous, cannot thereby have referred to their observance of the ceremonial law, but to the justice, kindness, and love which they consistently practised in their dealings with their fellow-men.

The righteousness of the pious in the psalms is seemingly contradicted by the terrible curses which the poet levelled against the lawless, strongly reminiscent of Psalm 109, though not approaching in severity and bitterness the woes put into the mouth of Jesus in Matt. 23. The curses follow immediately after the description of the sinner in his

the malicious (39–42); the fifth is, Thou shalt love thy neighbour (43), extended to the enemy (44–48). So far go the examples introduced by Ye have heard, and all of them deal with man's attitude to his neighbour, his life, his wife, his property leading to lawsuits and oaths to support them, and his body. All this comes under the head of righteousness, as it was understood by Josephus, the Pharisees and their teachers. But in Matt. 3. 15 Jesus insists on being baptized by John, and says, Suffer it to be so now, for thus it becometh us to fulfil all righteousness. What is the meaning of the last word here? Not the correct attitude to the fellow-man, nor an action according to law; but it describes a dip in the Jordan, a purely ceremonial act to account for which somehow the commentators have to employ all possible and impossible means of so-called interpretation. If the same statement were found about a Pharisee of any description, the act and the declaration would be characterized with the usual vocabulary as Pharisaic empty, lifeless, meaningless ceremonial, as inward hypocrisy that ousted honesty, love, and God Himself from the heart of the Jew. Evidently the author of Matt. 3. 15 no longer knew the meaning of Jewish righteousness in Palestine, and by a wrong use of the term caused all the trouble (see Abelson in Hastings, *Encyclop. of Religion and Ethics*, X, 1918, 807 ff.). In his essay, 'Righteousness in the Gospels', *Proceedings of the British Academy*, vol. VIII, 1918, Dr. Abbott examined the passages in Matthew containing righteousness in Jesus' sayings. As he starts from the unwarranted assumption that Pharisee righteousness meant levitical purity and tithing, he barred for himself the plain understanding of Matt. 3. 15, and had to resort to an interpretation hardly in accord with the great scholar's scientific method. Even more forced is his explanation of Matt. 5. 6, Blessed are they that hunger and thirst after righteousness. Can there be any doubt about the meaning of the term, after all the passages in Philo and Josephus have been examined objectively? But the word here is, as has been suggested, an addition by Matthew; it was a year of drought and famine, and many hungered and thirsted, as Luke 6. 21 has it. To encourage them to hold out and not despair, the words, without 'after righteousness,' were addressed to them.

capacity as judge, when he sentences criminals (4. 1–6), and after that of his guile produced by greediness against innocent men (4. 7–15). As a judge acting in court he is accused by the psalmist of transgressions (1); while he is severe in speech in condemning sinners (2), and his hand is first upon them in zeal (3),[1] he is himself guilty of manifold sins and of wantonness. Two kinds of sin are mentioned here the second of which is sensuality; and also the first which represents a whole group of transgressions must have been grave, as the author seems to put it on the same level as that for which the judge imposes a severe sentence. As the continuation of the psalm fully explains, it was immorality and robbery (4–6, 11–15), as in the denunciation of the Pharisees (?) in Matt. 23. 25, extortion and excess. The second crime was directed against the property of a prosperous neighbour (11). The suggestion of Ryle-James, taken up by Kittel and Gray, that the misappropriation was brought about by the seduction of his good wife, is not favoured by the text and is in itself not probable; for how could the miscreant have in that way obtained the house of the deceived husband? V. 15 clearly says, 'He fills one (house) with lawlessness, and his eyes (are then fixed) upon the next house, to destroy it with words that give wing to (desire?);' and v. 23 reads, 'For they have laid waste many houses of men, in dishonour, and scattered (them) in (their) lust . . . (25) because with deceit they beguiled the souls of the flawless . . . (27) The Lord shall deliver them from guileful men and sinners, and deliver us from every stumbling-block of the lawless.' All these lines expressly mention words of guile

[1] The phrase is taken from Deut. 13. 10 (9), Thine hand shall be first upon him to put him to death, and afterwards the hand of all the people; and 17. 7, The hands of the witnesses shall be first upon him to put him to death, and afterwards the hands of all the people. This would suggest that the psalmist was referring to a grave crime punishable by death. But as the man concerned is acting as a judge and not as a witness, the phrase is to be taken figuratively: he is the first to give his vote for sentencing the accused person to death or some other severe punishment.

and deceit as the means by which the sinners misled the unsuspecting neighbour. By some clever suggestion the greedy man placed a stumbling-block in the way of the innocent, probably a political snare by which his property passed into the possession of the cunning schemer. Let us only remember that, when Aristobul II deprived his brother Hyrkanos II of his throne, Antipater the Idumaean began to intrigue for the reinstatement of the weak prince. The nation was divided; a supporter of Aristobul may have visited the house of a wealthy, inactive, and harmless Pharisee, and by cunning advice involved him into a hasty remark about the king or even into more serious trouble, and then betrayed him to the authorities. The unfortunate man had to flee for his life, and the obvious punishment was the confiscation of his property, by which the deceitful Sadducee was rewarded.[1] In any case, it seems clear that his words of perverse wisdom drew the unsuspecting owner of the house into the net of destruction. Such unscrupulous wickedness roused the just anger of the poet which he poured out in harsh curses (16–22). They are sad reading; but they were merely the retaliation in powerless, helpless words of the writer, wishing that the very same forms of distress and suffering might fall upon the head of the successful swindler as he had in terrible reality brought upon several innocent men, their wives and their children. The dishonour which recurs here several times (16, 18, 21, 23), means in the case of these men that, when they had to flee in order to escape death or other punishments, they wandered about homeless and suffering privations, till they died in the wilderness, and their bones lay there unburied, exposed to beasts and ravens (see 21). Against such political slanderers psalm 12 is directed, 'O Lord, deliver my soul from (the) lawless and wicked man, from the tongue that is lawless and slanderous, and speaketh lies

[1] Unfortunately v. 11 which described his machinations, is obscured by a textual mistake, see Gebhardt, 75 ff. Could the participle of δολιόω, δολιῶν perhaps be substituted?

and deceit . . . (4) to involve households in warfare by means of slanderous lips. May God remove far from the innocent the lips of transgressors by (bringing them to) want, and may the bones of slanderers be scattered (far) away from them that fear the Lord! (6) May the Lord preserve the quiet soul that hateth the unrighteous; and may the Lord establish the man that followeth peace at home.' The righteous man had no interest in conspiracies, he was for peace in his house and kept away from dangerous politics, as also Psalm 120 puts it; he was not a quietist, but a peaceful and peace-loving citizen.

7. There is, however, one idea that absorbed a considerable part of the author's attention and pervades all the psalms of the book: the interpretation of God's justice revealed in the recent sudden destruction of the sinners, the suffering of the righteous, and their religious attitude to the grave affliction during and after the conquest of Jerusalem by Pompey. When in the course of the terrible events many noble men and their families were killed and others degraded and sold into slavery; when King Aristobul himself was deposed and, along with his sons and his surviving supporters, was taken to Rome into captivity; and when on the day of the great disaster the lives and the substance of the wealthy inhabitants were annihilated: the author of our psalms was stunned and dumb (3. 1). He found no word to express his despair; for all that he could grasp was the fact of the downfall of his people, incapable of collecting his thoughts, and of searching for God's reason and object in sending so great a calamity upon His people. Only after a time he began to meditate, and he soon recognized that it was the work of God's punishing justice; and his old conviction of His perfect justice assisted him in the interpretation of His intentions. In looking round, he found that chiefly the active military and political section of the people had been crushed, while the pious had suffered comparatively less; and his religious explanation of the sad events was definitely formulated. Those

had openly and heavily sinned against God, and even more gravely in secret; hence their overwhelming destruction by which His justice was revealed to the earth (2. 36). For as rulers and priests they had sinned grievously against God, His Temple, and His holy things, against justice and morality, and against the righteous by oppressing him (2. 39). Though the approach of the Roman army and its progress, the conquest of Jerusalem, the desecration of the sanctuary, the mocking and the cruelties of the enemy, and the fearful humiliation of the Jewish heads and leaders by the conquerors had struck awe into the psalmist and had filled him with deep pain and grief, he still acknowledged the unequalled visitation as sent by God and as fully justified (2. 12; 4. 9; 8. 7, 8, 27, 30, 31, 40; 9. 3, 4), with uprightness of heart (2. 16).[1] As the king of Assyria

[1] Bousset, *Religion*², 473, says that the author of the Psalms of Solomon exulted over the punishment which God had decreed against the unlawful ruling house, a profligate race of priests, as also later against the arch-enemy of Israel, the dragon Pompey. First of all, I am unable to discover in the whole book a trace of exultation. Bousset misunderstood the fundamental idea of the book: to prove, perhaps against some writer who declared the catastrophe an undeserved and harsh punishment and questioned God's justice, that it was fully merited, and that God's justice was vindicated by having punished the sinners measure for measure. That is also the reason why the author dealt so frequently with the problem of punishment, and only very incidentally and casually with that of the reward of the righteous. In this connexion one of Hillel's difficult theological sentences deserves to be mentioned (Aboth, II, 6): 'He saw also a skull floating on the surface of the water: he said to it, Because thou drownedst others, they have drowned thee, and at the last they that drowned thee shall themselves be drowned.' Only a natural death in old age required no explanation; but death by drowning must have had a reason in a specially grave sin of the victim. As God alone guides man and, as the judge of the world, punishes sinners, we must try to understand His principles of justice. Hillel and others before him found that God punished measure for measure, so that the punishment revealed the sin for which the man was drowned: he had drowned somebody. Though he may have been God's instrument in executing His punishment, he knew nothing of his employment as God's instrument and committed a crime of his own free will, for which he deserved to be drowned. Of course, the first case of drowning, as Abel's death, must have had in God's providence a special reason. See also Testam. Zebul. 5. 4; *Jubil.* 4. 31, and Oppenheim in *Kobak's Jeschurun* V, 1866, 102 ff.

in Isa. 10, so the Roman conqueror executed God's charge too zealously and far beyond the orders given to him; therefore he will also be punished by God, the King of the Universe, the judge of kings and rulers (2. 34); and here again God's justice will be made manifest to the world (2. 36). It is true, in the catastrophe also the righteous suffered; it was, because they also had sinned. But as their sins had been committed only in ignorance and error, God separated between the pious and the wicked (2. 38) by marking them differently (15. 8, 10) and by showing mercy to the righteous (2. 39, 40), so that they were not destroyed (13. 1–11) by the sword, famine, and pestilence, and by poverty (15. 6–8; 4. 19; 16. 13; 18. 3). Without the faintest inclination to self-righteousness the pious patiently submitted to God's visitation (2. 40; 10. 2; 14. 1), without murmur (16. 11) and without losing their faith in Him (16. 9–12). They, moreover, recognized their sufferings as a sparing punishment for their sins (10. 1; 16. 11; 18. 4, 5) committed in ignorance (13. 6)[1] and blotted out by God's chastening after their confession and repentance (9. 12, 15). God's object in His visitation was also to awaken the pious from temporary sloth (16. 4), and to warn him as a beloved son (13. 8; 18. 4), and to restore his soul to salvation (16. 4, 11). Therefore the righteous not only did not despise chastening (3. 4), but justified God by their own errors (3. 5; 10. 6), and in their distress praised God full of trust in Him (15. 1–8; 6. 1; 2. 40) and His mercy (2. 37, 40; 6. 9; 9. 15; 13. 11), thanking Him in the assembly of the people (10. 7, 8) for rousing their soul by affliction from torpor (16. 4–6), and because suffering brought God's mercy (2. 39; 10. 3); and they called him whom He chastised, happy (10. 1).

[1] 18. 4: Thy chastisement is upon us as (upon) a first-born, only-begotten son, (5) to turn back the obedient soul from folly (that is wrought) in ignorance, ἀπὸ ἀμαθίας ἐν ἀγνοίᾳ (in 13. 6 only ἐν ἀγνοίᾳ). The phrase is evidently taken from Ezek. 45. 20: מאיש שגה ומפתי, where LXX is in a hopeless condition; see Cornill, and the second tradition about Symmachos' translation in Field's *Hexapla*.

8. Strange appears to be the psalmist's attitude to the Temple and the sacrifices. Unlike the biblical Psalms, the Psalms of Solomon never mention a vow in distress or any sacrifice, which in a pious man who lived in Jerusalem between 70 and 40 B.C.E., seems rather strange. In his prayer for the future king of the house of David (17. 23 ff.) he refers to the purging of Jerusalem (32) 'making it holy as of old: (34) so that nations shall come from the ends of the earth to see His glory, bringing as gifts her sons who had fainted, (35) and to see the glory of the Lord, wherewith God hath glorified her'. Here a reference to the Temple and its sacrifices would not only have been natural, but is even demanded by the context in Isa. 66. 18–20 whence v. 34 was taken. Why did he leave out the offering? Did he disapprove of the Temple and its sacrifices on principle, or was there some special reason for his attitude? It was noticed by scholars that not in a single passage did he even allude to the high-priest Hyrkanos II who was in charge of the Temple before the Roman invasion, and was reinstated by Pompey after the Temple had been cleansed by the latter's order. Or did all the blame in 2, 3 ff. refer to him and his management, and was the writer not reconciled to his high-priesthood, when the terrible catastrophe had atoned for the sins of the past? Was he opposed to the Temple, as was suggested, because he considered the Maccabean high-priests usurpers of the dignity, and therefore the altar and its sacrifices disqualified? This seems hardly warranted, as, in connexion with the sins of the Sadducean priests committed in the service of the Temple, he refers to 'the holy things of the Lord which they polluted (1. 8), the sons of Jerusalem had defiled the holy things of the Lord, and profaned with iniquities the offerings of God (2. 3), they plundered the sanctuary of God (8. 12), as though there was no avenger. They trode the altar of the Lord, (coming straight) from all manner of uncleanness; and with menstrual blood they defiled the sacrifices as common flesh (13). They defiled

Jerusalem and the things that had been hallowed to the name of God' (8. 26). In all this he blames the noble priests ministering immediately before Pompey's invasion. And though once (8. 25) he says, 'They did according to their uncleanness, even as their fathers (had done): (26) they defiled Jerusalem and the things that had been hallowed to the name of God', extending the blame to their fathers, it is almost certain that he is referring to the immorality and the Sadducean indifference to holy things prevailing under Alexander Jannaeus. Had he objected, as the author of the *Assumptio Mosis* (6. 1) did, to the whole race of the Maccabean high-priests, he would not have described the sanctuary as of God, the altar as of God, the offerings as of God, the things of the Temple as holy, but defiled and polluted by their *occasional* uncleanness, as he would have considered them permanently unholy. It is from the same point of view that he says of the Roman conqueror (2. 2), 'Alien nations ascended Thine altar, they trampled it proudly with their sandals; (3) because the sons of Jerusalem had defiled the holy things of the Lord, had profaned with iniquities the offerings of God'. Should he not have rather said: (3) Because unworthy priests had ascended Thine altar and had defiled the sacrifices and the Holy of Holies?

Again, the attack of our author on the assumption of the royal title by the Hasmonaean high-priests (17. 5–12) also shows that he did not assail their high-priestly position. (5) 'Thou, O Lord, didst choose David (to be) king over Israel, and swaredst to him touching his seed that never should his kingdom fail before Thee. (6) But, for our sins, sinners rose up against us; they assailed us and thrust us out; what Thou hadst not promised to them, they took away (from us) with violence. (7) They in no wise glorified Thy honourable name; they set a monarchy in place of (that which was) their excellency; (8) they laid waste the throne of David in tumultuous arrogance. But Thou, O God, didst cast them down, and remove their seed from the earth, (9) in that there rose up against them a man that was alien to our race . . . (11) God showed them no pity; he sought out their seed and let no one of them go free'. As Ryle-James rightly pointed out, according to v. 14, 'In the heat of his anger he sent them away even to the west . . .', only Pompey's treatment of Aristobul and his family can be referred to here, as he took all the members of the royal family, except Hyrkanos, to Rome into captivity. Consequently, the whole group of the verses quoted above blames the Hasmonaean high-priests for their assumption of the royal title since Aristobul I in 104 B.C.E. But the interpretation of the individual sentences, as Ryle-James's notes show, is very difficult. The author does not object on principle to a monarch, as he prays for the restoration of David's dynasty in accordance with God's promise; but he opposes the Hasmonaean kings as usurpers. And the way in which he refers to the treatment of David's descendants by the Hasmonaeans, sounds rather strange. Was there an obvious possibility of restoring the old dynasty? Was there, besides the line living in Babylonia and descended from King Jehoiachin, any representative of the family in Judaea?[1] Would Aristobul I and his successors have allowed him to live in that country? The pronouns of the first person plural are certainly strange (6), and are accounted for by Ryle-James in this way: 'We believe that he represents not only the Pharisees, but the priests who had been alienated by the setting aside of the legitimate line of the High Priesthood. It is noteworthy that the fourfold repetition of the first Person Pronoun is followed by the mention of this spoliation'. But not in a single word is there a reproach raised against their priesthood; and also the introduction (1–4) emphasizes only God's kingdom to lead over to David's eternal rule, and v. 7 speaks only of *βασίλειον*, and there is not even a faint allusion to their high-priesthood. Was the author himself a descen-

[1] The Mishnah Ta'an. IV, 5 mentions בני דוד בן יהודה in the last years of the second Temple; but were descendants of David meant?

dant of one of the lines of the Davidic dynasty?[1] That would certainly make the attack and the pronouns clear. But did Aristobul I assail and thrust out a Davidic representative? or are those verbs merely poetical expressions for Aristobul's usurpation?[2] Only Testament Levi, 8. 14 asserts that God promised the kingship to Levi; and against such attempts at legitimation our author protests, and declares that the priests violently appropriated the dignity, and destroyed David's throne. Up to that time they had ὕψος for which, however, they substituted βασίλειον; the first may be an allusion to the title of the high-priests, כהן גדול לאל עליון,[3] in which God's name occurs, 'they in no wise glorified Thy honourable name'. Here the author, if he had objected to the high-priestly dignity of the Hasmonaeans, could have added that even that was usurped. As they were legitimate priests just as others, there could have been no objection to their ministration; and Josephus reports that the priests who were on duty, when the Romans under Pompey penetrated into the Temple, continued the sacrificial service, and were cut down before the altar.[4] So it was not on this head that our author never vowed a thank-offering, and that he eliminated from his messianic picture a reference to the Temple and sacrifices. The author of the book of Enoch 89. 73 declared all sacrifices offered in the second Temple unclean, and added that in the messianic

[1] Interesting is 15. 5: 'A new psalm with song in gladness of heart, the fruit of the lips with the well-tuned instrument of the tongue, the firstfruits of the lips from a pious and righteous heart—(6) he that offereth those things shall never be shaken by evil.' As it seems, the imagery is taken from the bringing of the firstfruit or of an offering with joy, song, and music, and the realities of the offering are turned into a song of gratitude. He knew all these details, but did not refer to a real sacrifice. Cf. Hebr. Psalm 119. 108.

[2] Two usurpers, John Hyrkanos and Herod, are reported to have opened David's grave (Josephus, *Antiquit.*, VII, 15. 3. 393; XIII, 8. 4. 249; XVI, 7. 1. 179) for money; perhaps they tried to obtain the insignia of the ancient royalty.

[3] *Assumptio Mosis*, 6. 1; *Jubil.* 32. 1; (36. 16); Josephus, *Antiquit.*, XVI, 6. 2. 163; Charles on Test. Levi, 8. 14; Rosh haShan., 18 b bottom; Geiger, *Urschrift*, 32 ff.

[4] *Antiquit.*, XIV, 4. 3. 167.

times that building would be removed and a new one erected in its place.[1] But our author, as just mentioned, does not refer at all to the new Temple in his messianic picture. *Assumptio Mosis*, 4. 7, in referring to the return of the Jews from the Babylonian exile says, 'Then some portions of the tribes shall go up and they shall come to their appointed place, and they shall anew surround the place with walls. (8) And the two tribes shall continue in their prescribed faith, sad and lamenting because they will not be able to offer sacrifices to the Lord of their fathers.' Charles remarks, 'For the low value set on the worship of the restored Temple, cf. 2 Baruch 68. 5, 6,[2] "not as fully as in the beginning". The sacrifices were unacceptable, cf. "the polluted bread" of Mal. 1. 7, and 1 Enoch 89, 73. The objection here indeed is not an Essene one to sacrifice as such, but to the imperfection of the worship of God's people as long as they were subject to heathen powers. God would restore their glory and freedom when they repented, 1. 17, but on no other condition, IX'. But all this is in the case of our author beside the point, as he did recognize the Temple, the altar and its sacrifices; and the reasons of his attitude must be sought elsewhere. His poverty could account for the absence of vows and voluntary sacrifices, but certainly not for that of a reference to the Temple and the public offerings.

9. The psalms refer several times to the relations between God and Israel, and their point of view is the biblical. (7. 1) 'Make not Thy dwelling afar from us, O God; lest they assail us that hate us without cause. (5) While Thy name dwelleth in our midst, we shall find mercy'. God Himself, or, as also the Bible expresses it, His name dwells in Israel.[3] But, as this, as a rule, refers to His presence in the Temple and in the city of Jerusalem, the prayer would suggest that

[1] 90. 29; *MGWJ.* 39, 1895, 20 ff.

[2] The words of Baruch do not criticize the sacrifices, but merely state that the number of the worshippers will be smaller, which is no criticism.

[3] Lev. 15. 31; 26. 11; Deut. 12. 11, &c.

God was about to leave His sanctuary; as in connexion with the destruction of the second Temple the Apocalypse of Baruch 8. 1 says, 'A voice was heard from the interior of the Temple, after the wall had fallen, saying: (2) Enter, ye enemies, and come ye, adversaries, for He who kept the house has forsaken it'.[1] Accordingly, the prayer was written when the poet had reason to fear that the Temple might soon be taken and entered by the Romans under Pompey. Wellhausen refers it to the siege of Jerusalem by Sosius for Herod; but Ryle-James adduced cogent arguments against that explanation. In addition, v. 2 is difficult to understand: 'For Thou hast rejected them, O God; let not their foot trample upon Thy holy inheritance'. If this refers to the Romans, as Ryle-James suggest, 'rejected' is not appropriate, and too strong. More probable is their other explanation that it refers to the rejection of Aristobul II and his followers by God, who are now trying to come back and to take possession of Jerusalem and the Temple; the danger is that their return might bring a new siege by Pompey, who could not allow an overthrow of the Roman conquest, and the destruction of the city and the sanctuary. Now, Josephus[2] reports how Aristobul's son Alexander with ten thousand men tried to regain Judaea and the capital; but he retired before Gabinius to the neighbourhood of Jerusalem where he was defeated. From the statement (5. 4) that Gabinius brought Hyrkanos to Jerusalem and handed over to him the care of the Temple, it follows that the high-priest had left the city during the military operations. Immediately after Alexander's failure Aristobul escaped from Rome, came to Judaea, and gathered many Jews round him;[3] and though he also was soon defeated, the poet of the psalm might have trembled lest, if Aristobul succeeded in entering Jerusalem, the Romans would soon follow him. In any case, God was still dwelling in Jerusalem.

[1] Charles refers to Tacitus, *Hist.*, V, 13: 'Et apertae repente delubri fores et audita maior humana vox, excedere deos'.

[2] *Antiquit.*, XIV, 5. 2.

[3] Ibid., 6. 1.

Ryle-James see in this an emphasis on Israel's privileged position with God.[1] 'But the universality of Divine mercy and justice in no way affects the peculiar relations of Israel with God. He is the God of Israel, 4. 1; 9. 2; 12. 6; 18. 6; cf. 8. 37; 9. 16, and the God of Jacob, 16. 3. Israel is His portion and heritage, 14. 3. The seed of Abraham was chosen above all the nations, the Divine name set upon it, the holy covenant established with the patriarchs, 9. 17–20. God's love and mercy are always towards Israel, 5. 21; 7. 8; 18. 2–4. Israel is His servant, 12. 7; 17. 23, for whom He hath promised blessings, 11. 8; cf. 17. 50. Jerusalem is the holy city, 18. 4.' This is all quite correct: the spokesman of his down-trodden nation still believes in his Bible, all parts of which taught him and every Jew those ideas; and also many a warning and, at the same time, several reassuring messages of the prophets told him that Israel would for all times and in all circumstances remain God's people. The universality of Divine mercy and justice did not affect in his mind Israel's privileged position with God. But the two commentators of the psalms did not pursue their inquiry into the close relations of Israel with God, though Amos could have given them the clue to it. Does He grant Israel special protection even when it is sinning, or the favour of a remission of iniquity? Does not, moreover, the author of the short psalm 7 that emphasizes the presence of God in Jerusalem and His protection of it (7. 5, 6), at the same time tremble at His anger at Israel (7. 4), at His impending withdrawal from the capital, His rejection of His people, and His most severe punishments (7. 4)? God's presence in Jerusalem not only condones no failings, but, on the contrary, brings with it quicker visitation for them, and even the righteous feel His stern justice. God sends against privileged Israel the punishing enemy, and it does not occur to the psalmist, just as little as to Amos 7, to pray to Him to withdraw all affliction; but all he requests with King David in 2 Sam. 24. 14,

[1] L. ff.

is that God may execute the severe punishment Himself and not employ the Romans. Again and again he prays for God's mercy, but for no privilege; only His mercy will have the effect that the nations will not prevail over Israel (7. 5, 6), and He will pity the seed of Israel for ever and not reject them (7. 8). The prayer concludes with the self-assurance (9), 'Thou wilt establish us in the time that Thou helpest us, showing mercy to the house of Jacob on the day wherein Thou didst promise (to help them).' Sins provoke the God of Israel (4. 1), and their consequences for every individual Israelite are emphatically stated again and again. Even when God will remember His people (11. 2), it will be due to His mercy; and the prayer for the messianic redemption (11. 9) reads, 'The mercy of the Lord be upon Israel for ever and ever'. And as throughout the book, as Ryle-James note, Israel includes only the pious part of the nation, the servant of God, even His mercy is granted in the first instance only to such as merit it by their piety.

The special love of God for the seed of Abraham (18. 1–6) deserves a short consideration. (1) 'Lord, Thy mercy is over the works of Thy hands for ever; Thy goodness is over Israel with a rich gift. (2) Thine eyes look upon them, so that none of them suffers want; (3) Thine ears listen to the hopeful prayer of the poor. Thy judgements (are executed) upon the whole earth in mercy; (4) and Thy love (is) toward the seed of Abraham, the children of Israel. Thy chastisement is upon us as (upon) a first-born, only-begotten son, (5) to turn back the obedient soul from folly in ignorance. (6) May God cleanse Israel against the day of mercy and blessing, against the day of choice when He bringeth back His anointed'. These lines were composed after God had accepted the prayer of the starving and poor righteous men, and everybody had food again. God is merciful to all His creatures at all times (1 a), but to Israel with a rich gift (1 b), which, in the grateful and exaggerating words of the humble poet, merely means, as he himself explains, that everybody has sufficient. God judges the whole earth in mercy (3 b), but towards Israel there is love (4 a); and what does that great distinction imply? The next line explains it as clearly as possible. According to Prov. 3. 12, 'For whom the Lord loveth He correcteth, even as a father the son in whom he delighteth'; and Deut. 8. 5, 'As a man chasteneth his son, so the Lord thy God chasteneth thee , our author states, (13. 8) 'For He correcteth the righteous as a beloved son, and His chastisement is as that of a firstborn'. The only expression of God's love and its special object is correction for the purpose of cleansing the beloved pious man from sin. This is what the pious Pharisee saw in his God's special love to him, and, as he suffered, in his own love to God: he not only readily submitted to His chastening, but bore it patiently and without a murmur, as he saw in it the love of his Father in heaven. This deeply religious idea of the Pharisee would have deserved, on the part of the commentators and of the historians of Jewish-religious thought, greater attention and appreciation.

Another instance is 8. 29, 'Worthy to be praised is the Lord that judgeth the whole earth in His justice. (30) Behold now, O God, Thou hast shown us Thy judgement in Thy justice; (31) our eyes have seen Thy judgements, O God. We have justified Thy name that is honoured for ever; (32) for Thou art the God of justice, judging Israel with chastening. (33) Turn, O God, Thy mercy upon us, and have pity upon us; (34) gather together the dispersed of Israel, with mercy and goodness; (35) for Thy faithfulness is with us. And (though) we have stiffened our neck, yet Thou art our chastener; . . . (38) and we will not depart from Thee, for good are Thy judgements upon us. (40) The Lord is worthy to be praised for His judgements with the mouth of the pious ones'. The last lines quoted praise God for His special goodness to Israel; and again, what favour did it bestow upon them? Sparing punishment! Special thanks are offered by the poet for God's judgments which are acknowledged by the people as just and fully deserved for their sins, and because towards Israel

He exercises special kindness by judging it with chastening; and He keeps His promise to the patriarchs by not allowing Israel to perish completely. And all that the poet is praying for, is mercy and pity in the catastrophe that threatens to swallow up the people. The beautiful prayer of the Pharisee writer deserves special attention, as it is full of deep sentiment and true inwardness (31–8). Again, whenever the psalmist stresses the special love of God to Israel in the past, it is in distress. (9. 16) 'And now, Thou art our God, and we the people whom thou hast loved: behold and show pity, O God of Israel, for we are Thine; and remove not Thy mercy from us, lest they assail us. (17) For Thou didst choose the seed of Abraham before all the nations, and didst set Thy name upon us, O Lord, (18) and Thou wilt not reject (us) for ever. Thou madest a covenant with our fathers concerning us; (19) and we hope in Thee, when our soul turneth (unto Thee). The mercy of the Lord be upon the house of Israel for ever and ever'. The author's whole mind is sunk in the terrible suffering of his people, caused by Pompey's cruelty; he points to no merit of his own, to no privileged position or claim of Israel. At the time of the prayer he saw nothing favourable in the life of the nation by which to support his supplication; and amid the depression and the despair of his heart and the prevailing distress his mind turned to the past, and he reminded God of all that he knew of the glorious position of his ancestors. There is no trace of pride at the descent of Israel from the patriarchs or at God's particular measures for the people; nothing but the humble cry of an anguished heart for mercy, that Israel may not be rejected. And the same spirit is evident in 14. 3, 'For the portion and inheritance of God is Israel', where Deut. 32. 9 is applied to the pious men who loved God in truth, endured patiently His chastening, and obeyed His commandments; they will not be uprooted, for they are God's portion. No idea of Israel's distinctive position or its closer relations with God was intended here.

Neither in his meditations nor in his prayers does the poet ever refer in the same definite way to a reward merited by the righteous as he refers to the punishment incurred by the sinner. Though incidental reference was repeatedly made in these notes to his conception of God's intervention on earth, a short explanation of his connected statement about the problem (2. 32–40) will give a clearer view of it. 'He (Pompey) reflected not that he was a man, (32) and reflected not on the latter end; (33) he said: I will be lord of land and sea; and he recognized not that it is God who is great, mighty in His great strength. (34) He is king over the heavens, and judgeth kings and kingdoms. (35) (It is He) who setteth me up in glory, and bringeth down the proud to eternal destruction in dishonour, because they knew Him not. (36) And now behold, ye princes of the earth, the judgement of the Lord, for a great king and righteous (is He), judging (all) that is under heaven. (37) Bless God, ye that fear the Lord with wisdom, for the mercy of the Lord will be upon them that fear Him, in the judgement; (38) so that He will distinguish between the righteous and the sinner, (and) recompense the sinners for ever according to their deeds; (39) and have mercy on the righteous, (delivering him) from the affliction of the sinner, and recompensing the sinner for what he hath done to the righteous. (40) For the Lord is good to them that call upon Him in patience, doing according to His mercy to His pious ones, establishing (them) at all times before Him in strength. (41) Blessed be the Lord for ever before His servants.' Most of the ideas referring to the arrogant conqueror are familiar from Isa. 10 and 37, and Ḥannah's psalm in 1 Sam. 2. The poet reminded Pompey that not he, but God alone was the ruler of the Universe, and that kings and kingdoms were called to account by Him for their wantonness. Also the Roman conqueror had been raised by Him for His own purposes, as He brought low the Jewish king and his supporters, because they had not known God. The same sin had been committed by them

(4. 24) '(In robbing people of their houses and driving them away), they have not remembered God, nor feared God in all these things; (25) but they have provoked God's anger and vexed Him,' and they were punished by Him through the Romans. His justice was manifest, and should be recognized by rulers. But the chief interest of the poet was in those of his own section, the pious, and their religious convictions. They should thank God, for they would be rewarded by Him for their deeds by His mercy in judgment, by giving them the strength to stand firm in the catastrophe and not be crushed; that is His great goodness to them.

So we see that God watches, on the one hand, the deeds of the righteous and the sinners in Judaea, on the other the treatment of both sections by the Romans whom He called from the ends of the earth to execute His punishment. The principle of God's providence and of man's free will the poet explains in 9. 5, 'For from Thy knowledge none that doeth unjustly is hidden, (6) and the righteous deeds of Thy pious ones (are) before Thee, O Lord; where, then, can a man hide himself from Thy knowledge, O God? (7) Our works are subject to our own choice and power to do right or wrong in the works of our hands; and in Thy righteousness Thou visitest the sons of men.' And in 14. 4, 'But not so are the sinners and transgressors, who love (the brief) day (spent) in companionship with their sin; their delight is in fleeting corruption, (5) and they remember not God. For the ways of men are known before Him at all times, and He knoweth the secrets of the heart before they come to pass. (6) Therefore their inheritance is Sheol and darkness and destruction, and they shall not be found in the day when the righteous obtain mercy; (7) but the pious of the Lord shall inherit life in gladness.' This emphatic statement seems to have deliberately set out one of the essential differences of religious doctrine between the Pharisees and the most advanced among the Sadducees. As in Psalms 10. 4; 14. 1; 36. 2; 53. 2, and Job 22. 12 ff., so in the passage quoted the wicked maintains that God cares nothing for, nor sees, the doings of man; so that there is before Him neither account nor responsibility, neither reward nor punishment for anybody, and life may be enjoyed without any restraint as long as it lasts. Against that, probably fairly general, teaching our author stresses the conviction that God does see and know every deed of man and even the intention rising in his heart, and that He does take an interest in man's actions, as He recompenses good and evil. On the other hand, there seem to have been others who held that man was not responsible for his deeds, as they were not a matter of his choice, but probably of fate.[1] Against those our poet emphasizes our free will and power in our actions, and the consequences for the sinners of their transgressions. When they, not thinking of God, enjoy life too freely, they will suffer for it; for God sees even their secret sins (8. 9–15), their hypocrisy, their injustice in judgment, their dishonesty, their immorality and their enormities, and their contempt for things holy to God. Without respect for any person, meaning the nobles and the king, He punishes them justly, even, where possible, measure for measure.

All classes of the population were sinful (17. 21, 22), and the righteous lived among them as innocent lambs and remained pious, though associating with the sinners; they were poor, modest and humble, and acted always in accordance with God's will, His commandments. Their prayers were submitted in humility, accompanied by the admission of sin committed in ignorance, by repentance, and by fasts to humble themselves. Even in the greatest affliction their faith in God never wavered; for they knew that His justice even in their own case of suffering was unassailable; therefore they bore it with resignation as a punishment not as full as deserved, and as the father's chastisement of his beloved son. In true devotion and inwardness, and from a pure and obedient heart they

[1] Schürer, *Geschichte*, II⁴, 463, about free will.

thanked God for His sparing visitation, and prayed for mercy for themselves and their people. He showed them pity, fortified their souls to endure suffering, saved them, and prolonged their lives, while the sinners were crushed before their eyes. On that day God distinguished between the pious and the transgressors, for He is just and kind for ever (10. 6), merciful and good for ever (10. 8), the hope and the refuge of the poor (15. 2; 5. 2), has mercy upon the needy (10, 7), He is good, gentle, merciful, sparing, helping the poor and the humble in loving-kindness, feeding the hungry in a famine, keeping away all the forms of destruction from the pious, and delivering the righteous from deceitful and sinful men (4. 27). When speaking of God, the poet often says name of God; this tendency, marked already in the biblical Psalms, grew in the course of the succeeding centuries, though in our psalms it is not used as frequently and as consistently as we would have expected. It seems that the author resorted to it only in certain definite phrases (8. 31), 'Our eyes have seen Thy judgements, O God. We have justified Thy name that is honoured for ever. (10. 6) Just and kind is our Lord in His judgements for ever, and Israel shall praise the name of the Lord in gladness. (8) For good and merciful is God for ever, and the assemblies of Israel shall glorify the name of the Lord.[1] (15. 1), I called upon the name of the Lord; (4) in giving thanks to Thy name; (17. 7) they in no wise glorified Thy honourable name; (7. 5) while Thy name dwelleth in our midst. (11. 9) Let the Lord raise up Israel by His glorious name, and (5. 22) Blessed be the glory of the Lord, for He is our king,' were preparing the ground for, or perhaps already presupposing, the formula ברוך שם כבוד מלכותו used in the Temple service on the Day of Atonement.[2] (6. 2) 'When he remembereth the name of the Lord, he will be saved; (8. 26) they defiled

[1] So 5. 1; 6. 6, 7.

[2] Yoma, III, 8; IV, 1, 2; VI, 2; and in the service of the public fast on the Temple Mount, Baraitha Ta'an. 16 b.

Jerusalem and the things that had been hallowed to the name of God; (9. 17) and didst set Thy name upon us, O Lord'.

God only in extreme cases brings great catastrophes to punish the sins of kings and of the leaders of the people; in the normal course of life He employs the affliction of drought with which Deut. 11. 17 threatens disobedience. Our book refers to such a calamity once; after a statement of Pompey's cruelties, he proceeds (17. 17), 'And the children of the covenant in the midst of the mingled peoples surpassed (?) them, there was not among them one that wrought mercy and truth in the midst of Jerusalem. (18) They that loved the assemblies of the pious fled from them, as sparrows that fly from their nest. (19) They wandered in deserts that their lives might be saved from harm, and precious in the eyes of them that lived abroad was any that escaped alive from them. (20) Over the whole earth were they scattered by lawless (men). (21) For the heavens withheld the rain from dropping upon the earth, springs were stopped (that sprang) perennial(ly) out of the deeps, (that ran down) from lofty mountains. For there was none among them that wrought righteousness and justice; from the chief of them to the least (of them) all were sinful; (22) the king was a transgressor, and the judge disobedient, and the people sinful.' The wording of the whole passage is not at all clear, and the historical references were not sufficiently elucidated by the commentators; and as they bear on the problem of sin and punishment in question, a few words of explanation are necessary. As v. 17 follows immediately after the description of the Roman conquest of Jerusalem and the offensive Roman practices, Pompey's garrison is stationed in Jerusalem, and the new administration is at work (17). As Aristobul and his followers were gone, who were now the leaders of whom the author expected loving-kindness? *Οἱ υἱοὶ τῆς διαθήκης ἐν μέσῳ ἐθνῶν συμμίκτων* are at first sight obscure, and Ryle-James offer as the only help to understanding LXX on Ezek. 30. 5: *καὶ πάντες οἱ ἐπίμικτοι καὶ τῶν υἱῶν τῆς διαθήκης μου* for וכל הערב וכוב ובני ארץ הברית. The similarity is indeed very close, and may contain the clue to a satisfactory interpretation of the line. From Josephus [1] we learn that Antipater was already in 63/2 assisting, at Hyrkanos' order, the Roman representative of Pompey in Syria, Aemilius Scaurus; so that he was, from the day of Hyrkanos' reinstatement by Pompey, by his side in Jerusalem as in former years, and governed Judaea on his behalf.[2] He, his sons, and his friends could in a twofold sense be referred to as the sons of the covenant, as they were circumcised, and were Hyrkanos' allies and friends. The Romans who were also represented, might have been described as בני הערב, the sons of the west, Italy being termed the west (17. 14), and the translator took the words, as in Ezekiel, to mean mingled people. The poet expected Antipater to be more kind to the Jews than the Romans, but he proved worse. The adherents of the pious,[3] from reasons not indicated, were forced to flee from Jerusalem; they scattered in various directions, and wandered for safety in deserts, probably hoping to be allowed soon to return. At this point (19) some new persons are introduced by the poet, called *παροικία*, Jews who had settled outside Judaea, and who valued every life of those who wandered in the deserts and who succeeded in escaping, as most precious. To those sojourners in countries outside Judaea the next lines are devoted. As the king who was never referred to before, was still in power, when the lawless drove out those men, it was before Pompey's invasion; perhaps they were identical with those who were deprived of their property by guile (4. 11–15)

[1] *Antiquit.*, XIV, 5. 1. 80.

[2] 'And Gabinius settled the affairs of Jerusalem according to Antipater's wishes,' *Antiquit.*, XIV, 6. 4. 103; *Wars*, I, 8. 7. 175; Schürer, *Geschichte*, I, 343, 14; Wellhausen in *Göttinger Gelehrte Anzeigen*, 1899, 245.

[3] In 10. 7, 'And the pious shall give thanks in the assembly of the people,' we see that those who loved the assemblies of the pious, belonged to the people.

and driven out from Jerusalem. At first they fled probably to the mountains of Judaea where, for some time, they found the most necessary food and water; but on account of a long drought the water supply failed them, many perished, and others emigrated to neighbouring countries. Naturally, they took deep interest in the safety of their former adherents and friends who under Antipater's administration were compelled to flee for their lives from Jerusalem. The drought was, in the opinion of the writer, due to the sinfulness[1] of the whole population of Judaea; not only of the king, the rulers and the judges of whose injustice and lawlessness other psalms speak, but even of the ordinary men of the people to whose sins no other passage refers. Was this addition necessary to account for the terrible drought by which many pious men and others of the people had perished, as without the sin of the ordinary man the calamity would not have been so general?

10. The author of the psalms and his friends were bitterly disappointed in their expectations that the reinstatement of Hyrkanos by Pompey as the ruler and high-priest would inaugurate conditions more fair and just to the section of the pious. Antipater saw his own interests best served by an absolute support of the Roman rule and by the unconditional suppression of everybody and everything opposing him, whether political or religious; and consequently many a pious man was expelled. Such violence only strengthened the messianic longing and hope which the recent catastrophe and the Roman yoke had again

[1] The words δικαιοσύνη καὶ κρίμα cover the sins of all, as they correspond with צדקה ומשפט in Gen. 18. 19 and elsewhere, and, as was shown above, p. 160–64, refer neither to ceremonial law nor to charity, but to the general good conduct of every individual in his own sphere in conformity with the Torah. The judge was reproached by the poet not for his neglect of the ceremonial rules, but, as in 4. 1–7, with partiality in his public and with immorality in his private life. The king's sins are nowhere mentioned; but if what is said against the priests and leaders, refers also to him, he treated the altar and the holy things with irreverence, and was immoral.

aroused. The impressive and clear picture of the messianic king was fully analysed by Ryle-James;[1] but as their chief interest centred round the person of the Messiah and his character, one eminently characteristic quality of the essential figures in the picture, holiness, though mentioned several times, did not attract their attention, and its meaning was not sufficiently realized. Holy is the adjective of Jerusalem, of the people of Israel and of the king. The author says of the messianic king (17. 32), 'And he shall have the heathen nations to serve him under his yoke; and he shall glorify the Lord in a place to be seen of (?) all the earth; (33) and he shall purge Jerusalem, making it holy as of old: (34) so that nations shall come from the ends of the earth to see his glory, bringing as gifts her sons who had fainted, (35) and to see the glory of the Lord, wherewith God hath glorified her. And he (shall be) a righteous king, taught of God, over them, (36) and there shall be no unrighteousness in his days in their midst, for all shall be holy and their king the anointed of the Lord'. In describing the attitude of the king to the nations, the author distinguished between the heathen whose cruel and offensive conduct he had recently witnessed in Jerusalem, and other peoples outside Judaea. Of his attitude to the Romans he said (24), 'And gird him (the king) with strength, that he may shatter unrighteous rulers, (25) and that he may purge Jerusalem from nations that trample (her) down to destruction. Wisely, righteously (26) he shall thrust out sinners from (the) inheritance, he shall destroy the pride of the sinner as a potter's vessel. With a rod of iron he shall break in pieces all their substance, (27) he shall destroy the godless nations with the word of his mouth; at his rebuke nations shall flee before him, and he shall reprove sinners for the thoughts of their heart'. That he sincerely wished such conquerors to be shattered and Jerusalem purged of them, is only natural. He places, however, the Jewish violent and sinful rulers on the same level, and his first

[1] p. lii–lviii, cf. Bousset, *Religion*², 260–77.

wish was that they might be removed from the Jewish inheritance; for he was, in the first instance, thinking of the Idumaean Antipater and his non-Jewish followers. Their power and their pride with which they oppressed[1] their fellow-Jews, deserved the same thorough destruction, and their evil plans frustration. His hope of the removal of the Romans and of Antipater, one would think, would appeal as obvious to every fair-minded commentator. When these foreign oppressors have been purged away by the messianic king, he will proceed to gather together the exiles, and place the returned all over Palestine, so that no room will be left in the territories of the various tribes for the sojourner and the alien (28–31). The psalmist did not apply to the inhuman, blood-thirsty conquerors the words of Isa. 52. 1 about the Babylonians: 'O Jerusalem, the holy city; for henceforth there shall no more come into thee the uncircumcised and the unclean'. Though the opportunity for it would have been most appropriate, no adjective except 'lawless' is applied to the Romans; for it was not any uncleanness attaching to his person, but the cruelty and the haughty conduct that were to the pious man unclean in the Roman. And when he said (17. 51), 'May the Lord hasten His mercy upon Israel! May He deliver us from the uncleanness of unholy enemies, *ἀπὸ ἀκαθαρσίας ἐχθρῶν βεβήλων*', he meant their desecration of the Temple and of the Holy of Holies with reference to which even the pious layman was only little less unclean;[2] and Ryle-James's remark, 'notice the prominence given to the uncleanness of the oppressors,' is entirely misleading. The word *ἀκαθαρσία* is applied three times in ch. 8, once or twice not to any non-Jews, but to the leading priests; them (13) the writer accuses of having gone up to the altar coming from every uncleanness, meaning immorality and

[1] Pride, or more correctly haughtiness and presumption revealed in the oppression of others, 17. 46; 4. 28.

[2] Josephus, *Antiquit.*, XIV, 4. 4. 72: Pompey and not a few of his companions went inside (the Temple) and saw the things which no other men but the high-priests only are permitted to see.

sin. And (24) 'He led away their sons and daughters, whom they had begotten in defilement (ἐν βεβηλώσει). (25) They did according to their uncleanness (κατὰ τὰς ἀκαθαρσίας), even as their fathers (had done)'.[1] And that Pompey should have appeared to the author of the psalm more moral and purer than those priests, could not possibly be expected. When, in the progress of the messianic king, the whole of Palestine is free from all non-Jews, the heathen nations submit to the rule of the king of the Jews, as they see him from all parts of the earth glorify God on the high mountain of Zion. He only now purges Jerusalem in holiness or sanctification (ἐν ἁγιασμῷ), as of old; probably in the same sense as King Josiah purged the city of all idolatry to the last vestige, so he removes all that Roman and Idumaean worship and their unjust and violent administration left behind. In the now holy city no wrong will be done, everybody will be holy (36). This last statement shows the moral and spiritual meaning of holiness which excludes every kind of wrong-doing.

The same is expressed in 17. 28, 'And he shall gather together a holy people, whom he shall lead in righteousness, and he shall judge the tribes of the people that has been sanctified by the Lord his God. (29) And he shall not suffer unrighteousness to lodge any more in their midst, nor shall there dwell with them any man that knoweth wickedness, (30) for he shall know them, that they are all sons of their God'. The Israelites gathered from abroad are termed here a holy people, as also in v. 48, 'In the assemblies he will judge the peoples, the tribes of the sanctified. (49) His words (shall be) like the words of the holy ones in the midst of sanctified peoples'. God sanctified, that is, purified them, as in the messianic prophecy in Ezek. 36. 24–9 God will bring the people back from the

[1] In 8. 23, 'He poured out the blood of the inhabitants of Jerusalem like the water of uncleanness', is, no doubt, a wrong rendering of 'unclean water'; for the water used for the purification of a person defiled by a corpse in Num. 19. 9, 17, 18, 21; 31. 23 is holy and not unclean.

exile, and purify them from all their impurities, and give them a new spirit; and in 37. 23, 'But I will save them out of all their dwelling-places, wherein they have sinned, and will cleanse them; so shall they be My people, and I will be their God. (24) And David my servant shall be king over them'. Again we see that holiness implied the exclusion of unrighteousness and even the knowledge of wickedness, and that the holy man is a son of God. The king will see to it that that spirit continue in the holy people, (41) 'he will rebuke rulers, and remove sinners by the might of his word; (46) he will lead them all aright, and there will be no pride among them that any among them should be oppressed'. And his qualifications are, (35) 'he (shall be) a righteous king, taught of God, over them, (36) the anointed of the Lord, he will not increase horses, riders and bows, nor gold or silver nor big armies (37), but (38) God Himself is his king, the hope of him that is mighty through (his) hope in God'. The contrast here clearly shows that God Himself will be Israel's protector, as in 1 Sam. 12. 12, making all other means of defence superfluous. Consequently, the king will have to use only his word (39), and wisdom and righteousness for the removal of sinners (17. 25, 31, 42; 18. 8), and bless the people with wisdom and gladness (40). He will be pure from sin (41),[1] that is, he will be holy, so that he may rule a great people. (42) 'God will make him mighty by means of (His) holy spirit, and wise by means of the spirit of understanding, with strength and righteousness'. There is no doubt that the author used Isa. 11. 2 here, but introduced some very interesting changes. It is very probable that for the spirit of the Lord he put the spirit of holiness, an expression occurring already in Isa. 63. 10, 'But they rebelled, and vexed His holy spirit; (11) where is He that put His holy spirit in the midst of them'? and in LXX Dan. 4. 5, 15; Susanna 44. Accordingly, it was used already a generation before Hillel in whose time it denoted the prophetic gift,

[1] See Apoc. Baruch, 9. 1.

called in the Bible the spirit of the Lord. By that holy spirit the messianic king will be the ideal ruler of his people (37–46), and, like David (2 Sam. 15. 2–4; Ps. 122. 5) and Solomon (1 Reg. 3. 16, 28; 7. 7),[1] the chief judge who (48) decides disputes in the assembly[2] and instructs the people (47); his words will be wisdom as precious as the teachings of Wisdom (Prov. 8. 10–21). As a good shepherd he will tend the flock of God faithfully and in righteousness (45), his spirit will be that of wisdom and righteousness (25, 28, 31, 42; 18. 8), 'that he may direct (every) man in the works of righteousness by the fear of God, that he may establish them all before the Lord (9), a good generation (living) in the fear of God in the days of mercy' (10). Even Ryle-James do not refer the righteousness of the messianic king to ceremonial rules, but concede here a wider and fuller meaning to it. As the king, however, directs every man in the works of righteousness, and the meaning of the virtue which he teaches others, must be the same as he himself also possesses, it follows that the works of righteousness are of the highest moral character. It was only natural that the writer applied the virtues that characterized the actions of the pious, righteousness and the fear of God, to the lives of those who under the messianic king would be free from sin and holy, and would possess the most perfect righteousness, the highest possible piety.

For the comparison of the piety of the pious men in the Psalms of Solomon with that of the Ḥasids and of Hillel

[1] Cf. 2 Reg. 15. 5; Prov. 29. 14; Jer. 21. 12; 22. 15, 16; Ps. 72. 4, 14.

[2] *Ἐν συναγωγαῖς διακρινεῖ λαούς*, he will judge peoples in assemblies; the peoples do not fit well in the context which is devoted exclusively to the king's activities within Israel. At a criminal trial 'the people' is mentioned not only in Deut. 13. 10; 17. 7, but 1 Reg. 21. 9, and the proceedings take place in an assembly, Jer. 26. 11, 16; Prov. 5. 14; Sirach, 23. 24; 42. 11; Ezek. 16. 37-40; 23. 22-6; *MGWJ.*, 55, 1911, 198, 207, 214. The king would hear cases either in the gate of the city or in some other open space and in the presence of the people constituting the assembly. His words will be accepted, as those of the most pious men are accepted, by the now sanctified people. A reference to angels would give no satisfactory sense in the context. But Gebhardt reads λαοῦ φυλάς.

there are, as stated at the beginning of this chapter, only few points of contact preserved in the respectively most characteristic traits. The psalms were occasioned by the terrible events of Pompey's conquest of Jerusalem and the subsequent destruction of the Sadducean rulers and nobles; and all the meditations and prayers of the author referred, as was shown, mainly to two subjects: the just punishment of the sinners and the protection of the pious men. On that line of thought nothing is recorded of the Ḥasids in the rabbinic literature, though they witnessed Jerusalem's conquest by Herod followed by a slaughter similar in its character and extent. Instead, the records inform us of their love of God as the guiding principle of their actions, their humility, their active love and kindness to their neighbours as the determining features of their character, their attachment to God and their close relations with Him expressed in their general piety, their devout prayer, their humble interpretation of their illness as a cleansing of sin, their overgreat fear of unknown transgressions, and the frequent atonement for such by sacrifices. The meditations of the psalmist fortunately extended to a number of religious subjects on which he held the same views as the Ḥasids, and which are sufficiently characteristic to prove that he belonged to the stock of the Ḥasids. God watches the actions of every individual, determines in His providence even his daily sustenance, rewards good deeds by protection from misfortune and by the prolongation of life, leaves no transgression unpunished, but punishes sometimes measure for measure or by a sudden and violent death for which He employs human agents or beasts. In His love God sends illness, poverty, and other sufferings upon the pious to purge him of his unintentional sins, and then rewards him for all his good deeds. God is ever present in the mind of the pious who in all adversity trusts absolutely in Him and is not discomfited by misfortune; but in his love of God patiently submits to, and even rejoices at, His trials, and in humility and devotion prays to Him.

Contented with his lot, he thanks God for his daily sustenance and protection. In strict obedience to His will, expressed in the precepts of the Torah, and in his love of God, he detests haughtiness and lawlessness, practises the commandments, especially works of righteousness which comprise scrupulous honesty, love of peace, and loving-kindness to the fellow-man, and also strict sexual morality, reverence for the Temple and all that is holy to God. Even the pious does not trust his own religious and moral firmness, as he discovered himself sinning in his dealings with his neighbour; he, therefore, continually searches his house for possible transgressions, and frequently atones for his errors: the psalmist for an established sin by confession, restitution, and fasts, the Ḥasid for suspected mistakes by frequent sacrifices of atonement. The pious men in Jerusalem formed a group of their own, met on certain special occasions to relate to each other their religious experiences, to thank God for His spiritual help, and to teach the people important religious truths derived from their own lives. The psalmist and his fellows met in assemblies in the city, the Ḥasids on the Temple Mount.

There were, accordingly, two schools of thought among the pious about the necessity of sacrifices for obtaining God's forgiveness and for rendering Him homage and thanks. One saw in the love and fear of God, in strict obedience to the life-giving Torah and its precepts, in the works of righteousness, in repentance and fast, in submission to suffering and in holiness the only right and, at the same time, sufficient means of atonement for sins of error, and of gratitude to God. Sacrifices of any kind were ignored; and the author went so far as to exclude the Temple and its sacrifices from the glorification of God by the nations on Mount Zion in the messianic age, when even the Jewish-Hellenistic Sibyl (III, 772–6) announced that incense and gifts would be brought from all parts of the earth to the house of God which will be the only one in the world. In determined opposition to that new tendency that contradicted the Torah, the other school of the pious men took a different stand. They not only clung to the ways of atonement by sin- and guilt-offerings prescribed by the Torah, but, as a conscious defence of established law and custom naturally would, overstressed the indispensability of the atoning sacrifices. They demanded as frequent a sin-offering as possible, and Baba b. Buta even brought every day a trespass-offering for sins only suspected. How much older than the year 63 B.C.E. this most important difference of opinion and practice was, cannot easily be proved. Professor Cheyne[1] and other Bible commentators found the two schools of thought in the biblical Psalms, in Proverbs and Job: and among the various passages quoted by him as evidence, Prov. 16. 6 expresses the tendency of the Psalms of Solomon most clearly, 'By mercy and truth (true loving-kindness, בחסד ואמת) iniquity is expiated (atoned for, יכפר), and by the fear of the Lord men depart from evil'.[2] But it would be a mistake to identify the first school with the Essenes; for there is in the Psalms of Solomon not only nothing to indicate an Essene as their author, but there is much to oppose it. Even if we take the statement of Josephus about the attitude of the Essenes to sacrificing in the Temple to be exact in all its details, they recognized the Temple and sent ἀναθήματα, gifts to it,[3] whereas our author never mentions any contribution of his or of the pious men to it; they would have also offered sacrifices, if their stricter purifications had been adopted in the sacrificial service. There is no reference in the psalms to the laws of purity which the pious observed, though the attacks on the

[1] *The origin and religious contents of the Psalter*, 1891, 364–8.

[2] See Sirach 35 (=32). 1 ff., He that keepeth the law bringeth offerings; he that taketh heed to the commandments offereth a peace-offering. (2) He that requiteth a good turn offereth fine flour; and he that giveth alms sacrificeth a thank-offering. (3) To depart from wickedness is a thing pleasing to the Lord; and to forsake unrighteousness is a propitiation. Cf. Schmitz, *Opferanschauung*, 65. 66 ff.

[3] *Antiquit.* XVIII, 1. 5. 19; Cheyne 375.

defiling priests would have afforded the author a very good opportunity for it. Leaving further negative arguments aside, the doctrine of the free will and man's responsibility for his actions[1] so strongly emphasized seems deliberately to oppose the view of the Essenes about the determination of all things by destiny. In his just anger at the violent and unscrupulous practices of the lawless, the psalmist not only did not pray for his enemies, but, as he expressly stated (12. 6), hated and cursed them most vehemently. He was not an Essene, but a pious man of the type described, distinguished by his strong attachment to God and by his righteous, loving attitude to his fellow-men, who, in accordance with the teachings of a school of the Ḥasids in Jerusalem, worshipped his Father in heaven without sacrifices.

[1] Ryle-James, 95 b ff.

IV

ḤONI THE ḤASID AND HIS PRAYER FOR RAIN

THE personality of Ḥoni the circle-drawer and his alleged Essenism have often been casually referred to; but his prayer for rain and his sacrifice which express very interesting and instructive religious thought and reflect important ideas of his school about God and His providence, have, to my knowledge, never been analysed and appreciated. It would be most important to ascertain the section of the population of Jerusalem or Judaea of 70–63 B.C.E. which he represented, and the religious doctrine which his words, spoken on a solemn occasion, implied. Both can undoubtedly be inferred at least with as high a degree of certainty from his purely personal and highly characteristic prayer as from one single detail of his external conduct in preparation for the prayer. Unfortunately, the information preserved in the rabbinic accounts about Ḥoni is too scanty to help to establish the share of the peculiar, personal contribution of the pious man to the characteristic features of his prayer and its distinctive religious thought, and the part representing the religious ideas common to all pious men of his type and his time. The censure which the official representative of Pharisaim, Simeon b. Shetaḥ passed on Ḥoni's conduct towards God on that occasion, would not necessarily imply that Ḥoni did not share fully the views of the Pharisees. But he certainly represented a characteristic type of Jewish piety that deserves greater attention than it has so far found.

1. A Baraitha reports,[1] 'Once they asked a Ḥasid to

[1] Tos. Ta'an. III, 1: מעשה בחסיד אחד שאמרו לו התפלל שירדו גשמים, התפלל וירדו גשמים, אמרו לו כשם שהתפללתה עליהן שירדו כך התפלל

pray for the rain to fall; when he had prayed and the rain fell, they asked him to pray for the rain to stop, as he had prayed for the rain to fall. He replied, Go and see whether a man standing at the corner of 'Ophel shakes his feet in the brook of Kidron; if so, we shall pray for the rain not to fall; but we are confident that God will not bring a flood upon the world according to Gen. 9. 15.'[1] ''Ophel was situated on the eastern hill on which Jerusalem is built, somewhere between the southern end of the Temple and Siloam. This is a spur which becomes narrow to the south until above Siloam it ends abruptly and precipitously'.[2] That the water of the Kidron could have ever risen 500 feet, is naturally out of the question; and to that impossibility the Ḥasid referred in order to reassure the anxious people. The reference to the 'Ophel and the Kidron is sufficient to show that the whole incident happened in Jerusalem before the year 70. A similar incident is reported of Ḥoni:[3] 'When once they asked

עליהן וילכו להם, אמר להם צאו וראו אם עמד אדם על קרן אפל משקשק את רגליו בנחל קדרון אנו מתפללין שלא ירדו גשמים אבל בטוחין אנו שאין המקום מביא מבול לעולם שנאמר ולא יהיה עוד המים למבול.

[1] The second part of this statement is quoted by R. Eliezer in jer. Ta'an. III, 67 a. 5; b. 22 b bottom: 'When they asked R. Eliezer, When do they pray for the rain to go away, he answered them, When a man is standing at the corner of 'Ophel and shakes his feet in the brook of Kidron; but we are confident that the God of mercy will not bring a flood upon the world according to Isa. 54. 9, For this is as the waters of Noah unto Me; for as I have sworn that the waters of Noah should no more go over the earth, so have I sworn, &c.' R. Eliezer quoted probably to his disciples, between 90 and 120, the rule of an earlier time in Jerusalem which was pronounced at the latest between 60 and 70, when he was a disciple of R. Johanan b. Zakkai in the capital; but it could be of an earlier date. b. reads משכשך, moving the feet in the brook to wash them.

[2] Warren in Hastings, *DB.*, III, 626 b.

[3] Ta'an. III, 8: מעשה שאמרו לו לחוני המעגל התפלל שירדו גשמים, אמר להם צאו והכניסו תנורי פסחים בשביל שלא ימוקו, התפלל ולא ירדו גשמים, מה עשה עג עוגה ועמד בתוכה ואמר לפניו רבונו של עולם בניך שמו פניהם עלי שאני כבן בית לפניך נשבע אני בשמך הגדול שאיני זז

Ḥoni the circle-drawer to pray for the rain to fall, he said to them, Go out and take in the ovens for the Passover sacrifice so that they may not be dissolved (by the rain). When he had prayed and no rain fell, he drew a circle (or dug a pit), stood up in it and prayed to God, 'Master of the Universe, Thy children have set their faces upon me, because I am before Thee like a son of the house; I swear by Thy great name that I shall not move hence until Thou hast had mercy upon Thy children.' When it began to rain in small drops, he said, 'Not such rain have I asked, but rain to fill pits, ditches, and caverns'; when now the rain fell in anger (storm), he said, 'Not such rain have I asked, but rain of favour, blessing and gift'. Then it rained normally, (but so long) that the Israelites went out on account of the rain from Jerusalem to the Temple Mount. When they came and asked him, 'As thou hast prayed for the rain to fall, pray now that it should go away,' he said, Go and see, whether the stone of the erring has dissolved.'[1] The account about the incident stops here, and is evidently incomplete, as also the parallels, to be quoted presently, show.

The continuation of the Mishnah describes Ḥoni as a contemporary of Simeon b. Shetaḥ. According to rabbinic

מכאן עד שתרחם על בניך, התחילו גשמים מנטפין אמר לא כך שאלתי אלא גשמי בורות שיחין ומערות, התחילו לירד בזעף אמר לא כך שאלתי אלא גשמי רצון ברכה ונדבה, ירדו כתיקנן עד שיצאו ישראל מירושלים להר הבית מפני הגשמים, באו ואמרו לו כשם שהתפללת עליהם שירדו כך התפלל שילכו להן, אמר להם צאו וראו אם נמחית אבן הטועים.

[1] This rock is mentioned again in Baraitha Baba meṣ. 28 b; jer. Ta'an. III, 66 d. 72: There was the stone of the erring in Jerusalem to which any one who had lost or found a thing, turned; the finder announced his find, the loser gave a description of his lost article and received it back. The position of the rock is nowhere indicated. Jerusalem in the account suggests a part of the city as opposed to the Temple Mount; and נמחית, as in the other report the reference to the 'Ophel, suggests the certainty of Ḥoni that either the rising floods could not reach the rock, or the rain was not sufficiently strong to dissolve it.

reports, Simeon was a brother of Salomé Alexandra, the queen of Alexander Jannaeus, and a leader of the Pharisees and a scholar under that king and his successor, Salomé Alexandra. Hence the correct and generally accepted view is that Ḥoni is identical with the Onias mentioned by Josephus,[1] who was in the camp of Hyrkanos II, when he with Aretas besieged his brother Aristobul II in Jerusalem. The account of Josephus says: 'A certain Onias, a righteous and God-beloved man who had once in a drought prayed to God for rain, and to whom God listened and sent rain. Owing to the prolongation of the war he hid, but was brought to the camp and was asked by Hyrkanos' followers to curse Aristobul and his supporters. He refused to do so; and when the crowd tried to force him, he stood up and prayed, O God, King of the Universe, since those who are standing around me are Thy people, and the besieged are Thy priests, I pray that Thou mayest not listen to these against those, nor realize that which these ask against those.' So far the interesting report of Josephus. The Jews attributed to Onias' prayer an immediate effect,[2] and, as far as the account goes, Onias did not protest against their belief. The two adjectives applied to him by Josephus do not suggest that Onias was an Essene[3]; for, as shown above,[4] 'righteous' was a comprehensive term for piety and was applied also to men who undoubtedly were not Essenes. 'Beloved by God' is a rare attribute, and refers to the acceptance of Onias' prayer by God. Josephus never misses an occasion to point to the Essenes and their wonderful gifts, and would not have failed to do the same here, if his source had even only alluded to the Essenic character of Onias; and to himself

[1] *Antiquit.*, XIV, 2. 1. 22.

[2] Goldziher, *Abhandlungen*, I, 43, compares with it the force which, in the opinion of Balak, Balaam's curse in Num. 22. 6 had.

[3] Kohler in *J. Q. R.*, V, 1893, 415, and in Kohut's *Semitic Studies*, 284; Abrahams in *J. Q. R.*, 20, 1908, 291; Egers in Steinschneider's *Hebr. Bibliogr.*, 16, 1876, 17 ff.; Grätz, *Geschichte*, III, 4th edition, 157.

[4] p. 158–164.

neither the public intercession of the pious and recognized man, nor the acceptance of his prayer suggested such a character. An in many respects interesting rabbinic parallel which contains a Hebrew equivalent of 'God-beloved' in connexion with a prayer for rain, confirms the above conclusion. In a year of drought Nikodemos b. Goryon, one of the well-known wealthy citizens of Jerusalem in the last twenty years of the second Temple, on his own responsibility borrowed of a non-Jewish hegemōn for the great number of pilgrims who had come up to the capital for the festival, twelve cisterns of water on the condition that he would, by a certain date, return the water in kind or pay a very large sum of money. When the day arrived, the drought still continued unbroken, and Nikodemos was in great trouble. He went to the Temple, wrapped himself and prayed, 'Master of the Universe, it is known and manifest to Thee that I acted not for mine honour nor for that of my father's house, but in Thine honour, that the pilgrims for the festival might have water'. At once the skies were covered with clouds, the rain fell, and the twelve and even more cisterns were filled with water. But as the sun was already going down on the fixed day, Nikodemos went to the Temple, wrapped himself and prayed, 'Master of the Universe, show that Thou hast beloved men, אהובים, in Thy world!' At once the clouds dispersed and the sun shone.[1] We have here the intense prayer of an unselfish, good and pious man who prayed for himself, and incidentally obtained relief for the whole population of Jerusalem. He was an adherent of the Pharisee R. Joḥanan b. Zakkai and evidently not an Essene; and, according to the report, his personal character, his generous act, and his general worthiness induced God to break the drought. The whole account rests on the prevailing conviction that in a calamity God accepts the interceding prayer of worthy individuals, and even more readily than that of the whole community or congregation; for their supplication is

[1] Baraitha Ta'an. 19 b ff.

supported before God by their piety. For the further miraculous intervention of God Nikodemos referred to such men as were distinguished by His special love[1]; and the granting of his prayer showed Nikodemos, as also to Onias, that they were beloved by God.[2]

Nor does the fuller rabbinic account of Ḥoni's prayer afford any more definite evidence about his Essenism. As in various passages in the Pentateuch and in 1 Reg. 17. 1; Jer. 14. 1, 7, 20–22; Amos 4. 7, 8, so in Ḥoni's words the drought was a punishment inflicted by God upon the whole country for provocation by sin. The degree of the drought and its duration were commensurate to the sins of the people, and fixed by God beforehand, as in the days of King Ahab, 1 Reg. 17. 1; and unless mercy and forgiveness were granted to them, no prayer could reduce the sentence. But from their past history the Jews knew that the prayer of Moses had on several occasions averted the impending doom of Israel in the wilderness,[3] as also the intercession of Samuel,[4] of Isaiah,[5] Jeremiah,[6] and Noah, Daniel, and Job.[7] And in a drought Jeremiah had prayed for rain[8]; and though God refused to accept his intercession, he still continued his prayer. Such entreaty for rain was naturally attempted on many an occasion in post-exilic times, though no information about it and the various intercessors has been preserved; and even about the practice of the first century very little has been recorded. Two grandsons

[1] Josephus, *Wars*, I, 17. 4. 331. Sirach, 45. 1 says that Moses was loved by God and men, and in 46. 13 that Samuel was beloved of God; 4 Ezra 3.14.

[2] See Abrahams in *J. Q. R.*, XX, 1908, 273 ff. If Midr. Tanḥ. וארא B. 22, 19 a, which describes Ḥoni as a direct descendant of Moses, is to be taken literally, he was a Levite. *Yuḥasin*, ed. Philipowski, 63 b quotes from 'Arukh, s. v. מגלון R. Ṣemaḥ Gaon's statement that Ḥoni lived in a town called מגלו. In 'Arukh, V, 76 b the quotation is wanting, and Kohut refers to the explanation of R. Simeon b. Ṣemaḥ Duran, קבא מגלונאה קב של חוני המעגל.

[3] Exod. 32. 11; Deut. 9. 18, 26; Num. 14. 13 ff.; 16. 22; 21. 7.

[4] 1 Sam. 12. 19, 23; Jer. 15. 1.

[5] Isa. 37. 4.

[6] Jer. 42. 2, 9, 20.

[7] Ezek. 14. 13–20; cf. Job 42. 8; Gen. 20. 7.

[8] Jer. 14. 11, 19–22.

of Ḥoni were invited to pray for rain, but only in their houses and not in public; were they really Essenes, as was suggested? Two scholars were sent to one of them, to Abba Ḥilkiah, to ask him to pray for rain; as he was not at home, they went after him to the field where he was working as a hired labourer. He did not return their salutation, nor pay any attention to their presence, because every second of his time belonged to the farmer for whom he was working. The mantle which he wore on his way home, he treated with the greatest care, for he had borrowed it. His wife came fully adorned to meet him, thus to attract all his attention and to prevent his eyes from turning to another woman; and as she entered the house first, he would not allow the scholars to follow her before him, because he did not know them and their moral character. At the table he did not offer them of his food which was scantily measured for his wife and his children; for he would not utter an untruth even in the form of a social compliment. After the meal he and his wife left the room and prayed on the roof for rain, the wife being favoured by God with the first cloud which appeared over her head; and when the rain fell immediately, they claimed no merit in it.[1] Another grandson of Ḥoni, Ḥanan הנחבא, was also approached by the scholars; whenever rain was wanted,

[1] The report is in Aramaic, Ta'an. 23 a ff. Kohler in *J. Q. R.*, XIII, 1901, 571, not deterred by the humble circumstances of the man, ingeniously tried to identify him with Ḥilkiah the Great in Josephus, *Antiquit.*, XVIII, 8. 4. 273. But there is a very serious objection to that identification. Josephus introduces his Ḥilkiah by these words: 'Aristobul, a brother of King Agrippa, and Ḥelkias the Great, and other most noble members of the same house, and the leaders (of the community) with them', stating expressly that Ḥilkiah was one of the members of the royal house of Agrippa, who went at the head of a deputation to Petronius, the governor of Syria under Caligula; so that the suggestion has no foundation. In jer. Ta'an. I, 64 b. 63, the same is reported of a Ḥasid in K'far-Immé as of Abba Ḥilkiah, and it is of interest to find here a Ḥasid chosen by the scholars to pray for rain. If he is identical with Abba Ḥilkiah, the latter would have lived in a village or a small town; as also the fact that the scholars invited him to pray suggests that he lived not far from a school in the country. See Lévi, *R. É. J.*, 48, 1904, 275.

they sent school-children to him to invite him to pray for rain. He evidently lived in a village or a small town.

Where now is the character of the Essene evident in the two pious men? Is it in Abba Ḥilkiah's personal qualities, in his wife or his children, in his scrupulous honesty, in his extremely strict morality, or in his prayer? As we have seen, his title Abba was claimed by Dr. Kohler as characteristic of an Essene; but in his learned article not a single real proof is to be found for it. It is true, Abba Ḥilkiah neither knew nor trusted the scholars that visited him, because he did not belong to their ranks, nor probably to any school. The same would apply to some of the men who are quoted in the rabbinic literature with the title Abba; while others were scholars, like Abba Ḥanin, the disciple of R. Eliezer, and Abba Saul, the author of a considerable number of halakhic and haggadic sentences. As Abba Saul b. Batnith in Jerusalem, so Abba Ḥilkiah in some provincial town was a pious man, distinguished by several practical virtues, and as such was considered by public opinion, and therefore by the scholars in his neighbourhood, worthy to pray to God for the community; and his title may reflect the rare fact that he practised the virtues taught and realized in the schools without being a scholar. The same may have applied to Ḥoni who is not mentioned with the title Abba, probably because it did not yet exist, but who states himself the reason for his being called upon to pray: because I am like a son of the house before Thee. This means an intimate slave who enjoys his master's confidence[1] and may, without hesitation and

[1] R. Joḥanan b. Zakkai said of R. Ḥaninah b. Dosa whom he had requested to pray for his son who was seriously ill: He is like a slave before the king, while I am like a high official before the king, Berakh. 34 b bottom. Rashi explains this by בן בית, belonging to the household and going in and out without having to ask permission. It corresponds with the Latin *familiaris*, as *familia* appears in the Baraitha jer. Sotah, V, 20 c. 73 in R. Ishmael's sentence, and in Abba Saul's in Sifra Lev. 19. 1, 86 c for all the slaves in the household; also in Sifré Num. 25. 1. 131, 47 b; jer. Synh. X, 28 d. 12 בן בית.

fear, approach him and intervene for a friend who has been sentenced to death; his request is listened to and often granted. In addition, Ḥoni may have had a good knowledge of the special prayers for the exceptional occasion; as we find another Ḥoni who was probably his grandson acting as a reader of public prayers. A discussion took place between the two schools as to whether, on the festival that falls on the Sabbath, in the prayer usually consisting of seven blessings the special reference to the Sabbath should be inserted in the blessing about the festival, or should form a separate, eighth blessing. The Hillelites said to the Shammaites, Did not Ḥoni the Small act as the reader in the presence of all of you, elders of the Shammaites, and he recited only seven blessings, and all the people expressed their satisfaction? The Shammaites replied, Because there was reason for shortening the prayer; to which the Hillelites retorted, If there was reason for shortening the prayer, all the blessings should have been shortened![1] This happened undoubtedly before the year 70 in Jerusalem, not only because the elders of the Shammaites are referred to,[2] but because even the legendary Ḥoni III lived before the destruction of the Temple.[3] The service mentioned on that holy day was public, and was attended by the leading members of the two schools and by a large congregation. As far as can be seen from the Tannaitic accounts, the prayers even for the festivals were not yet written down, and, consequently, it required special knowledge to master them by heart, and even great learning to know the formulation of the occasional insertions which were a matter of learned tradition

[1] Tos. Rosh haShan. IV, 11: אמרו בית הלל לבית שמאי והלא במעמד כולכם זקני בית שמאי ירד חוני הקטן ולא אמר אלא שבע ואמרו לו כל העם נחת רוח הילך, אמרו להם בית שמאי מפני שהיתה השעה ראויה לקצר, אמרו להם בית הלל אילו היתה השעה ראויה לקצר היה לו לקצר את כולן.

[2] Cf. R. Joshua's reference in Baraitha Ḥagig. 22 b top; Tos. Ohal. V, 11; Sifré Num. 15. 38. 115. 34 a; Menaḥ. 41 b bottom; Sukkah II, 7.

[3] Jer. Ta'an. III, 66 d. 53, cf. Heller in *R. É. J.*, 49, 1904, 206.

and not yet fixed. For those reasons even after 70 scholars were acting as readers; and so this Ḥoni was either a scholar or a specialist on the prayers. As he recited them at a place of worship where the leading members of the two schools attended the service, he was considered a well-informed and reliable reader; and he, in that instance, formulated the special blessing in question according to the opinion of the Hillelites. He was evidently a member of neither school, as otherwise the Shammaites would not have accepted his formulation as a proof; and still he was recognized as an authority on the prayer, as both schools entered into a discussion of his formulation as correct. That his assumed Essenic character would have obtained for him such recognition on a question that constituted a matter of dispute between the schools of Pharisee teachers and was based on a principle and on learned argument, is very far from probable; and in addition, nothing whatever is known from any source about the special authority of the Essenes on the formulation of the prayers.[1]

2. The place in Jerusalem where in the drought Ḥoni I prayed for rain, is evident from the statement that, when later the people urged him to pray for the rain to stop, he asked them to bring him a bull for a sacrifice, and when they had brought one to him, he laid his hands upon it and prayed.[2] As the laying of the hands upon the sacrifice could only be performed in the inner forecourt of the Temple, Ḥoni must have spoken his last, and consequently also his first prayers in the same place, or close by it on the Temple Mount. This is in fact expressly stated about

[1] Though scholars refer Megil. IV, 8, 'He who says, I am not going to step before the ark in coloured garments (to read the prayer), must not read even in white garments; I am not going before the ark in sandals, must not read even barefoot', to the Essenes who on certain occasions dressed in white, it is just as probable that it refers to priests who performed the sacrificial service in white garments and barefoot. Kohler in *MGWJ.*, 37, 1893, 447 ff. ascribes the earliest prayers, without any proof whatever, to the Essenes.

[2] Baraitha Ta'an. 23 a.

another occasion for prayers for rain in Jerusalem. When once in the days of R. Ḥalaftha and R. Ḥananiah b. Teradyon a service was held on a fast-day and the congregation did (not) respond to the benedictions with Amen, the scholars who heard of their unusual procedure, remarked that such was the practice only at the eastern gates on the Temple Mount.[1] For both religious and political meetings were held in that place throughout the centuries of the second Temple, as already in Joel 1. 14 the whole nation was convened in the Temple to pray to God in the terrible calamity caused by locusts, 2. 16, 17. Ezra 10. 9 relates how all the men of Judah and Benjamin assembled in the broad place before the Temple.[2] The prayer-meeting in Neh. 8. 1 was held in the broad place before the watergate[3] which is rendered by Josephus:[4] in the open space of the Temple, which looks towards the eastern gate.[5] The assembly convened by Nehemiah for the building of the city wall was held, according to Josephus,[6] in the middle of the Temple. Joseph, the son of Tobias, went up to the Temple and called the people together to a (political) meeting.[7] Jonathan, the Ḥasmonaean, convoked the people to the Temple;[8] this detail Josephus did not find in 1 Macc. 12. 35, but added the same place here and to 1 Macc. 13, 2 about Simeon's assembly[9] from his own time. For during the revolution the high-priests assembled the people in the

[1] Ta'an. II, 5: לא היו נוהגין כן אלא בשערי מזרח ובהר הבית, see Rabbinovicz, RN. and RI. Trani; Halévy, דורות הראשונים, Ie, 76 a ff.

[2] Josephus, *Antiquit.*, XI, 5. 4. 149 renders it by the upper storey of the Temple.

[3] In Tos. Sotah, VII, 13; Baraitha Yoma, 69 b top, R. Eliezer b. Jacob who was well informed about the Temple, says that the king read from the Torah (Deut. 31. 10–13) on the Temple Mount and not in the inner forecourt of the Temple, and supports his statement by Neh. 8. 1.

[4] *Antiquit.*, XI, 5. 5. 154.

[5] In 2 Chron. 20. 5, 9 King Jehoshaphat assembled the people to a fast in the house of the Lord before the new court, and prayed to God, If evil come upon us, . . . we will stand before this house, and before Thee.

[6] *Antiquit.*, XI, 5. 7. 168.

[7] Ibid., XII, 4. 2. 164.

[8] Ibid., XIII, 5. 11. 181.

[9] Ibid., XIII, 6. 3. 197.

Temple,[1] and King Agrippa went up to the Temple and called the people together.[2] After the repulse of Cestius,[3] the leaders of Jerusalem held a meeting in the Temple in order to appoint additional generals for the war. The place is more exactly described, when the nobles and the high-priests assembled the people in front of the brass gate which was situated in the inner space of the Temple towards the east.[4] The same is meant by the eastern gates in the Mishnah about the service on the public fast quoted before,[5] and in the account about the agreement which in 67 B.C.E. Aristobul II and Hyrkan II made in the Temple and confirmed by an oath and joining of hands, and after which they embraced each other before the eyes of the assembled people.[6] After his return from Rome, King Herod went up to the Temple and gave to the people convoked an account of his success;[7] and his son and successor Archelaos, after a week's mourning for his father, put on a white garment and went up to the Temple where the people received him with many blessings, and he in his turn greeted the people from a golden throne.[8] As on all

[1] *Wars*, II, 15. 3. 320.

[2] *Wars*, II, 16. 2. 340; in II, 16. 3. 344 he assembled the people at the Xystos which was connected with the Temple by a bridge, placed his sister in such a way by his side that she could be seen by all, and addressed the gathering in front of the palace of the Hasmonaeans which stood over the Xystos on the border of the upper city. This was not a public meeting of the people, and for such scenery the Temple was not a suitable place.

[3] *Wars*, II, 20. 3. 562.

[4] *Wars*, II, 17. 3. 411; the same was intended in the obscure description in *Antiquit.* XI, 5. 5. 154 quoted above, as already 1 Ezra 5. 47 added to the words taken from Ezra 3. 1 the same explanatory note as Josephus: But when the seventh month was at hand, and when the children of Israel were every man in his own place, they came altogether with one consent into the open place before the east gate.

[5] Ta'an. II, 5; the Cambridge Mishnah, the Mishnah in the Palestinian Talmud, and Tos. Ta'an. I end, Rabbinovicz, 42 a, note, line 3, omit the words בהר הבית. The eastern gates are those of Nikanor in Midd. II, 3, see *J. Q. R.*, X, 1898, 714 ff., XI, 1899, 59, and Büchler, *Synhedrion*, 126, note on *Wars*, II, 16. 2. 340 ff., and 128.

[6] *Antiquit.*, XIV, 1. 2. 7; *Wars*, I, 6. 1.

[7] *Antiquit.* XVI, 4. 6. 132.

[8] *Wars*, II, 1. 1. 1; *Antiquit.*, XVII, 8. 4. 200.

those public occasions, when the people were present, so also at the public prayer of Ḥoni for rain, all were gathered on the Temple Mount and listened to the words recited, and probably joined in the service of the devout reader.

As to the time of the year, when Ḥoni was asked to pray for rain, his order to the people to remove under shelter the ovens prepared in the open yards for roasting the Passover sacrifices,[1] points to a date not far from Nisan 14th; and a note in the Palestinian Talmud thinks of that date only.[2] But a Baraitha quoted immediately after that says, On the 20th of the month everybody fasted for rain and it fell.[3] This is taken from the note in the Scroll of Fasts on Adar where, however, the entry itself, owing to its brevity, mentions neither the day of the occurrence nor Ḥoni's name. But there must have been known to the Palestinian teachers of the Talmud and to the glossator of the Scroll of Fasts a definite tradition that the entry referred to the day on which Ḥoni, with the people of Jerusalem, had successfully prayed for rain. For also the Baraitha[4] about Ḥoni's prayer opens with the words: 'When once the greater part of Adar had passed and no rain had fallen, they sent to Ḥoni and asked him to pray for rain'. This account would, at the same time, appear to imply that no public prayer and fast had preceded his intercession; this, however, seems most improbable, as the autumn rains were due towards the end of October, and the anxiety of the farming, that is the whole, population, must have grown daily, as the season advanced and the rain continued to fail. Is it probable that the intervening four or five months should have been allowed to pass without public fasts and prayers, and none were instituted by the religious authorities? Unfortunately, no early information on this point is afforded by the reports preserved. Only the Mishnah[5] records that, when the rain had not fallen by Marḥeshvan 17, the select men observed

[1] Ta'an. III, 8.
[2] Jer. Ta'an. III, 66 d. 51.
[3] ותני כן בעשרין ביה צמון כל עמא למיטרא ונחת לון.
[4] Ta'an. 23 a.
[5] Ta'an. I, 4–7.

three fast days, then on Kislev 1st the authorities decreed three general fasts which were followed by another three, and ultimately by another seven, each successive group of fasts increasing in the severity of observance. But as the source and the authors of the rule are not stated, it probably reflects only the custom which obtained in Galilee in the second half of the second century. On the other hand, Rabbi's, the Mishnah redactor's discussion with his father, R. Simeon b. Gamaliel II, as to why only thirteen fasts were instituted,[1] presupposes these fasts as a custom established for some time. And apart from several anonymous Baraithas all of which belong to the second century,[2] colleagues of R. Simeon b. Gamaliel II discuss some details of the observances and the services of the thirteen fasts.[3] But the father of R. Simeon b. Gamaliel II, R. Gamaliel II, and his colleagues (90–120) had already referred to the several fasts. 'The authorities must not decree public fasts on the day of the new moon, on Ḥanukkah or on Purim; but if the fasts began before one of those days, they need not be interrupted according to R. Gamaliel. R. Meir remarked, Though R. Gamaliel said that they need not be interrupted, he agreed that the fast observed on one of those days should

[1] Baraitha Ta'an. 14 b: תניא אין גוזרין יותר משלש עשרה תעניות על הצבור לפי שאין מטריחין את הצבור יותר מדאי דברי רבי, רבן שמעון בן גמליאל אומר לא מן השם הוא זה אלא מפני שיצא זמנה של רביעה.

[2] Ta'an. 13 b; 14 a; 14 b; Tos. Megil. I, 8; b. Ta'an. 13 b bottom.

[3] Baraitha Ta'an. 15 b: ורמינהי שלש תעניות ראשונות ושניות נכנסים לבית הכנסת ומתפללין כדרך שמתפללין כל השנה כולה ובשבע אחרונות מוציאין את התיבה לרחובה של עיר ונותנין אפר על גבי התיבה ובראש הנשיא ובראש אב בית דין וכל אחד ואחד נוטל ונותן בראשו, רבי נתן אומר אף אפר מקלה הן מביאין, where R. Nathan differs from an anonymous colleague of his on one point of the ceremonial during the last seven of the thirteen fasts; (the Mishnah Ta'an. II, 1 codified R. Nathan's view). R. José b. Ḥalaftha, a leading member of the school of Usha and Sepphoris between 137 and 170, fixed in the Baraitha Ta'an. 6 a, Tos. I, 3, jer. I, 64 a. 69 as the date of the first fast of the select Kislev 1st, differing from his anonymous colleague, either R. Jehudah or R. Meir whose view the Mishnah codified.

not be observed till nightfall; and the same applies to the fast of Abh 9th, when it falls on the Friday.[1] That this was not merely an academic rule, is evident from another Baraitha: 'It is reported that after the death of R. Gamaliel R. Joshua tried to carry the abolition of that rule, but R. Johanan b. Nuri prevented it'.[2] And it is stated expressly that, when R. Eliezer, the leading scholar in Lydda before 120, once decreed thirteen fasts, the rain did not fall.[3] As he was a very conservative Shammaite scholar, it may be assumed as very probable that those numerous fasts were not only not introduced by him, but would not have been decreed with his approval, if he had not known them as an institution established and practised in earlier times in Jerusalem.

Of its earlier existence the Mishnah gives evidence. 'On the first three fast-days the division of the priests (who

[1] Ta'an. II, 10: אין גוזרין תעניות על הצבור בראש חדש בחנוכה ובפורים ואם התחילו אין מפסיקין דברי רבן גמליאל אמר רבי מאיר אף על פי שאמר רבן גמליאל אין מפסיקין מודה היה שאין משלימין וכן תשעה באב שחל להיות בערב שבת.

[2] 'Erub. 41 a; Tos. Ta'an. II, 5. The Talmud refers the controversy to the question about משלימין, whether on the days of joy enumerated the fast may be observed till nightfall; though it was only R. Meir who introduced the subject, and R. Gamaliel had not mentioned it. It seems more probable that the dispute referred to מפסיקין, whether a group of fast-days which was begun before one of those days of joy, might be continued on those days; so that R. Joshua differed on that point. Now Tos. Ta'an. II, 5; jer. III, 66 a. 43 reports: 'When once a public fast was decreed in Lydda for Ḥanukkah, R. Eliezer demonstrated his disapproval by having his hair cut, and R. Joshua by bathing, and the latter told the congregation that they would have to fast for the sin committed by fasting on Ḥanukkah. Immediately after this follows the report of R. Joshua's attempt to overthrow R. Gamaliel's rule; and the juxtaposition suggests that the fast in Lydda was based on R. Gamaliel's opinion. As in fact R. Joshua fully agreed with R. Gamaliel on the prohibition of decreeing a new fast for Ḥanukkah, his opposition in Lydda could only have referred to the continuance of a group of fasts begun before Ḥanukkah, so that the fast in Lydda was one of several.

[3] Baraitha Ta'an. 25 b; cf. jer. III, 66 c. 75.

are on a week's duty in the Temple) fasts, but not till nightfall, while the section of it (who are on the day's duty) did not fast at all; on the second three fast-days the division of the priests fasts till nightfall, while the section of the priests fasts, but not till nightfall; on the last seven fast-days the division and also the section fast till nightfall according to R. Joshua; but his opponents hold that on the first three fast-days neither fasts.'[1] It is true, this controversy may have been one of the numerous academic discussions carried on in the school of Jamnia after the year 90 about the priests and their services in the Temple. But R. Joshua was not only born in Jerusalem and attended there as a grown up disciple the school of R. Joḥanan b. Zakkai, but acted as a levitical singer in the choir of the Temple. As he had many an opportunity for observing things connected with the service of the priests, and the life and the customs of the capital, his references to an observance of the priests should not be treated as academic. His anonymous opponent here was, as in many instances, probably R. Eliezer who, though not born in Jerusalem, attended the same school, and acquired a good knowledge of old traditions about the Temple and the priests; according to his rule, he would not have contradicted R. Joshua without such information at his disposal. And so both teachers presuppose the observance of the thirteen fasts already in Temple times in Jerusalem in connexion with some serious calamity. It cannot, however, be denied that some reports about actual occurrences seem to refer to only one day's fast, and appear to know nothing of groups of fasts. When once a fast was decreed in Lydda, and the rain fell before noon, R. Tarfon told the congregation

[1] Ta'an. II, 6: שלש תעניות הראשונות אנשי משמר כתענין ולא משלימין ואנשי בית אב לא היו מתענין כלל, שלש שניות אנשי משמר מתענין ומשלימין ואנשי בית אב מתענין ולא משלימין, שבע אחרונות אלו ואלו מתענין ומשלימין דברי רבי יהושע, וחכמים אומרים שלש תעניות הראשונות אלו ואלו לא היו מתענין כלל . . .

to go home, to eat and to drink, and to have a holiday.[1] And the same seems to have been the case on the two occasions, when Samuel the Small decreed fasts, and when on one of them the rain fell before sunrise, and on the other after sunset.[2] But the formula גזר תענית could just as well refer to any day in the series of continued fasts, as in the incident of the fast in Lydda decreed for Ḥanukkah, where one of several fast-days was meant. Difficult, however, is the short and not at all clear account of a fast of R. Joḥanan b. Zakkai. 'When once R. Joḥanan b. Zakkai wished that the rain should fall, he said to his barber, Stand up before the Temple (and say), My Master is grieved, because he wants his hair to be cut and must not do so; and immediately the rain fell.'[3] This occurred in Jerusalem before 70, when the Temple still stood. Owing to the long drought R. Joḥanan must have observed for several days the same degree of abstention as a mourner; for had it been only one fast-day, even if he should have followed the custom of some persons of high standing and had his hair cut every week, he would not have felt it so heavily, as he could have had his hair cut next day. He sent his barber, and did not go himself to the Temple, perhaps on account of his weakness due to the fast; the barber did not fast, because it was one of the first three fast-days, when only the select fasted.[4] The message was intended for the congregation that was assembled at the service of the fast in front of the Temple, and was perhaps waiting for the rabbi to join in their prayer; and his reference to his own discomfort was intended to stimulate their devotion. But all this scanty information does not take us further back than the years 50–70; and it leaves without the support of earlier and direct evidence the very

[1] Ta'an. III, 9.

[2] Ta'an. 25 b bottom.

[3] Jer. Ta'an. III, 67 a. 46: רבן יוחנן בן זכיי כד הוה בעי יחות מיטרא הוה אמר לספריה קום לך קומי היכלא בגין דרבי בעי מספרא ולית בחייליה מצטער, מיד הוה מיטרא נחית.

[4] Ta'an. I, 4.

probable inference that, before Ḥoni was invited on Adar 20th to pray for rain, several public fasts had been observed with public prayers in the presence of congregations specially convoked, and that perhaps other pious men had already interceded before Ḥoni, though without avail.

3. For public prayers in connexion with a general calamity are known not only from Joshua 7. 6–9; Judges 20. 26; 1 Sam. 7. 5; Jer. 14. 11–22; 36. 9; Joel 2. 12–17; Judith 4. 9–15; 2 Mac. 13. 12, but even outside Palestine and from other sources.[1] In describing the terrible drought under King Ahab, Josephus quotes a statement of the Phoenician historian Menander about the same visitation to this effect:[2] Under King Ithobal of Tyre a drought prevailed for a whole year; . . . when he ordered urgent prayers, terrible storms are said to have come. And of a much later occurrence in Gaza Marcus Diaconus in the Life of St. Porphyry[3] reports that in a drought the inhabitants gathered in the temple of their god Marnas and for seven days offered up many sacrifices and prayers, and then went outside the city to a place called that of the sermon. And of Carthage Tertullian states:[4] 'But more than that: the heathen recognize every form of self-humiliation. When the heaven is rigid and the year arid, barefooted processions are enjoined by public proclamation; the magistrates lay aside their purple, reverse the fasces, utter prayer, offer a victim. There are, moreover, some colonies where, besides, the people, by an annual rite, clad in sackcloth and besprent with ashes, present a suppliant importunity to their idols, while baths and shops are kept shut till the ninth hour. They have one single fire in public, on the altars; and no

[1] The letter of Baruch to the ten tribes in Apoc. Bar. 86. 1, 2 asks these to read the letter in their assemblies with care, and to meditate thereon, above all on the days of their fasts. The author seems to have known a custom of reading appropriate literature on some definite fast days; Baruch 1. 3–6, Thackeray, *Septuagint and Jewish Worship*, 80 ff.

[2] *Antiquit.*, VIII, 13. 2. 324. [3] *J. Q. R.*, XIII, 1901, 593 ff.

[4] *De jejuniis*, 16, *Ante-Nicene Christian Library*, XVIII, 151.

water even in their platters. There is, I believe, a Ninevitan suspension of business! A Jewish fast, at all events, is universally celebrated; while, neglecting the temples, throughout all the shore, in every open place, they continue long to send prayer up to heaven. And though by the dress and ornamentation of mourning they disgrace the duty, still they do affect a faith in abstinence, and sigh for the arrival of the long-lingering star to sanction (their eating).' About the Jewish-Palestinian rites the rabbinic sources have more detailed accounts. Already in the course of the several fasts, according to a Baraitha,[1] on the last seven of the thirteen fast-days, when the ark was brought from the synagogue to the market, the place of these public prayers outside Jerusalem, an old man or a scholar, specially chosen for the occasion, addressed the congregation. 'The eldest among them[2] addressed them with words of humiliation: Brethren, of the people of Nineveh it says not, God saw their sackcloth and their fast, but God saw their deeds, that they turned from their evil way, Jonah 3. 10; and in the prophets, Joel 2. 13, it says, Rend your hearts and not your garments, and return to your God. (2) When about to begin the prayer, they send down before the ark an old man versed in the prayer, who has children and a house empty of food, so that his heart may be fully devout in the prayer;[3] and

[1] Ta'an. 15 b. [2] Ta'an. II, 1.

[3] In the Baraitha Ta'an. 16 a bottom R. Jehudah says, He should be a man with children and no means, who has work in the field and an empty house, who has an unblemished past, is humble and is liked by the people, who knows the tune and has a pleasant voice, is versed in the Torah, the prophets, and the holy writings, in Midrash, Halakhah, and Haggadah, and in all the blessings (in jer. II, 65 b. 74 much shorter). Accordingly, in the middle of the second century the rule may have been to select a poor and humble scholar; but R. Jehudah may have derived that rule from his experience in Judaea or in Galilee, as an interesting reference suggests. In jer. Berakh. V, 9 b. 18, R. Samuel b. Naḥman, of the second half of the third century in Tiberias, says, When Israel come to sins and evil deeds, and on account of those the rain is withheld, they take a scholar like R. José the Galilean, and when he entreats for them, the rain falls. Though very little has been preserved about R. José's

he recites before them the twenty-four blessings.[1] The words of the speaker aim at stirring up genuine confession of sin and repentance,[2] just as the fast is not imposed for its own sake, but as a means of humiliation. As some

personal character, one very instructive trait of it is important for our question (Gen. r. 17. 3 ; Lev. r. 34. 14 ; jer. Kethub. XI, 34 b. 62). His wife who was his sister's daughter, was very bad, and abused him before his disciples ; when they suggested to him to divorce her, because she did not honour him, he replied that he did not possess the means to pay her her marriage settlement, and therefore could not divorce her. When once he invited R. Eleazar b. 'Azariah to his house and his wife again behaved disrespectfully, R. Eleazar suggested to him to divorce her, and, on learning of his financial difficulty, offered to advance him the amount required. She then became the wife of a watchman of the town ; when he lost his eyesight, he had to beg and she had to lead him round. When she refused to go near the house of R. José, her husband beat her and caused public scandal in the town. When R. José heard of it and saw the shame of his former wife, he took the couple into his house and provided for them to the end of their lives. In Lev. r. 34. 14 and Gen. r. 33. 3 it is further reported, how, in a drought, R. Tanḥuma ordered a public fast; when two fasts had proved unsuccessful, he, on the third day, called on the congregation to distribute charity. One man then fetched all that he had at home, and, when about to distribute it among the poor, he met his divorced wife; when she asked him for assistance and he saw her poverty, he gave her some money. The morally objectionable conversation between them and the handing of money were reported to R. Tanḥuma who summoned the man and reproved him ; but when he learned the facts, he lifted up his face to heaven and prayed, Master of the Universe, this man who is mortal and had no obligation to maintain that woman, was filled with pity and gave her money: we who are Thy children, the sons of Abraham, Isaac, and Jacob, and whose maintenance depends on Thee, how much more shouldst Thou be filled with mercy for us! Then the rain fell and people were again relieved.

[1] According to the parallel in Baraitha Ta'an. 16 a the elder said to the congregation, Brethren, not sackcloth and fasting bring it about, but repentance and good deeds, as we find about the men of Nineveh. In another account in Tos. I, 8, jer. II, 65 a. 70 he said, My sons, let no one be ashamed (to admit) before his fellow-man, no one (to admit) his deeds ; it is better that a man be ashamed before his fellow-man and of his deeds than that he and his children should starve. . . . While a man is holding a dead insect in his hands, even if he bathe in the Shiloaḥ or any water, he will never become pure ; but as soon as he throws away the insect, a dip in a bath of forty Se'ahs will be effective, for it is said, Prov. 28. 13, Whoso confesseth and forsaketh them shall obtain mercy; and again it says, Lam. 3. 41, Let us lift up our heart with our hands.

[2] Lévi in *R. É. J.*, 47, 1903, 162.

superficial members of the congregation might be contented with the outward signs of mourning and fasting, the speaker did not fail to point to true repentance, and to the essential preliminary act of determination to cast off sin and to substitute good deeds for it.

The character of the second elder who was appointed to recite the prayer, is given in detail by R. Jehudah b. Ilai and an anonymous colleague of his;[1] this, however, would reflect only the conditions prevailing in Galilee about 150. But his master, R. Eliezer b. Hyrkanos, on two occasions took an active part in the service of a public fast; he ordered thirteen fasts, went down before the ark and recited the twenty-four blessings, but was not answered by God. Then R. Akiba went down before the ark; and when he said, Our Father, our King, we have no king but Thee, our Father, our King, for Thy sake have mercy on us, the rain fell.[2] It was on the last fasts that R. Eliezer acted as the reader; and before the last of the thirteen fasts had terminated and the congregation was dismissed, R. Akiba made a last effort on behalf of the suffering people. Though his intercession seems very similar to that of Ḥoni, it is in fact of the same character as R. Eliezer's. Not only because it is introduced in the same way by his going down before the ark; but even more so, because the comparison, in the contemporary account, of the prayers of the two teachers and of the different characters of the two intercessors presupposes that both acted on that occasion in the same capacity and had the same standing in the service. In addition, R. Akiba was the disciple of R. Eliezer, and in spite of his greatness would not, in the presence of his master, have accepted a superior office corresponding to that of Ḥoni. It seems, moreover, to have been the custom that at the service on a public fast more than one reader recited prayers. For a younger

[1] Ta'an. 16 a; jer. II, 65 b. 74.

[2] Ta'an. 25 b: אבינו מלכנו אין לנו מלך אלא אתה אבינו מלכנו למענך רוזם עלינו, see Rabbinovicz.

contemporary of R. Eliezer, R. Eleazar of Mode'im, interpreted Moses' words in Exod. 17. 9, 'To-morrow I will stand on the top of the hill', as decreeing in the straits of the Amalekite war a public fast for the next day; and as Moses, when going up, was accompanied by Aaron and Ḥur, an anonymous teacher, probably R. Eleazar himself, inferred that not less than three men should go before the ark on the public fast.[1] On the other occasion, as the Baraitha states, R. Eliezer ordered the full number of thirteen fasts to be observed, but they had no effect. When, at the conclusion of the service of the last of them, the congregation began to leave, R. Eliezer said to them, Have you prepared graves for yourselves? The whole congregation burst into tears, and immediately the rain fell. This clearly shows that R. Eliezer in that instance also must have recited the prayers up to the last day of the fast. But it did not occur to him in his despair to call in the assistance of a specially pious man who, in the opinion of the people, might, by his urgent prayer, have moved God to mercy. Either he did not countenance the type of piety, or there was no representative of it available in Lydda who would have enjoyed his and the people's confidence. Or the time of the men of prayer had passed; and R. Ḥaninah b. Dosa whose intercession was sought by R. Eliezer's master, R. Joḥanan b. Zakkai, and by R. Eliezer's brother-in-law and colleague, R. Gamaliel II, in the illness of their sons, was an exception, a single survivor of the past.[2]

[1] Mekhil. Exod. 17. 12, 54 b: מכאן אמרו אין פוחתין משלשה בני אדם עוברין לפני התיבה בתענית צבור, and 17. 9, 54 a. In jer. Ta'an. II, 65 a. 66; Threni r. 3. 40, R. Abba b. Zabda, R. Tanḥum b. Ḥanilai, and R. Joshia went to a public fast, and all of them addressed the congregation to move it to humility. Was it at the end of the third century, and perhaps already at an earlier date in Jerusalem, the custom to have at public fasts three preachers, as they had three readers?

[2] Similarly, Samuel the Small acted as the reader, when once he ordered a public fast; when the rain fell before the sun rose and the congregation claimed the merit for themselves, Samuel retorted by this parable: When the slave asked his master for food, the master told his household to give it to him, so that he might not have to hear the slave's

When R. Akiba's prayer was immediately followed by the fall of rain, the scholars who attended the service could not refrain from attributing the success to R. Akiba's personality; for it was so different from that of R. Eliezer whose long prayers had not obtained God's acceptance A heavenly voice, explained by Bacher[1] as authoritative opinion, declared both equally great, but R. Akiba of a yielding, R. Eliezer of an unyielding nature. Accordingly, the effect of the reader's prayer at the service of the public fast depended on his personality; and among the various good qualities found in scholars meekness and humility were essential in his equipment, just as important as the true repentance and contrition of the congregation. As these were the two indispensable factors of success, it appears natural that the speedy rain was claimed by the congregation as their merit, while a long delay or the failure of the rain was attributed entirely to the reader An incident, though of the middle of the third century in Galilee, vividly illustrates the open criticism and blame levelled by the suffering and disappointed community of Sepphoris against a teacher whose prayers were not answered. When once a drought prevailed in that town, R. Ḥaninah decreed a fast, but the rain did not fall, while the prayers of R. Joshua b. Levi in the Darom, Lydda, did bring the desired rain. On this the inhabitants of Sepphoris commented with the remark, 'R. Joshua b. Levi brings down the rain to the people of the Darom, whereas R. Ḥaninah keeps the rain away from the inhabitants of Sepphoris'. When another occasion for public prayers for rain arose, the people of Sepphoris invited R. Joshua b. Levi to pray who, in his turn, asked R. Ḥaninah to come out to the

voice any longer. When, on another occasion, Samuel decreed a fast and the rain fell after the sun had set, the congregation claimed the merit for themselves; but Samuel said that it was not their merit, and gave them this parable: When the slave asked his master for food, the master told his household to keep him waiting, until he was curbed and felt the pain.

[1] *Agada der Tannaiten*, I, 85, note.

service. When, in spite of the united prayers of the two teachers, the rain failed to fall, R. Joshua addressed these words to the congregation, 'Neither does R. Joshua b. Levi bring down the rain to the people of the Darom, nor does R. Ḥaninah keep it away from the inhabitants of Sepphoris; but the hearts of those of the Darom are tender and, on hearing words of the Torah, they humble themselves, whereas the people of Sepphoris are hard and, on hearing words of the Torah, they do not humble themselves'. When, on his way home, R. Ḥaninah saw that the skies were still clear, he said, After all that (the prayers) it is still so (and no rain)! When the rain immediately fell, he vowed not to act again in the same way and not to ask God, the creditor, not to exact His debt, punishment.[1] As here, so already about the year 100–120 the congregation of Samuel the Small claimed all the merit for themselves in favourable cases. But while that rabbi, by his illustrations, only hinted at the unsatisfactory conduct of the assembly, R. Joshua b. Levi expressly told the people of Sepphoris that the sole object of the preacher's address was to stir humility before God in the hearts of the fasting assembly, and that it had failed in their instance. Nor had R. Eliezer's prayer any result, because, in his opinion, neither their numerous fasts nor his impressive warnings had moved the congregation to contrition. And his assumption was proved right by the effect of his last attempt: to rouse such feeling, he, in his despair at the impending famine, asked the audience whether they had prepared graves for themselves; and by his terrifying words he succeeded in bringing about the attitude of the mind by which alone God is moved to mercy.

This is an old maxim of Judaism which already the prophet, Joel expressed clearly in his impressive warning at the public fast and prayer, when Palestine was in his days visited by locusts. (2. 12) 'Yet even now, saith the Lord, turn ye unto Me with all your heart, and with fasting, and

[1] Jer. Ta'an. III, 66 c. 50–61.

with weeping, and with lamentation; (13) and rend your heart, and not your garments, and turn unto the Lord your God; for He is gracious and compassionate, long-suffering, and abundant in mercy, and repenteth Him of the evil'. It is to be regretted that none of the addresses of teachers of Ḥoni's days and of the century and a half after his time has been preserved, to acquaint us with the ideas by which they strove to stir in the hearts of the fasting congregations feelings of humiliation before God. Fortunately, the short prayer of R. Akiba informs us at least of the thoughts which filled him, when he tried to intercede for his people, and hoped to obtain God's grace that had been refused to R. Eliezer. In the first of his two sentences he called upon God as 'our Father'; not in his own name, but on behalf of the whole congregation he turned to the Father of Israel.[1] As was shown above, the conception of God as our Father was familiar to the rabbis, and its religious force was especially manifest in prayers. Here 'our Father' is followed by the invocation 'our King'; already the association of King with Father suggests that they were synonymous, and the stress laid in the great calamity on God as our only King makes it clear that King means here one whose help alone can free his people from the oppressive distress.[2] To Him R. Akiba addresses his fervent, insis-

[1] In Midr. Tann. Deut. 26. 3, 172 it is reported: When once R. Gamalie[l] and his disciples were caught in a terrible sea-storm and they asked him to pray for them, he said, *Our* God, have mercy on us! The disciple[s] said to him, Thou art worthy that the name of God fall upon thee (to cal[l] on God in thy own name). He then prayed, *My* God, have mercy on us It was considered immodest to invoke God's help for others in one's own name, for it would suggest that he thought himself sufficiently importan[t] to have a claim on God. It is more appropriate to include onesel[f] in the congregation or among those for whom one is praying.

[2] Even in some passages of the Bible this special meaning of king a[s] saviour is evident, as Isa. 44. 6, Thus saith the Lord, the King of Israel, an[d] his Redeemer. Here it cannot possibly signify the ruler and master, but standing next to Redeemer, it means the Defender, as next to שופט i[n] Isa. 33. 22, For the Lord is our Judge, the Lord is our Lawgiver, the Lor[d] is our King; He will save us. Here the verb attached to it defines th[e] King as Saviour. The same in Psalm 44. 5; 74. 12 where He bring[s]

ent prayer, for He alone can deliver them; and unless He helps them, they will perish. He appeals to His mercy; for not only can the people point to no merit to support their supplication, but, by his asking for mercy for His sake, he admits their sinfulness and their unworthiness of consideration by God. So his words expressed, on the one hand, the recognition that God alone and nobody else could save them, and, on the other hand, the deepest humiliation and contrition in R. Akiba's mind; and it is certain that, if the terse declarations were understood and fully realized by the already crushed congregation, they must have penetrated with their full force to every heart.

4. When Ḥoni, at the request of the authorities, prayed for rain, his prayer might as to its contents have been a free composition, wholly dictated by the inspiration of the moment; and as to its form, it either followed the structure and expression of earlier prayers of a similar character like those in Jer. 14. 19–22; Joel 2. 17; 1 Reg. 18. 36, 37, or was shaped in his individual style. As droughts and other serious calamities were not infrequent in Judaea, and, as the prophetic instances show, the spokesman's prayer was an old institution, it might have, in the course of time, evolved, at least in its main lines, a definite trend of thought and of form. As Ḥoni's second prayer was, as will be shown, in its daring attitude to God and in its presumptuousness exceptional and even unique, the early report hastened to present the strange details of the unparalleled scene, and had no word left for his first prayer which was probably built on familiar lines. Consequently, there is for the establishment of the contents of Ḥoni's first prayer and of its formulation no other way open but an examination of the earliest statements available about other prayers for rain. As in Lydda R. Eliezer and R. Akiba,

salvation to His people; therefore the psalmist turns to God as King in his prayer for help in distress, 5. 3; 89. 19; Isa. 43. 15. In Zeph. 3. 15 God has removed the oppressor, and is now in their midst as their mighty protector.

and probably in Jamnia Samuel the Small, so in Galilee, at the same time, two well-known rabbis are mentioned in connexion with the prayer on public fasts. 'In the days of R. Ḥalaftha and R. Ḥaninah b. Teradyon a man went before the ark and recited the first blessing to its end, and the congregation responded (not) by Amen. The attendant then called on the priests to blow the trumpets; and when they had blown the trumpets, the reader proceeded to recite another sentence of the same paragraph of the prayer, the attendant called on the priests to blow an alarm, and they blew an alarm; and then the reader began to recite the second blessing. When the rabbis (of the central school) learnt of the way (in which the blessings were recited), they remarked that such had been the custom only in the eastern gates (on the Temple Mount)'.[1] According to the last statement some formulated prayers for the public fast were already recited in Jerusalem on the Temple Mount before the year 70, when the Temple still stood; they were recited in sections which were followed by the responses of the congregation. Perhaps, as in Galilee, even an ark containing a scroll of the Torah was brought out in front of the eastern gates for the service, as the two scholars in Sepphoris and Sikhnin seem to have followed, certainly in more than one detail, the practice on the Temple Mount. In the above account only two paragraphs of the prayer are mentioned, and even the wording of these is evidently not quoted in its original entirety. The same is the case in the several, older, parallel Baraithas which, while giving additional information about other details, also quote only two paragraphs of the prayer. The third of those Baraithas states the constituent parts of the two paragraphs in full. In examining the second part of the Baraitha[2] which deals

[1] Ta'an. II, 5, 16 b.

[2] תנו רבנן על הראשונה הוא אומר ברוך ה׳ אלהי ישראל מן העולם ועד העולם ברוך גואל ישראל והן עונין אחריו ברוך שם כבוד מלכותו לעולם ועד וחזן הכנסת אומר תקעו הכהנים תקעו וחוזר ואומר מי שענה

with the second blessing, we find that the reader opened it with the praise of God to which the congregation responded with an appropriate formula; then the attendant of the synagogue called on the priests to blow an alarm, and they blew an alarm; the reader recited a sentence beginning with 'He who answered', after which the priests blew three blasts of which the first was an alarm, the second a plain blast, and the third again an alarm. The repeated blowing of the trumpets in the course of the recital of one paragraph of the prayer is not mentioned in the other parallel Baraithas, but is stated also in the Mishnah's description of the services held in Galilee. As to the first benediction, the first part of the Baraitha states the same arrangement of the corresponding parts in it, and the same repetition of blasts; only the order of the blasts in the second group is a plain, an alarm, a plain blast.[1] So every paragraph of the prayer had the same structure: it opened with a doxology which closed by a benediction followed by the response of the congregation; then came the blasts of the priests followed by the reader's good wishes addressed to the congregation, and again the blasts of the priests.[2] As to the order of the various blasts in the two groups, the call

את אברהם בהר המוריה הוא יענה אתכם וישמע בקול צעקתכם היום הזה (והן תוקעין ומריעין ותוקעין), ועל השנייה הוא אומר ברוך ה׳ אלהי ישראל מן העולם ועד העולם ברוך זוכר הנשכחות והן עונין אחריו ברוך שם כבוד מלכותו לעולם ועד וחזן הכנסת אומר הריעו בני אהרן הריעו ואומר מי שענה את אבותינו על ים סוף הוא יענה אתכם וישמע בקול צעקתכם היום הזה והן מריעין ותוקעין ומריעין, וכן בכל ברכה וברכה באחת אומר תקעו ובאחת אומר הריעו עד שיגמור את הברכות כולן, וכך הנהיג רבי חלפתא בציפורי ורבי חנניא בן תרדיון בסיכני, וכשבא דבר אצל חכמים אמרו לא היו נוהגין כן אלא בשערי מזרח ובהר הבית.

1 The words are bracketed by R. Samuel Edels as incorrect, but are undoubtedly correct, as manuscripts and Tos. I, 14 also have them.

2 Note that ברוך גואל ישראל and ברוך זוכר הנשכחות have their places in the first halves of their respective paragraphs, which contradicts the above analysis; they were shifted to the end at a later stage of development, see below.

of the attendant to blow was carried out by a plain blast, an alarm and again a plain blast; while his call to blow an alarm was followed by an alarm, a plain blast and again an alarm, as several manuscripts and texts expressly have it.

The words with which the first paragraph of the prayer opened in Temple times, read in all the three Baraithas: 'Blessed be the Lord, the God of Israel, from eternity to eternity, blessed be the Redeemer of Israel'. It seems strange that a prayer in distress should begin with 'blessed be', and that immediately after the doxology another shorter sentence beginning with the same word should form the conclusion. To my knowledge, such repetition has no parallel in early short prayers, except in the opening paragraph of the Eighteen Benedictions [1] And our blessing appears all the more difficult, as an early report [2] states that in all the closing formulas of benedictions in the Temple מן העולם was originally said, but when the heretics went astray and taught that there was only one world, the authorities instituted that מן העולם ועד העולם should be said instead. Though ours is not a closing, but an opening formula, the assertion in the statement is strange, as already the closing doxologies of several Psalms contain

[1] Only 1 Chron. 29. 10 is a similarly characteristic instance of God's praise, and exceptionally begins with 'Blessed art Thou', but has no concluding formula; but, as the king continued without a break to v. 19, it became necessary to repeat in v. 20 that David invited the assembly to praise God. As the response contains a description of God as the God of our fathers, different from the king's call, it would seem that in the days of the author there existed a fixed formula like: Blessed be the Lord, the God of our fathers, and its recital was followed by a prostration. In Neh. 8. 6 the response of the people consisted only of a double Amen, in 1 Chron. 16. 36; Psalm 106. 48 of Amen Hallelujah. In Neh. 9. 5 the Levites, after the prayer of the public fast, call on the congregation to bless the Lord their God from everlasting to everlasting, but the response is not stated; evidently it is contained in the next sentence where a slight change has to be introduced, see the commentaries.

[2] Berakh. IX. 5: כל חותמי ברכות שהיו במקדש היו אומרים מן העולם, משקלקלו המינים ואמרו אין עולם אלא אחד התקינו שיהו אומרים מן העולם ועד העולם.

not only Amen which according to the Baraithas in Ta'an. 16b was not used in the Temple, but also the very formulas which are stated to have been a new and late institution in the Temple.[1] The shortest and the longest of these doxologies at the ends of the books of the Psalms have in common the formula: 'Blessed be the Lord for evermore', and the reponse of the congregation: Amen and Amen, or Amen Hallelujah; only Psalm 72 has two doxologies, the second being: 'And blessed be His glorious name'.[2] With the formula in 1 Chron. 16. 36 agrees the benediction in the first paragraph of the prayer spoken on the Temple Mount on the public fast. And just as the response of Amen, so that of 'Blessed be the name of the glory of His kingdom', was not created by the rabbis, but both were the responses of the congregation to certain Psalms sung by the choir of the Levites in the sacrificial service of the Temple, and used also in the service of the public fast. Consequently, the statement in the Mishnah and the Baraitha[3] that in the Temple Amen was not usual as a response, must refer to some services held independently of the sacrificial service; namely to such as were held on the Temple Mount in front of the eastern gates, just as was that on the public fast.

To the doxology of our prayer which concluded with 'Blessed be the Redeemer of Israel', the congregation re-

[1] So Psalm 89 closes: Blessed be the Lord for evermore, Amen, and Amen; 41 with Blessed be the Lord, the God of Israel, from everlasting and to everlasting, Amen, and Amen; 106 with Blessed be the Lord, the God of Israel, from everlasting even to everlasting, and let all the people say, Amen, Hallelujah; and in its parallel in 1 Chron. 16. 36 the last word appears as two: praise to the Lord. 72 ends with the longest formula: Blessed be the Lord God, the God of Israel, who only doeth wondrous things; and blessed be His glorious name for ever; and let the whole earth be filled with His glory, Amen, and Amen. See the commentaries, and Grätz in *MGWJ.*, 21, 1872, 482 ff.; Lehmann in *R. É. J.*, 31, 1895, 34 ff.

[2] Grätz compares it with Neh. 9. 5: Let them bless Thy glorious name; see further.

[3] Ta'an. 16 b; jer. II, 65 d. 56; b. Berakh. 63 a; Tos. VII, 22; jer. IX, 14 c. 12; Blau in *R. É. J.*, 31, 1895, 188; Grätz in *MGWJ*, 21, 1872, 483.

sponded not by Amen which became the rule in the service of the synagogue, but by 'Blessed be the name of the glory of His kingdom'. About this and various other responses a report of the second century supplies some information;[1] but, as R. José b. Ḥalaftha expressly stated, the responses discussed were in vogue in the synagogue in his own days. To the call of the reader (at the beginning of the daily morning and evening prayer) to praise God, the fixed response was ברוך ה׳ המבורך לעולם ועד; in another, unknown case[2] to the call 'Bless' the otherwise rare response was ברוך שם כבוד מלכותו לעולם ועד. When the reader recites a benediction, as e.g. one of the Eighteen Benedictions, the response is the familiar Amen; when he recites a certain part of the Kaddish, which is otherwise known only as a response, the congregation responds by 'For Eternity of Eternity', an unfamiliar response. In a parallel account[3] Ḥaninah, the nephew of R. Joshua and an older contemporary of R. José, also terms the reader המברך, as one who recites a blessing and praises God, and refers to the response quoted by R. José first; then he says, When he calls on God's name, the response is ברוך שם כבוד מלכותו לעולם ועד. Though here also the occasion of the call is not stated, it seems obvious

[1] Sifré Deut. 32. 3. 306, 132 b: כי שם ה׳ אקרא הבו גדל לאלהינו, רבי יוסי אומר מנין לעומדים בבית הכנסת ואומר ברכו את ה׳ המבורך שעונים אחריו ברוך ה׳ המבורך לעולם ועד תלמוד לומר כי שם ה׳ אקרא הבו גדל לאלהינו . . . ומנין שעונים [אמן] אחר המברך תלמוד לומר כי שם ה׳ אקרא הבו גדל לאלהינו, ומנין לאומר ברכו שהם עונים אחריו ברוך שם כבוד מלכותו לעולם ועד . . . ומנין לאומר יהא שמיה רבא מברך שעונים אחריהם לעולמי ולעולמי עולמים . . .

[2] In pointing to Ta'an. 16 b, Friedmann (see Rashi on Deut. 32. 3) suggests as the occasion a prayer in the Temple; but there is, to my knowledge, no such or similar call mentioned in connexion with any service in the Temple, nor would R. José, the historian, have failed to refer to the Temple.

[3] Mekhil. Exod. 13. 3, 19 b: רבי חנינא בן אחי רבי יהושע אומר כי שם ה׳ אקרא זה המברך, הבו גדל לאלהינו אלו העונים אחריו ומה הן עונין אחריו ברוך ה׳ המבורך לעולם וכשהוא קורא בשמו יהו עונין אחריו ברוך שם כבוד מלכותו לעולם ועד וכן הוא אומר גדלו לה׳ אתי ונרוממה שמו יחדיו.

to think of the Temple service on the Day of Atonement, when the high-priest pronounced the name of God, or of the priestly blessing at the conclusion of the daily morning and afternoon sacrifice. But, as already stated, it is not at all likely that the rabbi of the beginning of the second century who, in the other parts of his statement, dealt only with the service of the synagogue, should, without special indication, have referred to a response in the Temple. On the other hand, R. Akiba's example of a response in the Synagogue service to a call ending with the name of God,[1] as in Pss. 103. 20, 22; 135. 19, 20, is not ברוך שם כבוד מלכותו. To think of the recital of the first verse of the שמע which, as the reliable R. Jehudah b. Ilai reported,[2] was already in Temple times followed by ברוך שם כבוד מלכותו, is hardly admissible, as the call to which the same words were the response in the synagogue, was according to the express statement of R. José 'Bless'.

In the prayer of the public fast the doxology and the response of the congregation were followed by three blasts of the priests; as the same was the case also after the second sentence of the prayer, it is evident that the blasts were an essential part of each section of it. Was, in the first half of the paragraph, the praise of God to be enhanced by the sounding of the horn (Ps. 98. 6), or was it the closing 'Blessed be the Redeemer of Israel', which, though in its form a statement, was in reality an urgent appeal to God as the Redeemer?[3] According to Num. 10. 9 the trumpets were to be blown by the priests as a pressing cry in distress, to remind God of His people's suffering. And so in 1 Macc. 3. 46–50 it is reported: 'Wherefore the Israelites assembled themselves together, and came to Maspha, over against Jerusalem. (47) Then they fasted that day, and

[1] Berakh. VII, 3: אמר רבי עקיבא מצינו בבית הכנסת אחד מרובים ואחד מועטים אומר ברכו את ה׳, רבי ישמעאל אומר ברכו את ה׳ המבורך.

[2] Pesaḥ. IV, 8; Tos. II, 19; jer. IV, 31 b. 27; Blau in *R.É.J.*, 31, 1895, 186, 188.

[3] See Oppenheim in *Beth Talmud*, III, 1883, 176 ff.

put on sackcloth, and cast ashes upon their heads, and rent their clothes . . . (50) Then cried they with a loud voice toward heaven, saying, What shall we do with these, and whither shall we carry them away? . . . (52) And, lo, the heathen are assembled together against us to destroy us: what things they imagine against us, Thou knowest. (53) How shall we be able to stand against them except Thou, O God, be our help? (54) Then sounded they with trumpets, and cried with a loud voice'. And in 1 Macc. 4. 37: 'Upon this all the host assembled themselves together, and went up into Mount Sion. (38) And when they saw the sanctuary desolate, and the altar profaned, and the gates burned up, and shrubs growing in the courts as in a forest, or in one of the mountains, yea, and the priests' chambers pulled down; (39) they rent their clothes, and made great lamentation, and cast ashes upon their heads, (40) and fell down flat to the ground upon their faces, and blew an alarm with the trumpets, and cried toward heaven'.[1] So were also at the public fast in Ta'an. II all the signs of mourning applied, prayers of distress were spoken, and after the second sentence an alarm was sounded. And though neither the Mishnah nor the Baraithas mention the prostration after the blasts of the trumpets, it seems to be understood, as also several instances of a similar character in the sacrificial service suggest. So 2 Chron. 29. 27 says, 'And when the burnt-offering began, the song of the Lord began also, and the trumpets, together with the instruments of David, king of Israel. (28) And all the congregation prostrated themselves, and the singers sang, and the trumpets sounded; all this continued until the burnt-offering was finished'.[2] Even more definitely in Sirach 50. 15: 'He (the high-priest) stretched out his hand to the cup, and

[1] In Judith 4. 9–15 a public fast with all its rites is described in detail; but, as in 2 Macc. 13. 12, the sounding of an alarm with the trumpets is missing, while the prostrations are mentioned. See also the prayer of Izates of Adiabene in Josephus, *Antiquit.*, XX, 4. 2. 89.

[2] *ZATW.*, 19, 1899, 335 ff.

poured out the blood of the grape; he poured out at the foot of the altar a sweet-smelling savour unto the most high King of all. (16) Then shouted the sons of Aaron, and sounded the silver trumpets, they made a great noise to be heard, for a remembrance before the Most High. (17) Then all the people together hasted, and fell down to the earth upon their faces to worship their Lord, God Almighty, the most High'. And in its description of the daily morning sacrifice the Mishnah[1] says of the song of the Levites at the libation: At every break a blast, and on every blast a prostration.

As on none of those occasions did the priests pronounce the name of God,[2] the prostration was not, as on the Day of Atonement and at the daily priestly blessing,[3] due to the name of God. It seems to have marked, just as the blowing of the trumpets, the importance of the wine-offering and the adoration of God who was thought of as present in the Temple at the moment of the libation; as in Neh. 8. 6, 'And Ezra blessed the Lord, the great God; and all the people answered, Amen, Amen, with the lifting up of their hands; and they bowed their heads, and fell down before the Lord with their faces to the ground'.[4] The closest parallel to our prayer on the public fast is the description of the public fast in Neh. 9. 1–3: 'And they stood up in their place, and read in the book of the Law of the Lord their God a fourth part of the day; and another fourth part they confessed, and prostrated themselves before the Lord their God.' Rabh, the Babylonian teacher of the first half of the third century, ordered the family of R. Aḥa, and R. Ammi directed his own household, when they went out (to the market) to the service of the public fast, not to lie down in the usual way, when carrying out the old custom of the prostration.[5] R. Samuel in Tiberias reports

[1] Tamid VII, 3: על כל פרק תקיעה ועל כל תקיעה השתחויה.

[2] See, however, Ginzberg in *Oriental. Studien in honour of Nöldeke*, 625.

[3] Sirach, 50. 21, and R. Tarfon in Kohel. r. 3. 11 end; Tosafoth Sotah 40 b, s.v. וכל.

[4] *ZATW.*, 19, 1899, 338.

[5] Jer. ʿAbod. zar., IV, 43 d. 6–19.

that he saw R. Abahu lie down in the usual manner; R. Assi questioned R. Abahu about it, as Lev. 26. 1 prohibited the prostration upon a stone which had figures carved on it. R. Jonah and R. Aḥa lay on their sides. R. Joḥanan remarked to his disciple R. Ḥiyya b. Abba who had emigrated from Babylonia to Tiberias, 'Babylonian, two things have come to us from your country: the stretching out of the limbs at the public fast, and the taking of willows on the seventh day of Tabernacles'.[1] R. Joḥanan did not mean that the whole custom of the prostration at the service of the public fast had recently been introduced from Babylonia, but merely the stricter form of it, the stretching out of the arms and the legs, while lying flat on the ground, as is evident from the word מפשוטיתא; but the prostration at the service of the fast was an old established custom in Palestine. The stricter observance of the Babylonian Jews is proved by another incident. When Rabh once came to a service on a fast-day in Babylonia, he rose from his place, recited the prescribed blessing over the Torah and read therefrom; and when, on finishing his reading, he did not recite the blessing after it, the whole congregation immediately prostrated themselves, but Rabh did not follow their example.[2] The Talmud tried to account for his attitude in various ways. As Rabh had spent many years in the school of R. Jehudah I in Galilee, he had learnt to prostrate himself on the public fast only in the market and only after the prescribed blessings and prayers; whereas the service which he attended in Babylonia, seems to have been held in the synagogue, just as that arranged during the revolution in 67 in the synagogue in Tiberias and described by Josephus.[3] The Jews in Babylonia had their own and stricter rules regarding that custom.[4]

[1] מפשוטיתא דתעניתא וערובתא דיומא שביעיא.

[2] Megil. 22 b.

[3] Vita, 56. 290–93.

[4] If Jerome may be trusted, he once or several times saw the annual mourning of the Jews on Abh 9th before the wall of Jerusalem, *Ad Zephan.*

5. In the days of the Mishnah, whenever the rain continued to fail after Kislev 1st, thirteen fasts were prescribed by the authorities to be observed by the community. Of those the last seven were stricter than the first six, for on them an alarm was blown and the shops were closed.[1] It was after each of the six blessings of the prayer that three blasts were blown, altogether eighteen, on every one of the seven fasts. When before the year 135 R. Akiba and his colleagues discussed the public and private calamities which affected only one town and for which an alarm should be sounded,[2] they defined the various kinds of visitations in which the trumpets should be blown; consequently, the continuation of the anonymous Mishnah III, 5 belongs to R. Akiba. As this teacher only defined the details,[3] the general rules themselves and the custom of sounding an

1. 15 ff.; Schürer, *Geschichte*, I, 703 ff.: Habent enim et in luctu tubas, et juxta prophetiam vox sollennitatis versa est in planctum; they blew the trumpets at those prayers of mourning in the same way as in 1 Macc. 4. 39 ff. and at the service of the public fast.

[1] Ta'an. I, 6; Baraitha, 14 a bottom: שבאלו מתריעין; instead of the denominative verb Tos. Megil. I, 8 has the noun תרועה, b. also התרעות.

[2] Ta'an. III, 3: וכן עיר שלא ירדו עליה גשמים . . . אותה העיר מתענה ומתרעת וכל סביבותיה מתענות ולא מתריעות, רבי עקיבא אומר מתריעות ולא מתענות. (4) וכן עיר שיש בה דבר או מפולת אותה העיר מתענה ומתרעת וכל סביבותיה מתענות ולא מתריעות, רבי עקיבא אומר מתריעות ולא מתענות, jer. III, 66 c. 42: וכל סביבותיה מתענות ולא מתריעות שכן מצאנו ביום הכפורים מתענין אבל לא מתריעין, רבי עקיבה אומר מתריעות אבל לא מתענות . . .

[3] Sifré Num. 10. 9. 76: רבי עקיבא אומר אין לי אלא . . מלחמת שדפון וירקון ואשה מקשה לילד וספינה המטרפת בים מנין תלמוד לומר על הצר הצורר אתכם על כל צרה וצרה שלא תבא על הצבור; Ta'an. 22 a: תנו רבנן על אלו מתריעין בכל מקום על השדפון ועל הירקון ועל ארבה וחסיל ועל חיה רעה, רבי עקיבא אומר על השדפון ועל הירקון בכל שהו, ארבה וחסיל אפילו לא נראה בארץ ישראל אלא כנף אחד מתריעין עליהן. (22 b) תניא מתריעין על הדבר בשבת ואין צריך לומר בחול, רבי חנן בן פיטום תלמידו של רבי עקיבא משום רבי עקיבא אומר אין מתריעין על הדבר כל עיקר.

alarm at public fasts must have been established before him.[1] This, in fact, is evident from the description of the service held in two Galilean towns before 135, and of those held on the Temple Mount before 70,[2] and, what is of special weight for our investigation, of that expressly recorded in the Scroll of Fasts on Adar 8th, as here we read: 'On Adar 8th and 9th was a day of blowing the alarm for rain.[3] And it may be assumed with the greatest probability that the alarm was sounded also on the two fasts which the Mishnah and Baraitha report of Temple times as illustrations of the rules quoted above.[4] 'When some elders were on their way down from Jerusalem to their towns and noticed some blasting of corn in Ashkalon, they ordered a fast'; and another fast was decreed because wolves had eaten two children on the other side of the Jordan; R. José said, 'Because wolves had merely been noticed there'.

The very fact that priests were chosen for the blowing, suggests that, as in Num. 10. 8 and 31. 6, the silver trumpets of the Temple, which only priests were permitted to blow, were used for the purpose. This was actually the case in the sacrificial service;[5] and, as also on other occasions connected directly with the Temple, priests blew the same trumpets,[6] it seems very probable that also at the service of the public fast, held in front of the eastern gates of the inner forecourt of the Temple, the trumpets blown by priests were the same. For not only at the actual morning-, evening-, and the additional Sabbath- and festival sacrifices which were offered within the inner forecourt, did the acting priests do so; but at the solemn procession that took place on the Feast of Tabernacles in connexion with the drawing

[1] See also jer. III, 66 c. 15; Tos. II, 8. [2] Baraithas Ta'an. 16 b.

[3] בתמניא ובתשעה יום תרועת מטרא, Grätz, *Geschichte*, III, note 1, 576, No. 30.

[4] Ta'an. III, 6.

[5] 2 Chron. 5, 12; 7. 6; 29. 26-28; Ezra 3. 10; Neh. 12. 35, 41; Sirach, 50. 15-18; Josephus, *Antiquit.*, III, 12. 6. 291-4; Tamid, VII, 3; Pesaḥ. V, 5; jer. V, 32 c. 40; cf. Tosafoth Sukk. 54 a, s.v. שייר.

[6] Sukk. V, 5.

of water from the well of Shiloaḥ for the water libation,[1] and, as will presently be shown, also at the Sabbath signals. These occasions on which the priests are expressly stated as blowing the trumpets, are sufficient for the inference that also on the other occasions included in the same Mishnah, at the opening of the gates of the Temple court and at the Sabbath signals, the priests sounded the trumpets.[2] The same applies to another religious act that was performed on the Temple Mount outside the Temple where, as is expressly stated, the service of the public fast was also held. When R. Akiba once asserted that the priests who blew the trumpets had to be without a blemish, R. Tarfon, a priest of Temple times, in contradicting him said, 'By the life of my children, I maintain that I saw Simeon, my mother's brother, who was lame on one leg, standing and blowing the trumpet'. R. Akiba then asked him, 'I agree, but perhaps you saw him not at the sacrifices of which I am speaking, but at the great gathering of the people, הקהל?' R. Tarfon admitted the correctness of that suggestion.[3] At that great assembly, held at the conclusion of the year of rest on the Feast of Tabernacles, Deut. 31. 10–13, Agrippa II once read from

[1] Sukk. V, 4; *ZATW.*, 20, 1900, 111 ff.

[2] According to Baraitha Sukk. 53 b; Tos. IV, 10; jer. V, 55 c. 30 (cf. R. Eliezer b. Jacob in b. 54 a), the author of the list in the Mishnah which is not uncontested, was R. Jehudah b. Ilai.

[3] Sifré Num. 10.8.75; jer. Yoma, I, 38 d. 37; Tos. Sot. VII, 16; incidentally we learn that the priests who blew the trumpets in the sacrificial service, had to be without a blemish. Sifré has instead of the last words שמא בראש השנה וביום הכפורים וביובל, which, as Friedmann had already remarked, is very difficult to justify. A manuscript rightly reads: שמא בהקהל וביום הכפורים ביובל, perhaps it was at the great gathering or on the Day of Atonement in the jubilee year, Lev. 25. 9. Similarly, Yalkut has: בהקהל ביום הכפורים וביובל where in the last word the first letter must be struck out. Though Pesik. r. 39. 165 b: אמר רבי עקיבא בעל מום כשר לתקוע בראש השנה וביובל שנאמר והעברת שופר תרועה וגו׳ בכל ארצכם אבל על הזבחים לאו also had before it in R. Akiba's question to R. Tarfon the reading ראש השנה, it is undoubtedly a mistake, and cannot be justified in the presence of the only correct reading: הקהל.

the Torah in the inner forecourt of the Temple,[1] or on the Temple Mount where R. Tarfon's uncle blew the trumpet.[2] This was a non-sacrificial act, and the priests still blew the trumpets which, however, did not belong to the Temple. And the signals which informed the people of Jerusalem of the beginning and the conclusion of the Sabbath, were also given by a priest who blew the trumpet on the pinnacle of the Temple.[3]

[1] Sot. VII, 8; Büchler, *Priester und Cultus*, 14; see, however, R. Eliezer b. Jacob in Baraitha Yoma, 69 b; Tos. Sot. VII, 13, who names the Temple Mount instead. Cf. Halévy דורות הראשונים, Ie 4 b, note.

[2] Tos. Sot. VII, 15 describes the same very vividly: On that day priests stood in the breaches of the wall and in the closed parts of it (cf. Midd. II, 3: Within the wall of the Temple Mount was the Soreg ten handbreadths high into which Greek kings, jer. Shekal. VI, 50 a. 2, broke thirteen breaches; later on these were closed, and in their direction thirteen prostrations were instituted, Tos. Shekal. II, 17) with golden trumpets in their hands and blew a plain blast and an alarm; he who had no trumpet was criticized as appearing not to be a priest. The inhabitants of Jerusalem earned money by letting their trumpets. On the same day R. Tarfon saw a lame priest blow the trumpet and inferred from it that a lame priest was permitted to blow the trumpet in the Sanctuary. In the name of R. Nathan it is reported, The Jews incurred destruction by flattering Agrippa.

[3] Josephus, *Wars*, IV, 9. 12. 582; it is true, he speaks of σάλπιγξ and not of βυκάνη, so that the nature of the instrument may seem doubtful. But the parallel reference in Sukk. V, 5 where, as we have seen, the blasts of the priests were, on several occasions, sounded with trumpets, makes it almost certain that the signals of the Sabbath which are included in the same list of the Mishnah, were also blown with the same trumpets. This is clearly stated in Tos. Sukk. IV, 11, 12: כיצד שלש להבטיל את העם מן המלאכה, חזן הכנסת נוטל חצוצרות ועולה לראש הגג לגובהה של עיר . . . (12) כיצד שלש להבדיל בין קדש לחול, חזן הכנסת נוטל חצוצרת . . . הניח חזן הכנסת חצוצרת בראש הגג וירד ובא לו, רבי יוסי אומר . . . אלא מקום היה בראש הגג ששם חזן הכנסת מניח חצוצרות, cf. jer. Shabb. XVII, 16 a. 53. Here the attendant of the Synagogue announced by a trumpet blast the beginning of the Sabbath; but the name of R. José shows that the passage deals with conditions that prevailed in Galilee about the middle of the second century. In the parallel Baraitha Shabb. 35 b שופר is put instead of the trumpet, while another Baraitha again: והתניא שופר מיטלטל וחצוצרות אינם מיטלטלין . . . תניא כשם שמטלטלין את השופר כך מטלטלין את חצוצרות, mentions the horn and the trumpets side by side as used for announcing the Sabbath. It seems

But there is some additional and, as it appears, early information about the blasts at the service of the public fast, which mentions the horn also by the side of the trumpets. 'The horn for the New Year is extended and straight, and is of a gazelle, and its mouthpiece is overlaid with gold; by the side of the horn are two trumpets, the horn blows longer, the trumpets blow a shorter time, for on the New Year the horn is prescribed. (4) On the fast-days they blow [two] bent ram horns the mouthpieces of which are overlaid with silver; between the horns are two trumpets, the horns blow a shorter time, the trumpets longer, for the duty of the day are trumpets'.[1] All that we know otherwise from rabbinic literature about the use of the ram's horn on the New Year in the service of the Synagogue, contradicts the rule of the Mishnah just quoted. When a Babylonian scholar, R. Papa b. Samuel proposed to follow that rule, Rabha remarked to him that that Mishnah referred to the Sanctuary; and also a Baraitha says, 'That rule applied only to the Sanctuary, whereas outside it either trumpets only or a horn only are to be used'. So R. Ḥalaftha introduced it in Sepphoris and R. Ḥaninah b. Teradyon in Sikhnin; but when the scholars (of the central

that some authorities objected to the religious use of the trumpet outside the Temple; but in the Temple and on the Temple Mount, it is clear, the signal of the Sabbath was given with the trumpet. See also Revel in *J. Q. R.*, III, 1913, 386; Ginzberg in *R. É. J.*, 67, 1914, 150.

[1] Rosh haShan. III, 3: שופר של ראש השנה של יעל פשוט ופיו מצופה זהב ושתי חצוצרות מן הצדדין שופר מאריך וחצוצרות מקצרות שמצות היום בשופר. (4) בתענית בשל זכרים כפופים ופיהן מצופה כסף ושתי חצוצרות באמצע שופר מקצר וחצוצרות מאריכות שמצות היום בחצוצרות. Cf. Tos. Rosh haShan. III, 3: ובתענית תוקעין שבע שלש ושלש ובמסעות שלש לשלש שלש על כל דגל ודגל דברי רבי יהודה וחכמים אומרים שלש על כל מטה ומטה, ובמה הן תוקעין בחצוצרות שעשה משה, רבי יהודה אומר בראש השנה· תוקעין בשל זכרים וביובל בשל אילים, נתנו חכמים את המצוי למצוי ואת שאינו מצוי לשאינו מצוי. b. 26 b: תניא רבי יהודה אומר בראש השנה היו תוקעין בשל זכרים כפופין וביובלות בשל יעלים.

school) heard of it, they said that such a practice had been followed only at the eastern gates and on the Temple Mount.[1] Accordingly, the above Mishnah described an early custom followed before the year 70 on the Temple Mount, and transplanted by those two scholars to Galilee.[2] But in what connexion was the horn blown in the Sanctuary along with the trumpets on the New Year? With our present information it appears nearly impossible to detect in our sources any indication that in the Temple service a horn was at any time or ever blown, as at the sacrifices in Num. 10. 10 as well as in the passages discussed only trumpets are mentioned. It is true, the horn is included among the instruments used in the Temple in the statement of the Mishnah: 'In Jericho they heard from the Temple the sounds of the flute, the cymbal and the Shofar, and, according to some, also the voice of the high-priest, as he pronounced the name of God on the Day of Atonement'.[3] But the occasion on which the horn was blown, is not suggested. In his explanation of the passage Maimonides refers to Sukk. V, 5 where the word Shofar does not occur at all; so

[1] R. H. 27 a: תניא נמי הכי במה דברים אמורים במקדש אבל בגבולין מקום שיש שופר מקום שיש שופר אין חצוצרות וכן הנהיג רבי חלפתא בצפורי ורבי חנניא בן תרדיון בסיכני, וכשבא דבר אצל חכמים אמרו לא היו נוהגין כן אלא בשערי מזרח ובהר הבית בלבד. In jer. Rosh haShan. III, 58 d. 31 it is reported: 'In the presence of R. Joshua b. Levi they blew on the public fast (the horn). R. José asked, Why did they not blow the trumpets before him? Did R. José not know the Baraitha, Trumpets in the Sanctuary, but not outside it'? In jer. Ta'an. II, 65 a. 34; b. 14 a R. Jacob of the Darom said, Why do they blow the horns on the fast? All this shows that on the public fast the Shofar and not the trumpets were blown in the third and fourth centuries; see also Oppenheim in *Beth Talmud*, III, 1883, 175–8. Jerome's report about the mourning of the Jews before the wall of Jerusalem on Abh 9th, quoted above, 230, 4, speaks of *tubae*, trumpets, not horns.

[2] In Gaonic times at public fasts in Babylonia the horn was blown, see הצופה מארץ הגר, I, 1911, 153.

[3] Tamid III, 8: מיריחו היו שומעין קול החליל מיריחו היו שומעין קול הצלצל . . . מיריחו היו שומעין קול השופר ויש אומרים אף קול של כהן גדול בשעה שהוא מזכיר את השם ביום הכפורים.

that he must have identified it with the trumpet blown by the priests, which presupposes a loose use of terms in an early report about the service of the Temple. On the other hand, it must not be forgotten that this account of the miraculously loud sounds heard in Jericho does not fit in with the sober tone of the whole tractate of Tamid. It evidently belonged to another source which, as its interest in the musical instruments of the Temple suggests, was concerned with a subject for which the author of the tractate had little attention left. Did perhaps the Levites and not the priests, blow the horn?[1] Very curious is the statement quoted by R. Joshua b. Ḥananiah who was once a levitical singer in the Temple: 'A live ram has only one voice, but, when dead, it produces seven sounds: its two horns are made into two *trumpets*, its two legs into two flutes, its hide is made into a drum, its entrails are used for psalteries, and its viscera for (strings of) harps'.[2] As R. Joshua naturally knew that חצצרת denoted in the Bible and in the Mishnahs of Sukkah and Tamid a metal trumpet and not a horn, it must be assumed that he knew from his experience in the Temple that שופר and חצצרת were used promiscuously for the animal horn. The reverse is, however, found in a passage,[3] evidently a Baraitha, which explains the trumpets of the priests in Num. 31. 6 by שופר; while another reference, representing another school, emphasizes the distinction between the two.[4]

To the blowing of the Shofar in the service of the Temple on the New Year no other reference is to be found any-

[1] See 1 Chron. 25. 5. [2] Kinnim, III, 6.

[3] Sotah, 43 a top.

[4] Sifré zuta on Num. 10.8 ff., 72: יתקעו בחצצרות לא בשופרות; ver. 9: והרעותם בחצצרות לא בשופרות. The instruments enumerated by R. Joshua were levitical, or at least non-priestly; so that Tosafoth in Menaḥ. 28 a see in the trumpets such as were used by the Levites, as in 1 Chron. 16. 42 (cf. 1 Chron. 15. 19, and Sukk. V, 4; the parallel Tos. Sukk. IV, 7 does not mention the trumpets). Perhaps the Levites were at some time deprived of their privilege of using the trumpets in the Temple, and they transferred the name חצצרת to the horn. For R. Ḥisda's opinion in Shabb. 36a the Mishnah of R. Joshua offers no proof.

where, nor is it stated that at the special, additional offering of that festival the usual trumpets were not blown;[1] while in a question about the blowing on the New Year only the trumpets are presupposed as used on that day.[2] The designation of the festival as the day of תרועה in Num. 29. 1, Lev. 23. 24 is not conclusive, as in Num. 31. 6; 10. 9 the word is connected with the priests' trumpets, and in Lev. 25. 9 and several other passages with the Shofar.[3] If it were certain that Ps. 81. 4, 'Blow the horn at the new moon, at the full moon for our feast-day', referred to the New Year, as those interpreted it who instituted the psalm to be sung by the Levites on that festival at the sacrifice, the blowing of the horn should have been the custom in the Temple on the New Year. Philo's explanation of the character of that festival is very instructive. 'Then follows the festival of the sanctification of the holy month, on which at the offering of the sacrifices in the Temple it is the custom to blow the trumpet; on account of that this festival is rightly called the feast of the trumpet'.[4] This interesting description seems to have been derived neither from Num. 10. 10, where the blowing of the trumpets at the sacrifices is prescribed for all the festivals, nor from Lev. 23. 24, Num. 29. 1 where only the word תרועה characterizes the day, but from Philo's knowledge of the actual practice in the Temple of Jerusalem.[5] Again, trumpets and not horns are pointed out as characteristic of the day; and it seems impossible to reconcile with that the Mishnah[6] the

[1] Sukk. V, 5; Sifré Num. 10. 10. 77; Sifré zut. Num. 10. 9, 72 ff.

[2] Sukk. 54 a; jer. V, 55 c. 39 ff.

[3] The alarm blast with the Shofar is the signal of war and battle in Amos 2. 2; Zeph. 1. 16; Jer. 4. 19. The word תרועה, which means shout, sometimes refers to joy and accompanies the blast of the horn, 1 Chron. 15. 28; cf. Ezra 3. 13 and 1 Sam. 4. 5, 6; 2 Sam. 6. 15. In Ps. 47. 6 it is the greeting of the king by the people, as in Num. 23. 21, and is in Ps. 98. 6 followed by the combined blasts of the horn and the trumpets.

[4] *De Sabb.* 22 = *De spec. leg.*, II, 188 = *M.*, II, 295.

[5] See, however, Treitel's remark in *MGWJ.*, 47, 1903, 502 ff., and Heinemann in Cohn's German translation of *Philo*, II, 160, 2: 'It is derived from *μνημόσυνον σαλπίγγων* LXX.'

[6] Rosh haShan. III, 3.

correctness of which is borne out by a Baraitha and by the practice of the two Galilean scholars about the year 100–135 who ordered the horn and the trumpets to be blown at the same time at the service of the public fast. The Mishnah either represented a time and a practice different from those described in Sukkah, or, what is more probable, in spite of the word 'in the Sanctuary' did not refer to the sacrificial service of the Temple. As the parallel Baraitha expressly states that it was held at the eastern gates and on the Temple Mount, it would first follow that on the New Year a service was held outside the Temple, though close to it, at which two trumpets and one horn were blown, just as at the service of the public fast, held in the same place, the same two instruments were sounded. And it is of special interest that in the Baraitha about the New Year מקדש designates not the Temple itself and its sacrificial service, but the area in front of the eastern gates of the forecourt; and the same מקדש is used with reference to the service of the fast, and again the Mishnah substitutes for it the eastern gates and the Temple Mount.[1] And its bearing on the service on the New Year is corroborated by another statement. 'On the New Year that fell on the Sabbath, they blew in the Sanctuary, but not outside it; Jerusalem had this additional privilege over Jamnia that even a town in its close neighbourhood was permitted to blow on the Sabbath'.[2] A Baraitha reports: 'When once the New Year fell on the Sabbath and the inhabitants of all the places had gathered together, R. Joḥanan b. Zakkai said to the sons of Bethera, Let us blow! But they replied, Let us first argue it,

[1] Baraitha Ta'an. 16 b: במה דברים אמורים בגבולין אבל במקדש אינו כן לפי שאין עונין אמן במקדש, Ta'an. II, 5; see Zipser in Warnheim's קבוצת חכמים, 1–5.

[2] Rosh haShan. IV, 2: ועוד זאת היתה ירושלים יתירה על יבנה שכל עיר שהיא רואה ושומעת וקרובה ויכולה לבא תוקעין וביבנה לא היו תוקעין אלא בבית דין בלבד. This statement about the privileged position of Jerusalem contradicts the previous report about the exclusive right of the Sanctuary; evidently we have here the opinions of two different schools.

(whether it is permitted); R. Joḥanan answered, Let us first blow, and argue afterwards. When after the blowing they said to him, Let us argue it, he said, Since the horn has already been heard in Jamnia, you cannot refute it after the fact'.[1] As the arguments of the opposing parties indicate, the dispute occurred at the meeting of the highest religious authority whom the Mishnah describes as the בית דין; and as R. Joḥanan b. Zakkai had transferred to the beth-din in Jamnia the privileges of the highest beth-din, once in the stone chamber of the Temple in Jerusalem, he claimed for it the right to have the horn blown at its meeting on the New Year that fell on the Sabbath.[2] On the other hand, as, in addition to the official blowing in the beth-din, the trumpets and the horn were blown at the eastern gates of the forecourt of the Temple, as in the prayers of the public fast consisting of several blessings, there seems to have been held on the New Year in the same place a similar service in which the horn and the trumpets

[1] Rosh haShan. 29 b bottom.

[2] Cf. Rashi R. H. 30 a: When the New Year fell on the Sabbath, they blew only in the Great Synhedrion that sanctified the new-moon-days. With this agrees the early report in Tos. R. H. IV, 3: Simeon, the son of the vice-high-priest said, If the witnesses (who reported the appearance of the new moon on Elul 30th) only came after the afternoon-sacrifice had been offered up, the horn was blown, but the additional sacrifice of the festival was brought only after the sanctification of the new moon. As those witnesses had to give their evidence before the beth-din in Jerusalem, and the same authority sanctified the new moon, it seems most probable that also the blowing of the horn, characteristic of Tishri 1st and closely bound up with that evidence, was ordered by the same beth-din, just as this regulated the sacrifices to be brought on the New Year. A Baraitha in R. H. 30 a expressly states the fact that the horn was blown in the beth-din that sanctified the new moon. But as the people had on the day of the New Year gathered in Jamnia and before in Jerusalem, and could hardly have found room in the chamber of the meeting, the announcement of the beth-din must have been made in the Temple in the spacious inner forecourt, and the horn been blown before the large gathering (cf. Pesik. r. 41. 172 b: לפיכך ראש השנה שחל להיות בשבת אין תוקעים בכל מקום אלא בעינטב במקום שהיו בית דין יושבים ומעברים את השנים והחדשים for the time when the meeting for fixing the calendar was held in 'En-Tabh).

occupied a place of considerable importance. And as already the two schools of the Shammaites and Hillelites differed only on the detail as to the place of the special reference to the Sabbath in the prayer for the New Year, but were agreed without any doubt about the number of the blessings constituting the prayer for that festival,[1] it is certain that the additional blessings expressing the spirit of the New Year were already in existence in Temple times. On the other hand, in the discussion between R. Akiba and R. Joḥanan b. Nuri about the exact place in the prayer of the New Year where the horn is to be blown, מלכיות זכרונות ושופרות are referred to as fixed parts of that prayer, and R. Simeon b. Gamaliel II states that in the service held in Jamnia (in the days of his father Gamaliel II) the order suggested by R. Akiba was followed.[2] It seems most probable that the three additional insertions just mentioned already formed a part of the prayer for the New Year in Jerusalem, and that the blowing of the horn and the trumpets on the Temple Mount followed the recital of every one of those insertions, as in the prayer of the public fast held in front of the eastern gates of the inner forecourt of the Temple.

6. The prayer for rain itself has, strange to say, not been preserved in the Baraithas about the service of the public fast. All that is quoted, is the reader's wishes to the people which were similar to those of Eli to Ḥannah in 1 Sam. 1. 17, 'May He who answered Abraham on Mount Moriah, answer you and listen to the voice of your cry this day'.[3] But neither the prayer which God may answer, nor the cry sent up to Him is reported. As all the three Baraithas which describe the service, agree in all the details in the

[1] Tos. R. H. IV, 11: יום טוב של ראש השנה שחל להיות בשבת בית שמאי אומרים מתפלל עשר ובית הלל אומרים מתפלל תשע.

[2] R. H. IV, 5; Baraitha b. 32 a; jer. IV, 59 c. 11; Sifra Lev. 23. 24, 101 d; Tos. R. H. IV, 5.

[3] מי שענה את אברהם בהר המוריה הוא יענה אתכם וישמע בקול צעקתכם היום הזה.

two paragraphs, it seems that nothing has fallen out; so that the first blessing with its concluding benediction would have constituted the prayer proper. In support of the unusual form of the prayer as a blessing, 1 Macc. 4. 30 could be adduced: 'And when he saw that mighty army, he prayed and said, Blessed art Thou, O Saviour of Israel, who didst quell the violence of the mighty man by the hand of Thy servant David, . . . (31) Deliver this army into the hand of Thy people Israel'. Here also the prayer opens with the praise of God as the Redeemer in the past;[1] but the part corresponding with Judah's prayer to which the benediction was merely the introduction, seems to be missing. Again, R. Eleazar of Mode'im interprets Exod. 17. 9 as referring to a public fast at which (in the prayer) the history of the patriarchs and matriarchs, as that of Levi and Judah, is mentioned.[2] The prayer quoted in the Mishnah and the Baraithas refers to the acceptance of the supplications of Abraham on Mount Moriah, of the Israelites by the Red Sea, of Joshua in Gilgal, of Samuel in Miṣpah, of Elijah on Mount Karmel, and of Jonah, David, and Solomon; but there is no reference to Levi and Judah, nor to the matriarchs. And it would again appear that the prayer of the fast has in that part not been preserved in the complete form as R. Eleazar of Mode'im knew it. Again, in his description of a public fast for rain Jer. 14. 12 says, 'When they fast, I will not hear their cry, and when they offer burnt-offering and meal-offering, I will not accept them'; he presupposes that the people fasted, brought sacrifices, and called to God in רנה[3] which seems to denote the cry of the congregation at their prostration before God.[4]

[1] Imitated in Tobit 8. 5-8, and in the free composition in 'Azariah's prayer in LXX on Dan. 3. (26).

[2] Mekhil. Exod. 17. 9, 54 a top; Mekhil. R. Simeon, 17. 9, 82; Mekhil. 17. 12, 54 b.

[3] As in Isa. 58. 4, 'Ye fast not this day so as to make your voice to be heard on high'.

[4] *ZATW.* 19, 1899, 100 ff., 337 ff., and רנה ותפלה in 1 Reg. 8. 28; Jer. 7. 16; 11. 14; Ps. 17. 1; 61. 2; 88. 3; 119. 169; 142. 7; and the cry of

With this could be identified 'the voice of your cry' in our prayer, by which alone the congregation participated in the service,[1] as already in Joel 1. 14, 'Sanctify ye a fast, call a solemn assembly, gather the elders and all the inhabitants of the land unto the house of the Lord your God, and cry unto the Lord'.[2] Again, the Mishnah quotes as the parts of the reader's prayer six appropriate verses from various books of the Bible, Ps. 120. 1; 121. 1; 130. 1; 102. 1 which are termed זכרונות ושופרות,[3] known also from the prayer of the New Year discussed above, and 1 Reg. 8. 37; Jer. 14. 1. And if Jerome deserves credit, he once saw how hosts of

distress in Ps. 106. 44, as in 1 Macc. 3. 54: Then sounded they with trumpets, and cried with a loud voice.

[1] Cf. צעק in Ta'an. III, 7: על אלו מתריעין בשבת על עיר שהקיפוה גוים או נהר ועל הספינה המטורפת בים, רבי יוסי אומר לעזרה ולא לצעקה. Rashi explains the last part thus: We may call in people to come to help, but we must not pray on the Sabbath, as we are not certain of the effect of our prayer, to be permitted to cry on the Sabbath to God for them. In Baraitha Ta'an. 14 a bottom, the word is evidently used in the same sense: ושאר כל מיני פורעניות . . . לא היו מתריעין אלא צועקין; Berakh. IX, 3: הצועק לשעבר הרי זו תפלת שוא; IX, 4: הנכנס לכרך מתפלל שתים אחת בכניסתו ואחת ביציאתו, בן עזאי אומר ארבע שתים בכניסתו ושתים ביציאתו ונותן הודאה לשעבר וצועק לעתיד לבא, where it clearly means a prayer, as in Exod. 14. 15, 'And the Lord said unto Moses, Wherefore criest thou unto Me', which is rendered by R. Eliezer in Mekhil. 29 a by ואתה עומד ומרבה בתפלה. In Bab. meṣ. 75 b bottom: שלשה צועקין ואינן נענין, where, as in our prayer, נענין indicates that it means a prayer addressed to God. Rashi explains this as a complaint before a human court, as צעק actually means complaint in Exod. 22. 22; 2 Reg. 6. 26; Jer. 20. 8; but נענין hardly suits that meaning.

[2] Cf. 2 Chron. 20, 9, If evil come upon us, the sword, judgement, or pestilence, or famine, we will stand before this house, and before Thee, for Thy name is in this house, and cry unto Thee in our affliction, then Thou wilt hear and save.

[3] Ta'an. II, 3: ומוסיף עליהן עוד שש. ואלו הן זכרונות ושופרות, אל ה׳ בצרתה לי קראתי ויענני אשא עיני אל ההרים וגו׳ ממעמקים קראתיך ה׳ תפלה לעני כי יעטף, רבי יהודה אומר לא היה צריך לומר זכרונות ושופרות אלא אומר תחתיהן רעב כי יהיה בארץ אשר היה דבר ה׳ אל ירמיהו על דברי הבצרות ואומר חותמיהם.

locusts covered the soil of Judaea; and when a service of supplication had been held by the Jews at which Joel's prayer in 2. 17 was recited, at once a wind arose and carried the locusts into the sea.[1] Accordingly, instead of special prayers composed for such an occasion, appropriate passages from the Bible would have been recited. So R. Jehudah b. Ilai suggested 1 Reg. 8. 37 instead of the opening verses of four Psalms; though he might have more appropriately read 1 Reg. 8. 35: When heaven is shut up, and there is no rain, because they have sinned against Thee; if they pray toward this place, and confess (?) Thy name, and turn from their sin, when Thou dost afflict them: (36) then hear Thou in heaven.

The Baraithas about the service of the public fast quote only the wording of two paragraphs of the prayer. But the rule at the end of their statement about the alternation of the two groups of the three blasts of the trumpets reads: 'And so at every benediction, after one he (the attendant of the synagogue) says to the priests, Blow a plain blast, and after the other he says, Blow an alarm, until he finishes all the benedictions';[2] this presupposes at least two more paragraphs. According to the Mishnah the reader added six benedictions to the fixed prayer of the Eighteen Benedictions.[3] Similarly a Baraitha says, 'He recites before them twenty-four blessings, the eighteen of the daily prayer to which he adds another six'.[4] This combination was probably due to the fact that at the time which those sources reflect, the service for rain was no longer read as a prayer by itself, but, as R. Zeraḥyah haLevi suggested[5], as a kind of Musaf-service which was held in

[1] Comment. on Joel 2; *MGWJ.*, 41, 1897, 633. 2.

[2] Ta'an. 16 b: וכן בכל ברכה וברכה באחת אומר תקעו ובאחת אומר הריעו עד שיגמור את הברכות כולן.

[3] Ta'an. II, 2.

[4] Ta'an. 16 b: תניא אומר לפניהן עשרים וארבע ברכות שמונה עשרה שבכל יום ומוסיף עליהן עוד שש.

[5] In his *Ma'or* on Berakh. I; Herzfeld, *Geschichte*, III, 189.

the days of R. Joḥanan after nine o'clock in the morning.[1] R. Eliezer who died about the year 120, already recited the twenty-four benedictions on a public fast; so that the insertion of the six blessings of the prayer of the fast into the Eighteen Benedictions was then already an established custom.[2] Whether the insertion was effected before 70 in Jerusalem, or owed its origin to R. Joḥanan b. Zakkai after the destruction, we are not in a position to establish, as it is not even certain whether all the six benedictions were already in use before the year 70.[3]

All these details of the service of the public fast for rain prove that there was already in the time of the Temple such a service held on the Temple Mount in front of the eastern gates of the Temple court, that a prayer was there

[1] Jer. Berakh. I, 3 c. 49 ff. As already I. Lévi in *R. É. J.*, 47, 1903, 165 and Elbogen in *MGWJ.*, 46, 1902, 346 ff. noted, the list of the sentences beginning with מי שענה in Ta'an. II, 4 contains seven items, and counts the seventh of the daily Eighteen Benedictions to which the additional prayer is joined, as the first in the list; so also the Baraitha Ta'an. 16 b; jer. Berakh. I, 3 c. 59: בגואל ישראל מאריך. This represents a later development, when the six benedictions of the prayer for rain, constituting an independent prayer, were inserted into the daily Eighteen Benedictions after גואל ישראל, whereby two consecutive benedictions in the amalgamated prayers closed with the same formula: ברוך אתה ה׳ גואל ישראל. To avoid this, the two successive benedictions were combined into one which now formed the first of the special benedictions of the prayer of the fast. But some scholars regarded it even in its new and longer form as the seventh of the Eighteen Benedictions; and as they insisted on the addition on the fast day of six complete and separate benedictions, they had to compose a new sixth paragraph: על השביעית הוא אומר מי שענה את דוד ואת שלמה בנו בירושלים הוא יענה אתכם וישמע בקול צעקתכם היום הזה ברוך אתה ה׳ המרחם על הארץ, cf. Tos. R. H. III, 3: ובתענית תוקעין שבע שלש ושלש, which presupposes seven benedictions in the prayer of the fast, after each of which three blasts were blown. The concluding formula of this additional benediction differs entirely from those of the first six benedictions; and this alone is sufficient to indicate its later origin. As Symmachos, a disciple of R. Meir, in Ta'an. 17 a; jer. II, 65 d. 49; Tos. I, 10, תנא משום סומכוס אמרו ברוך משפיל הרמים suggested another concluding formula, it seems that the seventh additional paragraph was still fluid in the second half of the second century.

[2] Baraitha Ta'an. 25 b.

[3] Herzfeld, *Geschichte*, III, 135.

recited which consisted of four or six paragraphs, that after each of these priests blew trumpets and a horn, and that the assembled congregation responded and probably prostrated itself. But there is nothing in the sources extant to indicate how long before 70 that form of the service had been in practice in Jerusalem; and there is no possibility of proving that already in 70 B.C.E., when praying for rain on the Temple Mount, Ḥoni recited the same four or six blessings of the prayer preserved. He certainly differed in his conduct toward God from all those who, in the first and second centuries, acted on similar occasions as the spokesmen of the suffering community. When asked to pray, his ready acceptance, without any hesitation, of the office of an intercessor, offered to him, no doubt, by some responsible authority, seems to evidence too great a measure of self-reliance. And even more so his order which he gave to the people before his prayer, to remove from the open yards the earthen ovens set up for the roasting of the Passover lambs on the ensuing eve of Nisan 15th, shows his confidence, as he seems to have entertained no doubt about the immediate and full effect of his impending supplication. God reproved him for his immodest demeanour by not complying with his prayer of intercession;[1] and still he did not appear chastened, as God's refusal urged him on to even greater insistence. He drew a circle or dug a pit in the ground, and stood up in it; and, as though he intended or were able to force Him to yield and to send rain, he swore by His great name that he would not move thence until God had shown mercy to His children. Such self-confinement to a spot or a circle or a pit in connexion with prayer is nowhere reported in Jewish literature either of the Essenes or of anybody else;[2] and it is nothing else but

[1] Jer. Ta'an. III, 66 d. 53.

[2] Except in Targum on Ḥab. 2. 1 as an interpretation of the words of the prophet, 'I will stand upon my watch, and set me upon the tower'; probably the author took it from the Baraitha Ta'an. 23 a about Ḥoni. Schorr in החלוץ, VII, 1865, 33 ff. accepts the explanation that Ḥoni dug a pit, and declares his procedure as Persian, for which he refers to

a drastic illustration of his declaration, I shall not move from the spot in which I am standing. His prayer became now, at least in its opening words, less self-asserting: he apologizes to God for his acting as the intercessor by stating that it was the opinion of him held by the people that placed him in his present position, and that he is praying as its spokesman and on behalf of God's children. Acting in the capacity of His *familiaris*, he adjures God by His great name, as any one entreating a king for mercy would urge him by all that is dear to him and may weigh with him, not to persist in carrying out his strict and crushing judgment.

7. Many a characteristic detail of religious thought and belief is clearly implied by Ḥoni's words. He prayed for God's *mercy*, for he knew that the prevailing calamity was fully deserved as a just punishment for the people's sins; for God is just. Would it not have been appropriate for

Kleucker, III, 211 whose evidence I could not verify. Dr. Kohler in *J. Q. R.*, V, 1893, 415, 1 adduces only a late haggadic parallel which was undoubtedly based on Ḥoni's example, and stamps it a part of the mystic practice of the Gnostics, Dietrich, *Abraxas*, 158, where, however, no circle or pit is mentioned. In Neumark's *Journal of Jewish Lore and Philosophy*, I, 1919, 31, Dr. Kohler says, 'The best illustration of such an Essene wonder-worker is furnished in Ta'an. III, 8 in Onias, the Rainmaker, or, as the people called him, המעגל, the one who used to draw a circle around him for his prayer. . . . he shut himself up in the hole he had digged. . . . We have here . . . a striking characteristic of the typical Essene, who does not hesitate to force his will upon God by the use of the Great Name in his prayer.' Where do we find Essenes as wonder-workers? How do we know that Ḥoni was an Essene? Where is it stated that the people called him המעגל? Where is it reported that he *used* to draw circles? How do we know that that was typical of the Essene? Where and when did any Essene force his will upon God? A comparison of Ḥoni's method with the various magical and other practices all over the world for obtaining rains, in Frazer, *Golden Bough*[3], I, 1, 247–311, and Hastings, *Encyclopaedia of Religion and Ethics*, X, 1918, 562–5, shows that Ḥoni applied none of them, nor any magic at all; for even the circle which he drew and which reminds us of the circle drawn by Popilius Laenas round Antiochus IV Epiphanes in Egypt (Livy, XLV, 12; Schürer, *Geschichte*, I[3], 197), has nothing in common with the magical circle drawn by the conjurer for his own protection from the ghost (Hastings, *Encyclopaedia of Religion*, VIII, 321 ff.).

him, before appealing for God's mercy, first to try to move the congregation to repentance? It seems that in his first prayer which is not reported, he had already done so, and not only the long drought with its perils, but Ḥoni's admonition had stirred contrition in the hearts of the assembly; still the rain had not fallen. He addressed God as the Master of the Universe, the Ruler of the world to whose law every individual is subject, who watches and notes the actions of every person, especially in Israel, and who judges the deeds of His people; and as His omnipotence and providence give the rain or withhold it, He shows His anger at their sins by the terrible drought. Ḥoni called the Jews the children of God, thereby describing the intimate relation between Israel and their Father in heaven, as we found it among the early pious men seventy years later. His appeal was now addressed to God for His children; and it is for them that he most solemnly swore that he would not move from the spot until God had mercy on His children. In His justice God did not allow even His children to go on sinning without punishment; for they knew His will better than any other nation, as it was revealed to them in His Torah, therefore their disobedience was punished sooner and more severely. By his oath Ḥoni imposed upon himself the heavy restraint of having to remain within the circle for an indefinite period; and he added the solemn oath to bind himself firmly to his undertaking. As he did this for his people, he was confident and even convinced that God who loved His children and also him, would not allow him to suffer long for their sake; only in this his certainty has his oath any sense. Was it then again his great self-consciousness that had prompted those words, or was it his mission as Israel's representative, as the spokesman of God's children, who felt sure that their Father would not much longer withhold His mercy?[1]

[1] Is his oath Essenic? According to Josephus in *Wars*, II, 8. 6. 135; *Antiquit.*, XV, 10. 4. 371; Hippolytus, *Refut.*, IX, 18-28; Philo, II, 458; Kohler in *Jew. Encyclop.*, V, 229 a, the Essenes never took an oath; but

God accepted the more humble prayer, and it began to rain gently. But the scanty drops indicated to Ḥoni and his disciples that, while yielding to his supplication, God either did not grant to Israel more than a very partial measure of mercy, or still disapproved of Ḥoni's attitude in his prayer. In the account of the Baraitha which so far agrees with that of the Mishnah, a remark of Ḥoni's disciples expressed their interpretation of God's answer.[1] The disciples who were standing round him, said to him that they were looking to him for their rescue from death by famine, and they interpreted the poor rain as sent by God only to annul Ḥoni's oath. They meant to say that God did not like His beloved son to suffer in the circle drawn, and now enabled him to leave it. When, on his further request, the rain poured down in wild streams, the disciples interpreted it as sent by God to destroy the world. But who had just then sinned so gravely as to justify such an assumption? Not their master, as God had

when a new member was admitted, oaths of an awful character were administered to him and he had to swear that he would undertake the duties and obey the rules of the order. It is true, Ḥoni's oath was not to confirm and to support a statement, but to strengthen him in his own undertaking; but that an Essene would have used the sacred name of God even in such an oath is even less probable, unless Dr. Kohler adduces some evidence to the contrary.

[1] Ta‘an. 23 a: התחילו נשמים מנטפין, אמרו לו תלמידיו רבי ראינוך ולא נמות כמדומין אנו שאין נשמים יורדין אלא להתיר שבועתך, אמר לא כך שאלתי אלא גשמי בורות שיחין ומערות, ירדו בזעף עד שכל טיפה וטיפה כמלא פי חבית . . . אמרו לו תלמידיו רבי ראינוך ולא נמות כמדומין אנו אין נשמים יורדין אלא לאבד העולם, אמר לפניו לא כך שאלתי אלא גשמי רצון ברכה ונדבה, ירדו כתיקנן עד שעלו כל העם להר הבית מפני הנשמים, אמרו לו רבי כשם שהתפללת שירדו כך התפלל וילכו להם, אמר להם כך מקובלני שאין מתפללין על רוב הטובה אף על פי כן הביאו לי פר הודאה, הביאו לו פר הודאה סמך שתי ידיו עליו ואמר לפניו רבונו של עולם עמך ישראל שהוצאת ממצרים אינן יכולין לעמוד לא ברוב טובה ולא ברוב פורענות, כעסת עליהם אינן יכולין לעמוד השפעת עליהם טובה אינן יכולין לעמוד יהי רצון מלפניך שיפסקו הנשמים ויהא ריוח בעולם, מיד נשבה הרוח ונתפזרו העבים וזרחה החמה.

only a short while ago shown a sign of mercy to him; but the people that had in the drought experienced His punishing anger, and now continued to be punished by the threatening flood. His further prayer for a rain of favour and of gift made the rain more normal; but as it fell densely, the people had to seek shelter on the Temple Mount. There they asked Ḥoni to pray for the rain to stop;[1] he refused, as God whom he called בעל הרחמים, the Merciful, would certainly not destroy men, though they fully deserved it. Though God's justice would demand the extreme penalty to be inflicted, it would certainly not happen, as in His infinite mercy He had promised, even for the gravest sin never to destroy the earth by a flood again. The rain is a blessing, and even too much of it is still a blessing; and a tradition in his possession taught him not to pray for its stopping.

Still, in the end, he consented to pray; but not, as till now, by words of supplication only, but by entreating God over a sacrifice for which, at his request, they brought him a bull. He laid both hands upon the animal and prayed, 'Master of the Universe, Thy people Israel whom Thou broughtest out from Egypt, cannot exist either in the overgreat measure of blessing or in the overgreat measure of visitation; when Thou wast angry with them, they could not subsist, and when Thou showerest on them blessing, they cannot subsist. May it be Thy will that the rain stop, and ease prevail in the world!' Immediately a wind blew, the clouds dispersed, the sun shone and the people

[1] Here would follow suitably, as jer. Ta'an. III, 66 d. 71 actually has it, the statement of Tos. and partly of the Mishnah, that, in order to reassure the anxious people, he asked them to look whether the water of the Kidron had risen to, and flooded, the rock of the erring, or, as the parallel, without containing Ḥoni's name, has it, whether the corner of the 'Ophel was reached by the floods; and his further remark in jer. III, 66 d. 74, similarly understood as the reason for his refusal to pray again: Just as this rock cannot be dissolved by the rain, so I cannot pray for the rain to stop. He refuses to pray, unless the city be really threatened with destruction by the floods; but this cannot happen, as God assured humanity that He would never send a flood again.

went out into the fields to gather mushrooms and truffles. In this and the previous prayers no reference occurs to himself and his own person, but they all urge only the claims of Israel: it is God's people, as in Exod, 33. 13, Deut. 9. 29, the same that had enjoyed His special love, when He liberated it from Egypt, as in Exod. 32. 11; Deut. 9. 29. In his circumlocution in which he acknowledged the superabundance of the rain as a very great boon, Ḥoni actually avoided praying for the rain to stop,[1] but expressly declared that it made it impossible for the people to subsist, and he asked for relief. His sacrifice he called פר הודאה;[2] the difficult term is explained by Rashi: to confess sins over it,[3] but the prayer contains no reference to any form of confession, nor was there just at that moment any occasion for it. On the other hand, the word cannot here have its usual meaning of thanksgiving, as Ḥoni in his prayer expressed no thanks to God, but entreated Him for help in the trouble of the people. Now, in connexion with a prayer in a drought, in I Reg. 8. 35 we read, 'When heaven is shut up, and there is no rain, because they have sinned against Thee; if they pray toward this place, and confess Thy name, and turn from their sin, when Thou afflictest them; (36) then hear Thou in heaven, and forgive the sin of Thy servants and of Thy people Israel, when Thou teachest them the good way wherein they should walk; and send rain upon Thy land.' As in Ḥoni's prayer, so here the drought is God's punishment for the people's sins: it prays to Him and turns away from its evil ways, and, after having disregarded Him, again *acknowledges* both Him as the Master of its destinies and the justice of His visitations.[4] The same seems to have

[1] The words שיפסקו הגשמים are absent in jer.

[2] Jer. פר של הודיות.

[3] Similarly Samuel Edels: In any case, he was ungrateful, for at first he prayed for rain that was a blessing for the world, but now, as Rashi explains, he is going to confess that he will act wrongly in praying for the stopping of the great measure of good.

[4] So in Isa. 12. 1: I acknowledge Thee, O Lord, as the just Judge in visiting me in Thine anger with severe punishments.

been Ḥoni's idea in his declaration that both the oppressive drought and the now dangerous blessing of the rain have been sent by God, and were punishments which meant destruction to the people.

The report of the Baraitha continues, 'Simeon b. Shetaḥ sent Ḥoni this message, "If thou wert not Ḥoni, I should have decreed the ban against thee; for if the years (of the present drought) were like the years (of the drought) of Elijah, when the keys of the rain were in Elijah's hands, would not the result (of thine intercession) be a profanation of God's name? But what can I do to thee, since, though thou provest thyself a sinner against God, He still granteth thy request, just as a father granteth the wishes of a son who proveth himself a sinner against him. . . To thee applieth Prov. 23. 25, Let thy father and thy mother be glad, and let her that bare thee rejoice"'.[1] The leading Pharisee teacher knew Ḥoni as a man of importance who could not, without due consideration, be punished by the ban, even when his strange conduct seemed to merit it; for his past and his character made it clear that in his prayer neither his offensive words nor his blasphemous procedure had been intended to offend God or to profane His holy name. Assuming that an Elijah of the present generation had sworn, as the prophet in 1 Reg. 17. 1 had done, no rain would possibly have been permitted, in response to Ḥoni's prayers, to fall this year; and so his oath by God's great name that he would not leave the circle drawn by him until the rain fell, would in the end prove as uttered in vain, and thereby the name of God be profaned.[2] The

[1] Ta'an. 23 a: שלח לו שמעון בן שטח, אלמלא חוני אתה גוזרני עליך
נידוי שאילו שנים כשני אליהו שמפתחות גשמים בידו של אליהו לא נמצא
שם שמים מתחלל על ידך, אבל מה אעשה לך שאתה מתחטא לפני המקום
ועושה לך רצונך כבן שמתחטא על אביו ועושה לו רצונו . . . ועליך
הכתוב אומר ישמח אביך ואמך ותגל יולדתך.

[2] An anonymous statement in Gen. r. 13. 7, in interpreting Gen. 2. 5 haggadically, says: ואדם אין לעבוד את האדמה, ואדם אין להעביד את

parallel account bears out this interpretation of Rashi, and, at the same time, supplies very valuable information about the ideas of the two scholars concerning the influence of the righteous man upon God.[1] Simeon b. Shetaḥ sent Ḥoni this message, 'Thou deservest the ban, for had the same been decreed (by God) as in the days of Elijah, thou wouldst have brought the people to a profanation of God's name, and he who brings others to a profanation of God's name, deserves the ban.' To this Ḥoni replied, 'Does not God annul His decree in favour of the decree of a righteous man?' Simeon answered, 'Yes, God does annul His decree in favour of the decree of a righteous man, but does not annul the decree of one righteous man in favour of the decree of another righteous man. But what can I do, &c.?' If this most interesting part of the report is authentic in all its details, and, considering the source in which it has been preserved, there is no occasion for questioning it, the religious belief implied here deserves special attention. Ḥoni who applied to himself indirectly the epithet of 'righteous', used of him also in the account of Josephus, believed that the prayer of a pious man could persuade God to withdraw the visitation decreed by Him; for was not Moses' prayer in Exod. 32. 11–14; Deut. 9. 18, 19, 26–29 a convincing instance of such power?[2] Simeon, naturally,

הבריות להקדוש ברוך הוא כאליהו וכחוני המעגל, there was none to bring men to the service of God like Elijah and Ḥoni the circle-drawer. See Theodor's note on p. 117.

[1] Jer. Ta'an. III, 67 a. 9: שלח לו שמעון בן שטח אמר לו צריך אתה לנדות שאילו נגזרה גזירה כשם שנגזרה בימי אליהו לא נמצאתה מביא את הרבים לידי חילול השם שכל המביא את הרבים לידי חילול השם צריך נידוי . . . ואמר לו ואין הקדוש ברוך הוא מבטל גזירתו מפני גזירתו של צדיק, אמר לו הן הקדוש ברוך הוא מבטל גזירתו מפני גזירתו של צדיק ואין הקדוש ברוך הוא מבטל גזירתו של צדיק מפני גזירתו של צדיק חבירו, אבל מה אעשה לך ואתה מתחטא לפני המקום כבן שהוא מתחטא על אביו והוא עושה לו רצונו.

[2] Weiss, *Zur Geschichte*, I, 145, thinks that Simeon objected to Ḥoni's arrogant words against God and to his believing himself and his making

shared Ḥoni's view about the acceptance of such a prayer by God, as not only that of Moses, but those spoken in distress by various prophets, kings and psalmists supported it. In spite of Ḥoni's argument and defence, Simeon adhered to his opinion of the sinfulness of Ḥoni's conduct as deserving the severe disciplinary punishment which, at that time, as it appears, was only imposed on a public man for a grave and public sin. On the other hand, Simeon considered him a righteous man, and admitted that, in spite of his unreasonable, nay sinful conduct, God had accepted his prayer as that of a spoiled child; and this favour of God protected him from the imposition of the ban which he fully deserved. But whether, by this his admission and his illustration, Simeon credited Ḥoni with exceptional piety by which he was brought nearer to God than Simeon himself, is not at all evident. And even if we granted that, there is nothing to be discovered in his words that could be identified with any of the traits enumerated by Philo, Josephus, and Hippolytus as characteristic of the Essenes. The apparent presumption of Ḥoni that was, in his mind, fully compatible with his piety, but objectionable to the Pharisee teacher, is certainly contrary to all that can be thought of the Essenes; it is not in agreement with general Jewish principles, and rather reminds one of the methods of a magician or a heathen priest in praying for rain.

In another Baraitha a message of the members of the beth-din that met in the chamber of hewn stones in the Temple, is recorded.[1] It is an application of Job 22. 28–30

the congregation believe that he could force God to yield by his prayer; and that the reference to God's decree showed that Simeon held that against that the prayer of the pious man availed nothing. But the whole statement clearly shows that Simeon, without any hesitation, admitted Ḥoni's belief and only qualified it in one instance; on the main question and their mode of thought there was no difference between the two teachers.

[1] Ta'an. 23 a: תנו רבנן מה שלחו בני לשכת הגזית לחוני המעגל, ותגזר אומר ויקם לך ועל דרכיך נגה אור, ותגזר אומר אתה גזרת מלמטה והקדוש ברוך הוא מקיים מאמרך מלמעלה, ועל דרכיך נגה אור דור שהיה

to Ḥoni's prayer and its success, and to the relief which he brought to his contemporaries who had been oppressed by their sins and the consequent sufferings. If the message did not consist merely of the three verses, so appropriate to the occasion by themselves, the interpretation attached intended to express the unqualified recognition of Ḥoni's pure deeds by the highest authoritative religious body. They referred, by the biblical quotation and evidently also by their present application, to his honest, blameless dealings with his fellow-men. His uprightness and his piety were his equipment that had lent force to his prayer, commended it to God for acceptance, and saved his suffering contemporaries. Though the religious ideas embodied in the interpretation of the verses were, to a great extent, suggested naturally by the wording of the passage chosen, they still reflect some of the beliefs of that time, and agree with some of those expressed by Ḥoni and Simeon b. Shetaḥ. The prevailing long drought was decreed and sent by God as a punishment for the grave sins of that generation; but the will and the prayer of the pious man who was distinguished by virtues, induced God to revoke His decree and to send rain before it was, according to His will, due. Ḥoni's piety which is emphasized here, consisted neither in an ascetic life or that of a hermit, nor in frequent fasting, religious contemplation or mystic thought, but of pure deeds of the hands, of works of honesty, charity and loving-kindness. Though the stress laid on Ḥoni's deeds in the message of the learned body seems to suggest some superiority of his actions, it is only the degree and not the kind of work that distinguished him from others. The parallel account explains the purity of his hands more distinctly as his fulfilment of the positive commandments

אפל הארת בתפלתך, כי השפילו ותאמר גוה דור שהיה שפל הגבהתו בתפלתך, ושח עינים יושיע דור ששח בעונו הושעת בתפלתך, ימלט אי נקי דור שלא היה נקי מילטתו בתפלתך, ונמלט בבור כפיך מילטתו במעשה ידיך הברורין.

and the practice of good deeds to the fellow-man from the beginning.[1] The last word points to the fact that he began to realize such principles not in his later years, as among the pious men and the men of deed the repentant, but he followed that rule from his youth; and it was the practice of the two groups of positive duties, towards God and men, that made him a righteous man.[2] That those virtues were especially Essenic, cannot be proved from any record; whereas, according to express reports, they distinguished Hillel and his disciples, and there is nothing to suggest that they had learned them from the Essenes.

8. As it was the custom of all scholars of his time to be everywhere accompanied by their disciples, Ḥoni was at his public prayer surrounded by his, though their number is not evident. Thus there were not a few disciples with Judas the Essene, when, on the Feast of Tabernacles in the Temple, he referred to his prophecy of the impending death of Antigonos, the brother of Aristobul I.[3] As Hillel was accompanied by his students outside the school, so R. Joḥanan b. Zakkai, the Pharisee teacher, was in the company of his disciples, when in Ma'on in Judaea,[4] and again when, after the destruction of Jerusalem, he once came out from Jerusalem,[5] and when a heathen expressed to him his surprise at the strange procedure in connexion with the burning of the red heifer and the

[1] Jer. Ta'an. III, 67 a. 28: מהו ונמלט בבור כפיך, בברירות כפיך בזכות מצות ומעשים טובים שהיו בידך מראשיתך.

[2] The continuation of the report quotes the interpretation of vv. 29 and 30, and puts these into the mouth of God as addressed to Ḥoni: 'I said that I would bring them low, thou saidst to bring them high, and thy word was realized, and not mine; I said to lower their eyes by evil, and thou saidst to save them, and thy word was established and not mine; I said, the pure shall be saved, thou saidst, even the non-pure shall be saved, thy word was established and not mine'.

[3] In the year 103 B. C. E., Josephus, *Wars*, I, 3. 5. 78; *Antiquit.*, XIII, 11. 2. 311.

[4] Mekhil. Exod. 19. 1, 61 a, b.

[5] Baraitha Kethub. 66 b; Sifré Deut. 31. 14. 305, 130 a; Bacher, I, 42. 4.

purification of a defiled person with its ashes,[1] and also when a hegemon asked him about some difficulties in the Pentateuch.[2] In the last two instances, it is true, it would appear obvious that the conversations took place in his school where the students would naturally be with him. But the question of the non-Jew about the ashes of the red heifer was put to R Joḥanan before the year 70, when the heathen had not only read the law in Num. 19, but observed in Jerusalem the details, not stated in the Bible, of the pounding of the ashes and the declaration of the priest to the purified person that after the sprinkling he was now clean.[3] And it is not only not stated in the reports that the non-Jew visited the school, but it is not probable. In their continued personal intercourse with their teacher, Ḥoni's disciples desired, no doubt, to learn from him the order, the formulation and the wording of the special, and, as the instance of his grandson, Ḥoni the Small shows,[4] also of the festival prayers, and probably also his conduct on the solemn occasions. Similarly the disciples of the Essene Judas received practical training in the art of prophesying, even when he spoke to them about his alleged error in his forecast. Had corresponding information been preserved about Ḥoni's contemporaries', Simeon b. Shetaḥ's and Jehudah b. Tabbai's relations to their disciples, we should have learned that these also watched outside the school the religious decisions, the moral and social sayings and directions, and the conversations and actions of their masters, as we find it reported of teachers and students in the second half of the first and the beginning of the second centuries. It would be of great interest for the question before us to establish whether the three different kinds of teachers, the praying Ḥoni, the prophesying Essene Judas, and the Pharisee scholar Simeon b. Shetaḥ, confined themselves to their

[1] Pesik. 40 a and parallels noted by Buber.

[2] Ḥull. 27 b; jer. Synh. I, 19 b. 18; Bacher, I, 36 ff.

[3] R. Joḥanan b. Zakkai was present at the burning of a red heifer, Tos. Parah, III, 8; IV, 7, cf. X, 2.

[4] Tos. Rosh haShan. IV, 11, above, p. 204.

respective peculiar public activities reported, or whether each one of them practised two or all of them.

The Essenes who exceptionally prophesied and interpreted dreams [1], shared those acts, at least in the first century, with non-Essenes. Josephus, the historian, claimed to possess the knowledge of prophecy, and asserted that God had revealed to him in dreams of the night the impending misfortune of the Jews and the future fate of the Roman generals in the Jewish revolution; for he understood, when interpreting dreams, how to explain also such hints as God had left ambiguous, as he, as a priest and the son of a priest, was well acquainted with the prophecies of the holy books.[2] In comparing this with his statement that there were among the Essenes some who, having acquainted themselves from their youth with the holy books and various sanctifications and the utterances of the prophets, believed to know the future,[3] we note that both drew on the same books. Josephus claimed as a priest and not as a disciple of the Essene Banus,[4] to derive his prophetic information from the words of the holy books just as did the Essenes, though he applied it to the interpretation of his own prophetic dreams. And again he stated that a passage in the holy books about the quadrilateral form of the Temple, as well as an ambiguous prophecy in the holy books about the Messiah had been misinterpreted in the years 66–70 by the wise men of the Jews, and that various miraculous signs of warning had been interpreted by their ἱερογραμματεῖς and λόγιοι;[5] and here again not Essenes, but scholars are meant. Just as Josephus claimed to have foretold his future greatness to Vespasian,[6] so R. Joḥanan b. Zakkai was credited with the same prophecy [7] which he derived from an interpretation of Isa. 10. 34 b; as on the occasion, when the gate of

[1] Josephus, *Wars*, III, 8. 3. 351; *Antiquit.*, XVII, 13. 3. 346.
[2] *Wars*, III, 8. 3. 352. [3] Ibid., II, 8 12. 159.
[4] Montgomery in *J. Q. R.*, XI, 1921, 281, 291.
[5] *Wars*, VI, 5. 4, 3.
[6] Ibid., III, 8. 9. 401; Schürer, *Geschichte*, I[3], 75 ff.
[7] Threni r. 1. 5. 31; ARN. 4, 12 a.

the Temple opened of its own accord, he interpreted the portentous incident, according to Zech. 11. 1, to indicate the coming destruction of the Temple.[1] In the days of Herod some Pharisees prophesied to the eunuch Bagoas that he would have children,[2] probably from Isa. 56. 4, 5. So a few Essenes and some distinguished Pharisee scholars equally continued one of the activities of the ancient prophets. Again, not only Josephus reports that God conversed intimately with the high-priest and ruler Hyrkanos I, and that nothing about the future was hidden from him; for he knew beforehand that his two eldest sons would not reign long.[3] Also a rabbinic source states that a heavenly voice from the Holy of Holies informed him that his sons were victorious in Antioch.[4] And the high-priest Simeon the Just heard a heavenly voice from the Holy of Holies telling him of Caligula's death;[5] as also the scholars assembled in Jericho, one of whom was Hillel, heard a heavenly voice saying that one of them was worthy of the holy spirit. Accordingly, a few pious high-priests were, though only once, distinguished by God by a much higher and more direct form of revelation than the Essenes who, however, possessed the gift once acquired for many years. As the information at our disposal has only accidentally preserved just those references to a few instances of occasional prophecy, the fact could be established that the interpretation of dreams and the foretelling of future events were practised not only by Essenes, but by some learned Pharisees, pious high-priests, and even by the priest Josephus. Unfortunately, on the important point of Ḥoni's speciality of intercession no similar parallels of an early date have been recorded.

In conjunction with the revelation of God to some high-

[1] Baraitha Yoma, 39 b, and parallel in Bacher, I, 23. 2.

[2] *Antiquit.*, XVII, 2. 4. 41–5. [3] *Wars*, I, 2. 8; *Antiquit.*, XIII, 10. 7. 300.

[4] Baraitha jer. Sotah, IX, 24 b. 26; b. 33 a; Tos. XIII, 5.

[5] Jer. Sotah, IX, 24 b. 25; b. 33 a; Tos. XIII, 6. To Yaddua the high-priest God suggested in his sleep how he should receive Alexander the Great outside Jerusalem, *Antiquit.*, XI, 8. 4. 327.

priests, it should be noted that before the destruction of the first Temple a prophet, Jeremiah, prayed once for rain; while in Joel's days this prophet had no share in the prayer for the removal of the plague of locusts, but only the priests in the Temple interceded for the people in one single sentence, 2. 17. On the Day of Atonement the high-priest read a section from the Torah, recited all the prayers for forgiveness and mercy, and spoke a short prayer, while in the Holy of Holies; one of the high-priests who is not named, added once a special prayer for the preservation of the Temple and the people.[1] Josephus reports that, when the high-priest Yaddua learned of the hostile approach of Alexander the Great, he was terrified, ordered general prayers, offered sacrifices with the people, and prayed to God for help.[2] So to Josephus the high-priest seems to have been the intercessor before God not only in the sacrificial worship, but in the special prayers.[3] When there was no high-priest available, as in 1 Macc. 7. 36, when Nikanor threatened the Temple with destruction, the priests on duty went in, stood up before the altar and the Temple, and wept and prayed.[4] All this, however, was done within the Temple; but whether also outside it, when, on the Temple Mount, in front of the eastern gates of the forecourt, a prayer was recited for rain, the high-priest or a priest was the reader, as priests blew the trumpets, or a learned Pharisee, or a Ḥasid, or an Essene read, is nowhere stated, except in the case of Ḥoni.

The Apocalypse of Baruch which reflects the religious conditions prevailing immediately before and after the destruction of the second Temple, several times refers to prayers for the inhabitants of Jerusalem, when in distress, and may be used, at least for the first century, as a source of information on the point in question. God told Baruch to ask Jeremiah and all those who were like them, to leave Jerusalem (2. 2),

[1] Baraitha Yoma, 53 b; Tos. III, 5.

[2] *Antiquit.*, XI, 8. 4. 326; cf. Judith 4. 9–15; 3 Macc. 2. 1–20.

[3] See Philo, *De sacerd.* 6. 97, M. II, 227.

[4] Cf. 2 Macc. 1, 23–9.

'because your works are to this city as a firm pillar, and your prayers as a strong wall'. Several passages in the book make it clear that the author was referring to those whom he called righteous, as in the interesting statement in Baruch's letter to the ten tribes (85. 1), 'Know ye, moreover, that in former times and in the generations of old those our fathers had helpers, righteous men and holy prophets. (2) Nay more, we were in our own land, and they helped us when we sinned, and they prayed for us to Him who made us, because they trusted in their works,[1] and the Mighty One heard their prayer and was gracious unto us. (3) But now the righteous have been gathered and the prophets have fallen asleep, and we also have gone forth from the land, and Zion has been taken from us, and we have nothing now save the Mighty One and His law'. The righteous who trusted in their works[2] and who prayed for the people when in sins and distress, were men who not only refrained carefully from transgressing any of the prohibitions of the Torah, but carried out conscientiously the positive commandments of it, such actions constituting their works and deeds. In a further characteristic description of the same men, he says (51. 7), 'But those who have been saved by their works, and to whom the law has been now a hope, and understanding an expectation, and wisdom a confidence, to them wonders will appear in their time'. It is evident that he referred to scholars who, on the one hand, were filled with the desire and determination to carry out the commandments of the Torah, and, on the other hand, devoted their thought and their lives to the study of it.[3] And it is most instructive that for 'the vapour of the smoke of the incense of righteousness which is by the law' (67. 6), after the destruction of the Temple, when incense was no longer burnt on the altar, the observance of the law and its study were declared an equivalent and the

[1] The same is said of King Hezekiah in 63. 3.

[2] See the note of Charles on 14. 7.

[3] See 15. 5 and Charles's note.

full substitute for it. R. Joḥanan b. Zakkai declared to his disciple R. Joshua b. Ḥananiah who lamented over the loss of the altar as the means of the atonement for Israel's sins, that loving-kindness was an equivalent atonement.[1] And he interpreted the white garments and the oil in Eccles. 9. 8 as meaning the observance of the commandments, good deeds and the study of the Torah;[2] and he advised some priests in Jerusalem whose sons, on account of their descent from Eli, were dying young, to study the Torah, for it atoned for the gravest sin, when sacrifice was useless.[3]

R. Joḥanan b. Zakkai and his fellow-teachers were a strong protection for Jerusalem and its inhabitants, and by their instruction and their prayers obtained forgiveness for their sins. And their lay supporters, the councillors Kalba Sabu'a, ben-Ṣiṣith הכסת, and Nakdimon b. Goryon whose prayer was analysed above,[4] contributed by their religious deeds, their charity and loving-kindness an important share to the temporary preservation of the city. In any case, in the opinion of the author of the Apocalypse of Baruch, the prayers, private and public, of the learned Pharisees were eminently effective before 70; and though he may have referred only to the section of the population with which he sympathized and agreed, it may safely be inferred from his words that R. Joḥanan b. Zakkai and his fellow-scholars, and before them their teachers Hillel and Shammai and their colleagues, were called upon in Jerusalem to recite the prayers at the service of public fasts. The difference between the religious attitude of those scholars and that of Ḥoni was so slight that the people and the authorities considered all these teachers their equally worthy spokesmen before God.

For Hillel, as the first chapter endeavoured to demonstrate, was in Jerusalem not only a great scholar who expounded and applied all parts of the Torah, and a patient

[1] ARN. 4, 11 a. [2] Kohel. r. 9. 8. 1.
[3] Rosh haShan. 18 a; see Rosenthal, *Vier apokr. Bücher*, 57 ff.
[4] p. 200.

and impressive teacher of his disciples and of every man with whom he came in contact. He developed and practised the moral laws with special intensity, and strongly urged their vital importance. The goal of his instruction was gradually to turn by the Torah, indispensable for life and all piety, the uncultured into a sin-fearing, unselfish, kind, loving man; and some of his disciples were considered worthy of the holy spirit and of miracles. For his unusual degree of meekness and humility, his love of peace and of men, his unique altruism and loving-kindness, and his faith, his fellow-scholars described him as Ḥasid and worthy of the holy spirit. All his actions were in God's honour. Among his contemporaries, as the second chapter tried to prove, there were pious men of various forms of piety. In common with others, some consistently strove to avoid every kind of sin; but, in unparalleled fear of errors committed, they sought in the repeated vow of the Nazirite occasions for bringing sin-offerings for atonement, while others brought a guilt-offering daily. Other pious men appear by the side of the men of deeds of loving-kindness, who successfully fought against sin, and practised works of sympathy and love. One of the men of deed who survived the fall of Jerusalem, R. Ḥaninah b. Dosa, was poor, very humble, scrupulously honest, devout in prayer, and of great faith; he helped his fellow-men by deeds of sympathy, charity and loving-kindness, and his prayer of intercession as of a son of God for the sick, was sought by the great scholars of his time; but he never prayed for rain. Before Hillel's time there lived in Jerusalem the pious men of the Psalms of Solomon, whose piety was analyzed in the third chapter. They were humble, feared God truly, obeyed his commandments, and practised righteousness toward their fellow-men; as they expected no reward for their piety, they thanked God for every kindness. They acknowledged His justice in the terrible slaughter wrought by Pompey, and their own sufferings as fully deserved for their unknown sins or as God's trials of love; in unfaltering faith and humility they submitted to His visitations, and, in their love of God, were ready for more. They continually searched their hearts and their homes for errors, and humbly confessed their sins, repented in fasting, and, without atoning sacrifices, prayed for the grace of forgiveness. One of those pious men was Ḥoni, the only Ḥasid who was invited to pray for rain and against the enemy, for he was righteous and beloved of God. As the fourth chapter showed, he represented a peculiar type of the Ḥasid; but neither he nor the other pious men were Essenes, but strict Pharisees attached to God with all their heart, and serving their fellow-men with all their soul.

PRINTED AT THE UNIVERSITY PRESS OXFORD
BY FREDERICK HALL
PRINTER TO THE UNIVERSITY

Buchler, Adolph
Types of Jewish-Palestinian Piety.